I REMEMBER
TOM LANDRY

BY
DENNE H. FREEMAN AND
JAIME ARON

SPORTS PUBLISHING L.L.C.
WWW.SPORTSPUBLISHINGLLC.COM

Editor: Christopher Stolle
Director of Production: Susan M. Moyer
Dustjacket and photo insert design: Terry Hayden

ISBN:
hardcover:1-58261-302-8
softcover: 1-58261-459-8

SPORTS PUBLISHING L.L.C.
www.sportspublishingllc.com

Printed in the United States.

For Maxine and Judy, two splendid Texas ladies.—D.F.

*For Lori, who makes everything possible,
and Zachary, my superstar.—J.A.*

Contents

Acknowledgments

Tracking down more than 125 friends, relatives and other associates of Tom Landry couldn't have been done without the help and support of many people.

Frank Luksa got us started and Roger Staubach's early endorsement went a long way. Having the blessing of Tom Landry Jr. and the entire Landry family was the ultimate compliment.

The Dallas Cowboys provided unlimited access to their library and the pick of their photo reserves. The team's television production department helped make the second chapter and the epilogue complete.

Our project was greeted warmly throughout the NFL, including the league office and the NFL Alumni association. Pat Hanlon of the New York Giants deserves special thanks for his speedy help with every request made of him.

Denne H. Freeman and Jaime Aron

Sportswriting pals throughout The Associated Press came through, too, whenever we needed anything from their hometowns. Speaking of hometowns, current and former Mission, Texas, residents Gen Long, Marvel Deen Rhodes, A.B. Ward and Wade Spilman went out of their way to assist us.

Lew Holder was kind enough to be interviewed twice after a technical glitch wiped out the first one—then lent some personal items. No wonder Tom trusted Lew to set him up on that blind date, then made him his best man.

The respect for Landry among the Fellowship of Christian Athletes was evident in the way everyone involved in the organization treated us.

Everyone we dealt with at the Billy Graham Evangelistic Association—from headquarters to the Dallas offices—were all wonderfully courteous, too. Special thanks to former crusade executive Charlie Riggs for loaning us the videotape used for a key part of the epilogue.

Cal Lutheran officials have been honoring Landry's memory for nearly two decades through their Landry Medal. They showed their respect and appreciation for the coach again with their assistance in our project.

Lastly, we would like to thank everyone who took the time to share their memories of Tom Landry. It is what they remember that made this project possible.

Sincerely,
Denne H. Freeman and Jaime Aron

Foreword

by Roger Staubach

I was fortunate enough to play 11 years for an incredible football coach and an even more amazing man, Tom Landry.

Our relationship took us to the mountaintop of our profession. We won two Super Bowl titles and established a franchise that was so dominating, it became known as "America's Team."

Tom was the kind of person who never gave up. That's why the Cowboys had winning seasons for 20 consecutive years.

With Coach Landry, what you saw was what you got. Like Randy White said, "He walked the talk."

Coming to the Cowboys and Coach Landry was the best thing that could have happened to me. I guess it was fate and a little luck that brought us together.

Although I'd won the Heisman Trophy, I was the long shot of longshots to make the NFL: a 10th-round draft pick from the Naval Academy who still had a four-year commitment in the service. But Tom, Tex Schramm and Gil Brandt took a chance that I would play after I finished my tour of duty.

I quickly learned that Coach Landry was the kind of man we'd all like to be. He taught me so much about football and life.

There was somewhat of a shyness about him, but he was always there when you needed him. I don't know anyone who didn't have respect for him as a person. There was nothing phony about him. His Christian religion taught him to do the right thing, and he always did.

Some players might not have loved him, but they all respected him.

Coach Landry was so serious about winning that nothing could break his concentration.

One time, I came over to him on the sidelines and he was looking up through the hole in the roof of Texas Stadium. The joke is that when the stadium was built, Clint Murchison left a hole in the roof so Tom could communicate with God. Well, he took so long to give me the play that I figured that's what he was doing. I said, "I always wondered where you got those plays from." He didn't even crack a smile.

His image was that he was so serious about the game, but he had a dry sense of humor. If he'd say anything that was even halfway funny, to us it was like Don Rickles.

One of his happiest moments came after we won the Super Bowl against Miami in New Orleans. I can still see him being carried off the field with a big smile on his face. That victory wiped away all those bad memories of losing to Cleveland and Green Bay in championship games. He was so happy, and he was finally able to relax a little. We were no longer "Next Year's Champions," and he'd validated his system and his philosophies.

But Coach Landry always put football third in his life behind his faith and his family. His wife, Alicia; children (Tom Jr., Kitty, and the dearly departed Lisa); their spouses and his grandchildren were the team that meant the most.

Alicia was the Rock of Gibraltar that Tom stood on. She was always on road trips with us, celebrating wins in her classy way and enduring the losses with dignity.

They were a team in every sense of the word. Winning Super Bowls never changed them or their outlook on life.

Tom and Alicia were inseparable, the perfect couple. My wife Marianne and I will always treasure memories of their

Roger Staubach and Landry discuss strategy on the sideline. (Photo courtesy of Denne H. Freeman)

company, both professionally and socially.

Of course, their children were just the kind of offspring you would expect Alicia and Tom to bring into the world. They followed their parents' example to become bright, successful adults and warm, wonderful parents.

Tom couldn't have been prouder of his family. Likewise, Alicia and the kids couldn't have been prouder of him.

Through the years, I've learned that Tom was not only beloved by his family, players and fans in Dallas, he also was revered across the nation. Everywhere I travel, people always want to know about Coach Landry, the guy in the funny hat who never lost his composure.

In 1990, I had the privilege of introducing him at the Hall of Fame, just as he'd done for me.

Afterwards he said, "Roger, thanks for the nice talk. But you know, you shouldn't have mentioned this, and you could've said ..." And I said, "Coach, quit calling plays for me."

You know, I always did want to call my own plays.

But if I couldn't, I knew I had the best man I could think of doing it for me.

Prologue

---

by Denne H. Freeman

Tom Landry was the man who couldn't get his team to the top of the mountain in the late 1960s.

Two agonizing NFL championship game losses to the Green Bay Packers had critics labeling Landry as the coach who couldn't win the big one.

Although the Cowboys had become one of the major forces in the NFL, Landry was still seen by some as an underachiever. Only a championship ring would validate the stoic man from Mission as a true coaching genius.

My coverage of the Dallas Cowboys as The Associated Press Texas sports editor began at this time. I stepped into a tense atmosphere. Dallas was a talented team that had become the epitome of bad luck and big-game bobbles.

The heat was on Landry, although you never saw him sweat.

On January 1, 1967, the Cowboys nearly went to the first Super Bowl, although it wasn't called that at the time. Dallas fell behind Green Bay early, then Don Meredith led a late drive that stalled when offensive lineman Jim Boeke jumped offsides. With any luck, the Cowboys would've won.

On December 31, 1967, a Dallas team made for a dry, fast track was out of its element playing in minus-15 degree windchill at Lambeau Field. They lost the NFL championship game dubbed the "Ice Bowl" when Bart Starr dove into the end zone on a quarterback sneak with time running out. Once again, Landry's team came up just short.

I recall Landry being all business as I climbed aboard the Cowboys beat in those days. He was civil and professional, even while unhappy fans and critics pursued him as he tried to shake the demons haunting the team.

It got even worse after the Cowboys lost Super Bowl V. Dallas outplayed the Baltimore Colts only to succumb at the end on Jim O'Brien's chip-shot field goal after a costly Craig Morton interception.

Defensive tackle Bob Lilly almost hurled his helmet out of the Orange Bowl in disgust. The team was wondering if it would ever get a break.

This wasn't as much fun as I thought it was going to be. Covering that locker room was like attending a wake. The players knew that they would be hearing nothing but negative press the next year.

Landry was drained and frustrated. He had escaped death in World War II as a bomber pilot, but the flak in Dallas was getting just about as thick as it had been over Germany.

A book by Steve Perkins was released entitled *Next Year's Champions*. It gutted the Cowboys as underachievers who would never get over the top.

Second-guessers were taking their pot shots. Landry had a bull's-eye on his famed fedora.

Through it all, I recall Landry maintaining his sense of class. He wouldn't get down in the dirt with the newspaper boys.

"I don't have time to read the sports sections," he would say. "I'm too busy trying to get us over the hump."

Landry was also criticized for not being more buddy-buddy with his players.

"I have to keep my distance so I can make objective calls on tough decisions," he told me. "If they get too close, they might be tempted to use that friendship as a personal crutch."

Through it all, he never wavered from his game plan of discipline and hard work. He was a competitor, and nobody was going to make him lose his confidence, his sense of destiny.

A famous cartoon in the *Dallas Times Herald* by Bob Taylor showed several frames of a stoic Landry never changing expressions. In the last frame, Landry is saying, "Wanna see me do it again?"

Why was he so stone cold on the sidelines?

"My players had to believe I was under control," Landry said. "It would hurt the team for them to see me losing it."

Maybe Landry learned to be calm from his war experiences. He crash-landed a B-17 during World War II after it ran out of gas.

Which was harder, coaching a professional football team or belly-flopping a bomber?

"It's about the same," he laughed. "If you lose your cool in either situation, it's a disaster."

I never have seen such joy in a man's eyes as I witnessed when the Cowboys finally broke their jinx by beating Miami 24-3 in Super VI in New Orleans at old, broken-down Tulane Stadium.

Landry was as much relieved as he was excited. You could see it in his eyes when he was carried off the field.

No dressing-room celebration could have been more joyous. Lilly was smoking a big cigar. General Manager Tex Schramm got tossed in the shower.

And Landry got to say: "That 500-pound anvil is off our back."

Landry was a new man after that historic day.

He had never lacked confidence, but a team needs to win it all to totally believe in a coach's doctrine.

All the long film sessions and hard workouts and ignoring nagging injuries had finally paid off. The Cowboys went on to defeat Denver in another Super Bowl and lost twice to the Pittsburgh Steelers.

With the Landry legend secure, I found Tom to be a more warm and relaxed person, a lot easier to be around. Someone, I noticed, who had a sharp wit and a sardonic sense of humor.

Old Stone Face with a sense of humor? Now, there's a story that was hard getting a lot of people to believe.

Landry jumped my case one year at training camp in Thousand Oaks, California, because I was lying down on the sidelines without a shirt on while watching practice.

Nothing escaped Landry during the workouts.

He barked at a trainer through his bullhorn and salty old Buck Buchanan, a former Air Force sergeant, informed me I needed to stand up and get dressed.

Later, Landry, enjoying himself, said that as slow as I was, he was afraid I'd get run down and injured.

"You didn't have much recovery time," he said, then jabbed the needle hard and added, "Besides, you don't have enough muscles to go around without your shirt on."

I would sit by Landry at all his weekly press luncheons. We would talk about a lot besides football, particularly Western novels. Landry knew more about the Old West than most history professors.

"Give me a Zane Grey novel, and it beats newspapers and television," he would say. "It's one of my favorite ways of relaxing."

We played golf together several times in charity events, and the powerfully built Landry could really play. He boomed his drives about 275 yards and hit solid iron shots.

Landry played so well, I kidded him about neglecting the team and secretly practicing his golf game.

"No matter how much I play, I'll never play as much as sportswriters do," he kidded back. "My short game isn't that great. Does it look like I've been practicing?"

Landry was a fair man. He would always try giving as good an answer as he could to the most stupid of questions. I always respected him for that.

Of course, getting any information out of him was another thing. He'd tell you just what he wanted you to know and that was it. He would always dance around the starting quarterback question.

"Too early in the week to tell, OK?" he would say.

I once stumbled upon Schramm listening at the keyhole of Landry's door.

"Just trying to find out who my damn starting quarterback is going to be this week," Schramm said.

Landry kept his own counsel. He was busy preparing both the offensive and defensive game plans, something nobody is likely to ever see again in the NFL. He even took time to help the kickers, using golf swing keys to help them with their leg whips.

Landry was the first coach to use computers. He invented the 4-3 defense, then invented an offense to defeat it. He and Vince Lombardi were geniuses, which is why the New York Giants were so tough to beat when they were assistants together in the 1950s.

Personalized anniversary greeting to author's parents. (Photo courtesy of Denne H. Freeman)

The glory of five Super Bowl seasons made covering the Cowboys the plum assignment of any sportswriter in the country. They had become "America's Team," and Landry was "America's Coach."

Training camp in California could get dull, though. I recall one night when a member of our group stole Landry's oatmeal pan so he could cook a lobster in the media dorm.

Landry cooked oatmeal every morning of training camp. On this particular morning, he couldn't find his pan and sent a minion in search of it. The pan was found in the media dorm with lobster whiskers still in it.

Landry didn't say anything until a month later. Before one of the Tuesday luncheons began he said, "If my oatmeal pan gets stolen next year at Thousand Oaks, I'm going to make every one of you guys run laps. That should put an end to that."

Although some of the players he had to cut might not agree, Landry was a kind, thoughtful person.

Once, he overheard that my parents were going to celebrate their 50th wedding anniversary and that my father was a big fan of his.

"Can I do something for them?" he asked.

The late Doug Todd, the public relations director, got a picture of Landry and he wrote a note to my parents and signed it. It was one of their most prized possessions.

Things started going downhill with the team in the late 1980s, but Landry kept his sense of humor.

Suffering through his last season with a 3-13 team, Landry noticed that the Cowboys cheerleaders were on the cover of the *Dallas Cowboys Weekly* instead of a player.

"Does that tell you how far we've fallen?" Landry joked. "We can't even put a player on the cover."

Little did I know that only a few months later, I would be in his office with photographer Ron Heflin as Landry cleaned out his desk for the final time after being fired by new owner Jerry Jones.

Landry had the class to let Heflin and me inside his office, although you could tell he was hurting bad. His eyes moistened from time to time as he answered questions.

"That's the nature of the beast," Landry said. "It feeds on losses and eats you up, no matter how much success you've had."

On that bleak February day in 1989, Landry wasn't sure how long the fans would miss him.

"Oh, people will forget me pretty quick," Landry said at one juncture.

Later, the city of Dallas held a parade for Tom and wife Alicia. You could tell the Landrys were a little bit overwhelmed by it all.

The author and Landry inside the coach's office the morning after he was fired. Landry later added a personal note. (Photo courtesy of Denne H. Freeman)

It was an emotionally satisfying sight to see them going out on top down the canyons of Dallas, sitting in a convertible as fans shouted their thanks. Alicia waved until her arm wore out and Tom doffed his fedora hundreds of times.

I asked him later if he still felt he was going to be forgotten.

His smile was the answer.

Yes, Old Stone Face had a great smile.

Introduction

by Jaime Aron

Tom Landry knew how to smile. And laugh. And even cry. He also knew how to make others smile and laugh, and he lent a soft shoulder to anyone shedding tears.

That array of emotions might surprise people who only saw Tom Landry as the robotic coach of the Dallas Cowboys.

To those who knew him, the only surprise is that anyone would really think they knew Tom Landry just by watching him on the sideline.

In the pages ahead, you'll read stories about Landry that will cause you to smile, laugh and maybe even cry. Even those who knew him well will learn a few things about a guy who went out of his way to keep his good deeds quiet.

Landry never tooted his own horn. So, in this book, others will do it for him.

Respect is a word you'll read often. Impact is another word that comes up a lot. Sure, he had a tremendous impact on the game of football, but the kind of impact he's best remembered for is influencing lives, directly and indirectly.

For example, Bob Lilly credits his coach for teaching him the values he passed on to his own children, who are now parents themselves. Another former player, Mike Connelly, paints an even broader picture when he tells about seeing high school coaches cleaning up their language and trying to act stoically so they could be like Landry, which in turn made them better examples for their students.

I never had the privilege of knowing Landry. I moved to Dallas in 1992 and only once interviewed him one-on-one. Still, that one episode left a deep impression.

I had been assigned a story about the five-year anniversary of Jerry Jones' takeover in Dallas and had only a few days to do it. By the time I tracked Landry down, it was the afternoon before my story was due. I was told he was attending a banquet that night and wouldn't be home until after 10 p.m. I left my name and number anyway and said I'd be at the office until midnight.

Despite all the great stories I'd heard about Landry's accessibility with the media, I didn't expect to hear back from him that night. Would you call a reporter you didn't know after an evening on the town just to reflect on one of the worst days of your life?

Around 10:30 p.m., the phone rang.

"Hello, Jaime?" said a voice any sports fan in Texas would've recognized without further introduction. "This is Tom Landry."

Getting phone calls returned was not a problem during the three months Denne and I spent putting together this book.

Everyone was happy to share memories and stories about how Landry affected their life. Most people also gave advice. Some of the lines I heard the most were, "Make sure you include how great Alicia is," "You know, he really did have a great sense of humor," and "Don't forget about his parents. They were wonderful people."

The compilation of interviews in the chapters ahead forms a unique portrait of a unique man.

His priorities in life were faith, family and football, and those aspects and more are all covered.

You'll hear from Alicia, his wife for 51 years; his son and daughter; and his sister and brother. His minister describes being too awed by Landry to call him by his first name. Billy Graham talks about Landry's influence on his Crusades. The Fellowship of Christian Athletes also was a major part of Landry's life, and you'll discover the $108 million difference he made in that organization's growth.

As for football, many of his greatest players and top assistant coaches from the Cowboys share their memories, as do players and coaches from Landry's days with the New York Giants. Frank Gifford explains why he always defended his old teammate from the broadcast booth, and rival coaches such as Don Shula, Chuck Noll, and Bill Walsh reflect on what it was like facing a Landry-coached team.

Lifelong friends from Mission, Texas, chime in on their childhood together, and University of Texas teammates fondly recall the poise and power Landry showed upon returning from World War II. There are also stories from media who covered Landry and tidbits from a variety of others, from the son of a former teammate to his golf pro.

Plenty of people have coached football teams, and many more have been upstanding citizens and devout Christians. The way Tom Landry was able to do it all and remain true to his high standards serves as a model for all who were fortunate enough to know him and those who can only wish they had.

Chapter One

THE LANDRYS

Tom and Alicia Landry were the picture-perfect couple from the top of the wedding cake.

A blind date in college turned into a 51-year marriage. They had the pleasure of raising three children, then the joy of six grandchildren; sadly, they also endured the agony of burying a daughter.

Tom's death created a void in the lives of many, the deepest being in the hearts of his family.

Alicia Landry

Alicia Landry, the "first lady" of the Dallas Cowboys, had her world forever shaken on February 12, 2000.

Her beloved Tommy had died of leukemia, a disease she thought he would whip like he did every challenge he faced in his life, from being a bomber pilot in World War II to the demanding task of coaching America's Team.

She remembered her rush of emotions when doctors first said Landry was anemic.

"He was the most healthy person in the world," she said in early June 2000 in one of her first interviews since becoming a widow. "He worked out every day, had a perfect physique, didn't have any bad habits. Didn't smoke or drink. He didn't have high cholesterol or high blood pressure. He was a perfect physical specimen.

"How in the world could you say this person is anemic? I couldn't believe it. It was just incredible to me."

Leukemia, a blood disease, comes in different forms. Percentages of recovery range from high to low; the kind Landry had was 40 percent fatal.

A photo of Tom and Alicia Landry used as part of an invitation for their 50th wedding anniversary celebration. (Photo courtesy of Fellowship of Christian Athletes)

"I just knew Tommy would be in the 60 percent category," Alicia remembered.

Landry fought bravely. He handled the chemotherapy, which is extremely toxic to many leukemia patients, the way he handled most challenges in his life.

"It never bothered him," Alicia said. "Some drugs made him a little disoriented, but things were looking good.

"But the chemo never totally killed the leukemia, which kept coming back.

"He kept battling it. Five days before he died, things were looking good. Then doctors said it had come back again. It moved so unbelievably fast. Then he died.

"I couldn't believe Tommy didn't win."

In the weeks after his death, she still had trouble coping with the loss.

"Every time the telephone would ring," she said, "I would think it was Tommy."

Alicia Wiggs first met Tom Landry when she was a freshman at the University of Texas. Tom was a junior and a star on the football team following his war duty.

"I went to school early to pledge to a sorority, and my sisters set up blind dates for all the pledges with the big men on campus," Alicia said. "I drew Tommy, who had a black eye at the time from a football game.

"He still looked sharp and dressed well. He was still handsome, even with the black eye.

"From that point on, we had at least one date a week until we got married when Tommy was a senior. I guess you could say we had a date for the rest of our lives after that."

Alicia found out right away how disciplined her husband-to-be was.

"My dad wanted to make sure I didn't smoke as a teenager, so he paid me not to, because it was so smelly," she said. "I started dating Tommy when I was 17.

"When I turned 18, I told him I could start smoking now."

Tom's response: "If you do, I'm not going to kiss you."

"I never smoked," Alicia said, laughing. "And I didn't get paid by Tom either."

Landry signed with the New York Yankees of the All-American Football Conference under the goal posts after Texas beat Georgia in the 1949 Orange Bowl. He accepted the princely sum of a $6,000 salary and a $500 bonus.

"It sure looked like a lot of money to us," Alicia said. "It was enough to get married on."

So they did. On January 28, 1949, they exchanged vows in Houston, then honeymooned in Mexico.

In 1999, they had a big party to celebrate their 50th anniversary. They were a few weeks past No. 51 when Tom passed away.

Alicia loved life in the Big Apple.

"New York City was a great place to go, and it was a big adventure for us," she said. "Back in those days, you could ride the subways without any worries, and I rode it a lot. There was just so much to do. We'd eat at Toots Shor's and go to Broadway plays. We had a great time.

"Of course, I went to more plays than Tommy did. He worked almost all the time."

The NFL absorbed the old AAFC in 1950, and Landry became a New York Giant. He started as a player, then became a player-coach and eventually a full-time coach,

The happy couple always found time to spend together at least once a week for more than 50 years. (Photo courtesy of Wade Spilman)

working as the assistant in charge of the defense. While Landry launched his famous 4-3 defense, Vince Lombardi ran the offense.

Alicia, meanwhile, worked her way up to being invited along on the team plane on road trips.

"Me and Marie Lombardi were the only wives who got to go on road trips, and they were fun, particularly when we won," she said. "Tom and I were very fortunate in working for the two best owners in the NFL, the Maras with the Giants and, of course, Clint Murchison with the Cowboys."

Alicia liked Big D, too. She had lived in Dallas for a many years, then moved to Houston, where her father, Herbert, was chairman of the board of an insurance company.

She was delighted when Tex Schramm and Murchison talked Tom into becoming the first coach of the expansion Cowboys in 1960.

"We were happy to be settling down in Texas," she said.

Managing their three children—Tom Jr., Kitty, and Lisa—and keeping her husband happy kept Alicia going 24/7. Tom always tried to give the children some of his precious time during football season.

"He was never a stranger to me and the kids. Tom was always home for breakfast with the children and for the evening meal, although it would be kind of late sometimes," Alicia said. "Tommy didn't sleep at the office like some coaches do, but he brought a lot of work home.

"I loved football and tried to watch some films with him. I never got brave enough to try to give him any plays or anything, but I was knowledgeable about the rules. The thing that got me was that he was always stopping the film and running it backwards. I'd watch a play, then BOOM, he'd run it backwards again. I couldn't take much of that."

Life with the Cowboys was fun for Alicia, even during the tough times of the early 1960s when the team struggled to win.

"We knew it would take time to win until our draft picks started paying off," she said. "We knew that Tex and the Murchisons were behind us and would be patient. Of course, it didn't hurt any when Clint gave Tom that 10-year contract.

"He did it, I guess, to answer any potential critics. The media mostly was very good to us. There were just a few stinkers."

Then came the Cowboys' Super Bowl victory in January 1971.

"We had lost to Baltimore in the Super Bowl the year before in a game with a lot of bad breaks and it was hard to take," she said. "We also had that bad 'Ice Bowl' loss to Green Bay. We couldn't take another one of those losses. I think we all felt better when we beat Miami. It took the pressure off."

As the years went on, Landry began running more film backwards, and Alicia and Tom began missing out on some of their dates.

"Tom just got busier and busier," Alicia said. "We used to meet at the Chaparral club for lunch at least once a week, but Tom told me one day: 'We just can't do that anymore. I'm too busy. I'm sorry.'"

Alicia said Tom was good at masking his feelings, but she knew when things weren't going well.

"He was a cool guy, very much in control of his emotions, but I could tell things were serious when he got real quiet," she said. "I wasn't dumb enough to ask him what was the matter. I just went to my room or made myself busy until things got better."

Through the years, Landry was always impeccably dressed. He once earned a spot on a list of the nation's Ten Best Dressed Men.

Alicia confessed that, as rumored, she picked out some of his clothes.

"He didn't have time during the season, so I got them out for him," she said, laughing. "Tommy had great taste in clothes, and, with his build, he looked great in anything he put on."

Alicia was always a welcomed sight around the team. Players still talk about how much they respected and appreciated her support. The feeling was mutual.

"I enjoyed going to training camp for a few weeks and on the plane trips for road games," she said. "Back in the early days, we would go in on Friday nights and Tom and I would dine out. Once planes became much faster, we'd go on Saturday mornings. I liked the slow planes better.

"We had two different lives: the regular season and the off-season, which was the month of June. During the off-season, we would take vacation trips and do the normal things. I can remember once Tom and I stayed in Salado for almost a week and golfed and ate at the Stagecoach Inn almost every day. I must have gained five pounds, the food was so good.

A Landry family portrait from the 1970s. (Photo courtesy of the Dallas Cowboys)

"I never kept score when I played golf. Tom was the golfer in the family. Whenever we went on a vacation you could bet a golf course was going to be nearby."

Alicia didn't wish to dwell on Tom's firing by Jerry Jones in 1989, although she did say it gave the couple a new direction in their life and time to enjoy it.

For example, they took their first *real* vacation, a dreamy trip to Europe.

"We spent two great weeks in Paris and took the train to Switzerland," she said. "We had never really had time for a real long vacation and this one was just wonderful.

"We got back and played golf together and rode our boat at the lake house and swam together. It's been difficult to go to the lake house without him."

Tom's death was Alicia's second tragic blow. Their youngest daughter, Lisa, died of cancer in 1995 not long after giving birth to daughter Christina Alicia.

"I spend a lot of my days helping watch her," said Alicia, whose major at Texas was child psychology. "It's my calling now."

Alicia said she fully expects to see her husband again in the next life.

She already knows how Tom will greet her at their reunion.

He'll smile and say, "Don't I know you from somewhere?"

Tom Landry Jr.

Tom Landry Jr. relished growing up as the "junior" to one of the most famous coaches in NFL history. He looks back at his early years as being right out of a novel.

"I had the dream childhood of an American boy," he said. "I got to go to practice with the Dallas Cowboys. I got to go to training camp. I got to ride on the team plane. I got to meet all the players and get their autographs. It was great being a ball boy.

"It was pretty neat spending training camp with your father and the coach of the Cowboys, too."

If Tom Jr. missed missed anything, it was probably some extra time with his dad, who was always scheming ways to keep the Cowboys atop the cutthroat world of professional football. That didn't leave Tom Sr. much time to play catch.

"We didn't get to do a lot," Tom Jr. said, adding that he understood the situation. "When you grow up with a famous father, the words 'quality time' come into play. You don't spend a whole lot of time with him."

Tom Jr. remembers some of the early clues that his father had a different profession than most.

"I could turn on the TV and there he was," Tom Jr. said. "I found out not all the kids at school could do that.

"In fact, I was pretty popular at school. I wonder why?"

Football wasn't the theme to all of Tom Jr.'s happiest memories.

"We had family vacations, but they usually ended right around July 4th," he said. "When dad's parents were still alive, we would spend some time down in Mission. We were usually there on July 4th. I loved those trips. We would stop and hit the rapid rides in New Braunfels.

"We would also take long trips by car to Yellowstone and other places. When I was older, we would go skiing at Vail or Beaver Creek. People starting recognizing Dad more and more at those places.

"They really started recognizing us after we won the Super Bowl in the early 1970s. We started getting more television exposure, like the Thanksgiving Day games. It was hard to go somewhere without people wanting autographs. It was interesting to see the more games we won, the more popular we got."

Tom Jr. wasn't perfect, but he said he was no problem child for his parents.

"I never gave them much occasion for discipline," he said. "I sort of lived by my Dad's example. I just never had this vision of talking back to Tom Landry. He gave you the feeling you just didn't want to get out of line. I had a great childhood."

Tom Jr., an excellent athlete whose football career was cut short by knee injuries, remembers many fun times with his father on the golf course.

He especially recalls their final round together.

"It was over Easter weekend of 1999. Dad shot 82 at Hidden Hills down in Austin, which is pretty good on that golf course. He sank a lot of long putts. It was a wonderful time," Tom Jr. said. "Then, he went into the hospital for the first time in May."

When Tom Sr. left the Cowboys, he and Tom Jr. joined the business world together in the Landry Investment Group.

"We had 10 tremendous years," said Tom Jr., an attorney. "When you are in business together, you have a different relationship with your father, although your dad is always your dad.

"In this case, it was two grown adults working together. Your voice means more to him.

"Dad was a real good partner. I could handle most of his business relations for him. I didn't always have to go to him and ask if he wanted to do something. We had a lot of endorsements going on, but I knew what was appropriate and what wasn't. The same went with our business investments.

"He'd pretty much let me do things, although I would always ask his opinion. A lot of the details were left to me."

One of Tom Jr.'s most vivid memories is of his father's humbleness and dedication to doing the right thing.

"Dad was not one to tout his own accomplishments," the son said. "He always tried to do his best, no matter what he was doing. He always felt someone should be the best they can be at whatever they are trying to do. He was happy he made a difference in people's lives.

"He was an amazing man in that he did so many things in so many areas, but didn't broadcast those things. He would never say anything about it. He would just help someone or some organization and go on down the road. I'm still hearing stories from people about something that Dad had done and I'd never heard about it. Some of them were really neat."

Tom Jr. said his father came as advertised.

"He was such a tremendous person to just be around," he said. "It's so unusual today to find a person who is such a great role model and is consistent in their beliefs. He really was. He lived his life just like you would describe it.

"That's how he was. There was no charade to it.

"He had such a feeling for everybody. We were in New York City one time walking down Fifth Avenue. Porters were running out of the hotels and shoeshine boys quit what they were doing to come over and say hello.

"Dad loved it. He clapped them on the back and shook their hands and signed autographs. People can recognize when a person is genuine. You can't fool 'em.

"And they really loved dad."

Landry gave as well as he received.

"Dad accomplished so much in his dealings with people," Tom Jr. said. "I didn't know until recently that he would spend three hours a week just writing thank-you notes to different people. I don't know how he had the time to do it.

"I read one letter at the memorial service. It was from a father in New York who had a 14-year-old son dying of cancer in a hospital. He was a big Cowboys fan. One of his wishes was to talk to Dad.

"One day, in the middle of football season, the telephone rang, and it was Dad. Then, he put Roger Staubach on the telephone. You can imagine the boost it gave that boy."

"That," Tom Jr. concluded, "was my Dad."

Kitty Landry Phillips

On those nights when geometry was a little too difficult, Kitty Landry turned to her dad for help.

"I knew he'd be watching film, so I'd go back and knock on the door," Kitty said. "He'd immediately click off the projector and give me some help. He was great at math. He studied engineering at the University of Texas. I remember I made an A in geometry that year."

Kitty laughed and added, "I just hope I wasn't the cause of any losses by taking his time away from the football films for my math tutoring."

Kitty said that story is an example of the kind of doting dad she had.

"He never said he was too busy," she said.

Being the daughter of the high-profile coach of the Dallas Cowboys "seemed like a normal life to me," Kitty recalls.

"I guess I didn't know he was famous," she said. "I do know he was a great father, and now, as a mother, I realize how much patience he had. He had a lot of patience with us kids.

"He had a way of making us all feel so special, like there was nothing any more important than us."

Kitty, the second of Tom and Alicia's three children, said she doesn't recall a lack of quality time despite her father's hectic schedule.

"I don't remember him not being there much," she said. "I know he was always there for breakfast and dinner. Then, at night, he'd hit the film room."

As fate would have it, Kitty married a former University of Texas football star, just like her mother did.

Eddie Phillips was a Longhorn from 1969-71 and was the starting quarterback on the 1970 squad that went 10-0 and was No. 1 in the country before losing to Notre Dame in the Cotton Bowl.

"I think Dad was thrilled about Eddie being from Texas," said Kitty, who now helps run the Lisa Landry Childress Foundation, a charity named for her late sister that helps spread awareness of organ and tissue donation. "I know they had a lot of fun on family vacations. Dad was in great shape, and he could ski all day and beat my husband.

"Dad would beat him in tennis, while Eddie was really good and beat him for sure in golf. Dad was a great golfer. My dad was very competitive even in those family games. He liked to win.

"Dad would get a townhouse at the World of Tennis in Lakeway and we'd have the Landry Olympics."

Kitty recalled the fun of getting to go down on the field after games in the Cotton Bowl, then meeting her father outside the locker room.

"I guess that's when I first realized he must be famous or something," she said. "I can remember walking past a group of people and they started applauding. I wondered what they were doing that for.

"Then, it kind of dawned on me, 'Oh, we won the game.'"

Kitty also has lasting memories of Super Bowl trips.

"Now that was really fun," she said. "Things were really good the years we got to do that. The kids were really spoiled on those trips."

Kitty Landry Phillips and Alicia Landry (left) along with Tom Landry Jr. (far right), shown with longtime Cowboys assistant coach Jim Myers and his wife, Carolyn, in front of a bust of Landry given by the Dallas chapter of the Fellowship of Christian Athletes. (Photo courtesy of the Fellowship of Christian Athletes)

Chapter Two

REMEMBERING A LEGEND

Tom Landry pulled out so many fourth-quarter victories in his coaching career that family and friends were convinced he'd find a way to rally and beat leukemia, too.

The disease was diagnosed in May 1999. Landry endured rounds of chemotherapy and regained enough strength to go home from Baylor University Medical Center the Sunday before Thanksgiving. However, he soon returned and ultimately lost his fight the evening of Saturday, February 12, 2000. He was 75.

An immense outpouring of emotion followed.

The family held a private funeral and burial on Wednesday afternoon and a semi-private memorial at their church Thursday morning. Hours later, the city of Dallas played host to a public memorial service that was televised live on local stations. About the same time, yet another memorial was held in Mission, Texas, at the church where Landry grew up.

The funeral and burial were the most dramatic.

About 300 close friends and former players from Landry's days with the Cowboys and New York Giants gathered at a funeral home for a chapel service. Tom Landry Jr. told the guests that things were running behind schedule and invited everyone to relax and greet each other.

Intended or not, it was a great tension breaker. People who hadn't been together for years shared hugs, handshakes and memories of the man they were there to honor. They helped each other cope with the fact that a man they all considered indestructible was no longer with them.

Service of Celebration and Remembrance

for

Thomas Wade Landry, Sr.

September 11, 1924 - February 12, 2000

12:00 noon

February 17, 2000

Highland Park United Methodist Church

Dallas, Texas

Program from private memorial service.

ORDER OF WORSHIP

Organ Voluntary

Words of Greeting

Hymn 77   How Great Thou Art

Affirmation of Faith

   I believe in God the Father Almighty, maker of heaven and earth; and
in Jesus Christ his only Son our Lord: who was conceived by the Holy
Spirit, born of the Virgin Mary, suffered under Pontius Pilate, was
crucified, dead, and buried; the third day he rose from the dead; he
ascended into heaven, and sitteth at the right hand of God the Father
Almighty; from thence he shall come to judge the quick and the dead. I
believe in the Holy Spirit, the holy catholic church, the communion of
saints, the forgiveness of sins, the resurrection of the body, and the life
everlasting. Amen.

Gloria Patri 70

Scripture Readings

Pastoral Prayer

The Lord's Prayer

Personal Testimonies

Anthem   My Eternal King   Jane Marshall

Words of Faith and Remembrance

Hymn 378   Amazing Grace

Benediction

Closing Voluntary

*   *   *   *   *

Mark Craig and Kenneth M. Dickson, ministers
Bonnie Jean Coleman Mouton, director of the Chancel Choir
Ron Neal, violinist   Scott Warren, organist

(The family will greet friends in the Great Hall following the service.)

Many kind words were spoken during the service, but the lasting memory was a gesture made by Tom Jr. The younger Landry took one of his father's trademark fedora hats and gently placed it inside the casket, then closed it.

Everyone was then invited to the grave site for a burial befitting a World War II hero. There was a color guard, a 21-gun salute and a flag over the casket that was presented to the widow. There also was another dramatic moment.

What at first sounded like a rude interruption by a commercial airplane became a military flyover featuring the classic "missing wing" formation in tribute to a fallen pilot. Shortly after came a flock of vintage World War II planes.

When the service ended, Alicia Landry invited everyone back to her house to continue celebrating her husband's life—with the emphasis on celebration. As they'd begun during the delay at the chapel, guests caught up with each other and swapped old stories.

At noon on Thursday, the main sanctuary of Highland Park United Methodist Church was filled to honor one of the outstanding members of the congregation. A closed-circuit broadcast carried the service to an adjacent chapel.

The altar was typical Landry in that it was stylish yet simple. There was a hat, an open Bible and a large portrait. There was nothing to symbolize football or the Dallas Cowboys, except the dozens of former players and coaches sitting in the pews.

Captivating speeches by minister Mark Craig, Roger Staubach and Tom Jr. focused on all aspects of Landry's life.

Football was a prominent theme at the afternoon service held at the Morton H. Meyerson Symphony Center in downtown Dallas. Entitled "A Tribute To The Landry Legacy," the event featured 11 speakers with Cowboys ties.

Each was asked to limit themselves to three minutes, but few could. So with time running out, it was Staubach, of course, who came through in the clutch. He zipped through the speech he'd given at the previous service, leading to a sentimental finale.

One by one, a procession of former players crossed the stage and placed a yellow rose into an urn resting next to a classic photograph of Landry wearing a dark sports coat, tie and fedora, his arms crossed and just a hint of a smile.

CHURCH SERVICE

Roger Staubach

Roger Staubach knew Tom Landry as "a great husband, father, grand-father and friend." He also recalled that Landry was "a professional football player, an industrial engineer, a hero of World War II."

And, of course, there were those 20 consecutive winning seasons, proof that he was one of the greatest coaches in NFL history.

"How difficult it is to capture all these things in only a few minutes," Staubach said.

A passage from the Bible provided a good starting point.

"There's a quote from James that I've enjoyed. It says: 'You have faith, but I have deeds. Show me your faith without doing anything and I will show you my faith by what I do.'

"Tom Landry's faith and deeds, they went hand-in-hand. That's one reason he was so beloved. He was the essence of what Randy White has been saying: 'He walks his talk.' He lived his faith every day in so many ways.

"You could see it in his relationship with Alicia, his commitment to her, his love for his children and grand-children. You could see it in his respect for others.

"Many of Coach Landry's closest friends and relatives will tell you that they never heard him say a harsh word about anybody, not ever, including me.

"That's called good-ness. That's called integrity. That's called character.

A successful on-field relationship between Staubach and Landry turned into a lifelong friendship. (Photo courtesy of the Dallas Cowboys)

"I know this much to be true: Tom Landry's faith was his character. And he transferred that character to the players on his teams every day on the football field. He taught us stuff we didn't know and had never even heard of, as a matter of fact. But there was a lot of innovation and creativity, a lot of teamwork and a lot of leadership."

Landry was a master of preparation, especially when it came to football.

Because he oversaw the defense and the offense, Landry had to deal with one, then the other. So, if he spent the first part of the week with the defense, Staubach knew what that meant.

"On Friday night, we'd see him leaving the practice field and he'd have these cans of film under his arm. We'd say, 'Oh, we're going to have to change it on Saturday.'

"Sure enough, he'd come in on Saturday and there would be a few changes. Of course, on Saturday night, if it was an away game, we were flying to the game and he'd grab me on the plane. In fact, nobody would ever want to sit down next to me when we'd get on the plane because they knew their seat would be taken—and, sure enough, he would be back there because I was the starting quarterback. I know he had to do it with Don, Craig, Eddie, Danny—everybody, all his quarterbacks.

"But we'd be on the plane. He'd be isolated on me and we'd be talking. He'd be so focused, he'd be concentrating so much, that he wouldn't know what's going on around him.

"Coaches would be looking over at him wondering what was changing. But he wanted to make sure his quarterback knew what was going to happen. And there were a few changes.

"If it was a home game, I'd get a call at home. And it wouldn't be, 'Roger, this is Coach Landry.'

"First of all, I got used to it, so I had a game plan right by the phone. And I'd pick up the phone and he'd say, 'Roger, you know, on 67 pass, instead of doing the red flip, wing motion, we want the wing to short spy.'"

Staubach, though, knew Landry's intense preparation was behind the team's success.

"I think the best preparation that I ever encountered in his work was the first Super Bowl victory in January '72 against the Dolphins. In fact, I remember every single moment from the day we landed in New Orleans leading up to that game.

"It was a time when Dallas had had great teams. Don Meredith was a fantastic quarterback. He took the punishment to build Dallas . . . (emotional pause) to a great winning football team. And there we were in New Orleans. I had the load on my shoulders as the quarterback.

"The first night, I went out and celebrated in New Orleans. I went with Joe Williams. We went to a movie and saw Clint Eastwood in Dirty

Harry. I remember every moment, including that night, because the rest of it was camping out with Tom Landry.

"We'd be in his room and we'd both be watching film, going over game film, time and time again. We had team meetings, but I still had to be back in his room going over game films. Alicia would be sitting there and she'd say, 'Tommy, let him get to bed.' In fact, Alicia would walk me back to my room, trying to keep me motivated and inspired because she wanted this victory as much as Tom.

"He didn't want me to miss anything. And we were prepared."

The Cowboys won 24-3. Staubach threw two touchdown passes and was named the game's Most Valuable Player.

"Boy, did that victory ever make him happy. If you ever take a look at the game film, when he was being carried off the field, he had the biggest smile you ever saw on his face."

"Walt (Garrison) said it all one time. He was asked whether he'd ever seen Coach Landry smile. 'Nope,' he said, 'but I've only been here nine years.'

"But we did see him smile being carried off the field for that first world championship. It was preparation that won that championship for us, along with the character of Tom Landry.

"That's kind of a pattern to his life. He was prepared on the field, he was prepared off the field. He was prepared to leave his football team, he was prepared to leave his family. I believe he was prepared the moment he took his last breath on Saturday night. He didn't want to go, but he was prepared for what he knew would be his future: to meet his God, Jesus Christ, to have eternal happiness.

"Coach Landry was always able to keep things in perspective. He knew what was important in life and he helped us understand that his road was the high road. He didn't dwell on defeat. He looked at the next play, the next game, the next season.

"Sure, he was hurt when we lost a game or didn't have a good season. He'd give you that look, and it was tough at times. We knew that he was upset, but he went on. He'd get over it faster than anybody else, by far.

"He had tremendous perseverance. He was resilient. He was our rock, our hope, our inspiration. He was our coach.

"Probably, there were a few players who maybe didn't love him as much as some of the other players, but they all respected him. That's one of the reasons we as former players are here to honor him. We've experienced other relationships in our life and we keep going back to our relationship with him.

"Even though at the time we maybe didn't think he was listening or paying attention to us, we know he was. He was committed to us. You don't find that commitment in life very often.

"What's helped me deal with this loss and even to understand our mortality is the balance he had between his temporal life and spiritual life. I've tried to understand balancing the temporal and the spiritual.

"Corinthians tells something in scripture that represents Coach amazingly well. It says: 'So, we do not give up. We do not give up. Our physical body is becoming older and weaker, but our spirit inside is made new every day. We have small troubles for a while now, but they are helping us gain an eternal glory that is much greater than the troubles. We set our eyes not on what we see, but on what we cannot see. What we see will last only a short time. But what we cannot see will last forever.'

"This was the essence of Coach's faith. He did not give up. He set his eyes on what he could not see, but what he knew in his heart to be true. This is the way he lived here on Earth. One of the reasons why people loved and respected him was the reason we won for 20 consecutive seasons: He never gave up.

"This wise and relatively quiet, shy man wasn't much for small talk. He didn't seem to smile a whole lot. Somewhat stoic. But he could walk into a room and instantly become the center of attention. And it's why he's so beloved by his family, by the thousands of friends he made in his lifetime and by millions more who never had the honor and privilege to meet him.

"Tom Landry had a decency about him that was unsurpassed by anyone that I've ever known. He achieved great fame while never seeking that fame. Everyone knew that he was true.

"He didn't put on airs. He did things for the right reasons. That's what his Christian religion taught him: to do the right things, the things that help others. His dedication to the Fellowship of Christian Athletes, to the ministries of Billy Graham and so on and so on, his work for charity after charity, child after child, friend after friend and so many other things are testament to his character and his faith.

"He was there when people needed him. He was there for his country in World War II. He's been there for the city of Dallas, his teams, the Cowboys and, most importantly, his family.

"I'd like to close by reading a poem. It was one of Coach Landry's favorite poems, but I think it's appropriate as far as what it means based on why we're here today:

> *His love is greater than the expanse of the sea.*
> *He died a cruel death to save you and me.*
> *Although we continue to sin day after day,*
> *He forgives us and leads us back his way.*
> *His path is straight and narrow, you see.*
> *But if we follow his leading, in his will we'll be.*

This world gives no lasting pleasure,
But his kingdom is full of riches beyond measure.
Remember to always look above the sun,
Until that final day, when his will shall be done.
The Lord in his glory will ride on a cloud,
And trumpets will blast in the heavens so loud
To call his children home at last.
Never to look back to those things that are past,
Our bodies will become glorious and perfectly made,
For Christ made sure our ransom was paid.

"The author of this poem was Lisa Landry Childress. Coach, give Lisa our best. We miss you both."

Tom Landry Jr.

By working with his father from 1989-2000, Tom Landry Jr. gained even more respect and appreciation for "the finest man I've ever known."

"Tom Landry was everything the world believed him to be. He was a man of virtue, a man of high moral caliber, a man whose talents and hard work rose him to the top of his profession. He was a dedicated Christian and a wonderful husband, father and grandfather.

"In a world where often times the watchword is 'Do as I say and not as I do,' Tom Landry never strayed from his ideals. He remained a consistent, shining example to all of us. All those are things that, deep down inside, all of us would like to be.

"I had the privilege of being with and working with my father very closely from the time he left the Cowboys until he entered the hospital for the last time. This was such a privilege because I had grown older in my life, I had my own children, and I was better able to understand and appreciate the role model he was and the wisdom that he could impart to me.

"During that time, we had a number of activities. One of those was making speeches throughout the country. One of Dad's speeches was entitled 'Commitment to Excellence.' The theme of that speech was an ideal that was central to my father's beliefs. As he quoted: 'The quality of a man's life is in direct proportion to his commitment to excellence.'

"It was this commitment to excellence in all aspects of my father's life that made him great—it could be his job, it could be his family, it could be his Christian faith, it could be his compassionate dealings with other people. It was simply an effort to strive to do the very, very best at whatever it was a person was doing.

"As I look out at this crowd, I can't help but reflect on all the tributes and all the friends and people who were touched by my father. I can't help but think about the effect that he had on everyone.

"You've heard many of his players say that after they left football, they finally understood what he was talking about, and he became a man they loved like a father. He had tremendous compassion for his players and coaches, as well as for every person, no matter what their status in life.

"I can't tell you how many times we have received a letter, card or telephone call recounting some act of kindness unknown to anyone but Tom Landry and that person. I would like to read you one of those letters now because it represents countless others we have received through the years.

"This one is dated several months ago and I shared it with my father while he was in the hospital."

> *Dear Coach Landry,*
>
> *In the summer of 1979, my 14-year-old son Paul was dying of cancer in a New York City hospital. He was a Cowboys fan. And someone got through to you and told you about Paul and gave you the phone number of his room.*
>
> *Later, my wife was with Paul in the room when the phone rang and a man said, "Hi. I'm Coach Tom Landry. May I speak to Paul?"*
>
> *Paul's eyes opened wide as he said hello. You told Paul that you were rooting for him to beat his cancer, that you thought Paul was very brave. And you thanked him for being a Cowboys fan. You then introduced Roger Staubach, who also encouraged Paul to keep fighting.*
>
> *My wife told me that Paul hung up the phone and he was like a new person. He said, "Wow, Mama. That was Dallas Cowboys Coach Tom Landry and his quarterback. He knows about me and he wants me to keep fighting."*
>
> *Tom, your phone call did a tremendous contribution to Paul's determination. Later that year, my son died. And I know that he would want me to send this message to you.*
>
> *Now that you're fighting your own battle with leukemia, I'm confident that Paul is praying for you, Tom.*
>
> *You might think that your phone call was just a small thing, but my wife and I hold in our hearts the cherished memory of a moment of pure joy for Paul that brought him an enduring sense of strength.*
>
> *Mother Teresa said, "God does not expect us to do great things, only small things that bring love."*
>
> *Thank you for giving the blessing of your great love to Paul.*

"Incidentally, and coincidentally, my father's favorite figure in the Bible is the apostle Paul."

Like his father, Tom Jr. kept his emotions in check while others struggled with theirs. He then shared a story from their business relationship.

"I had been working on a very complicated deal and when I thought I had it all figured out, I went into Dad's office and sat down—somewhat proud of myself, I might add—to tell him how I felt we should proceed.

"Any of you who have been across the desk from Tom Landry know he is a great listener, even when he knows where you are headed—which is most of the time. He will be very patient. He'll listen. He won't interrupt. And he will let you finish what it is you have to say before he comments.

"Well, I sit down, and I start describing how I had this deal all worked out. I went through the whole complicated and somewhat tricky scenario. Then, I looked at Dad, and said, 'Dad, what do you want to do?' And he said to me these words: 'I want to do what's fair.'

"Think about those six words: I want to do what's fair. Think what our lives would be like if our actions were dictated as his were—by only trying to do what's fair."

Tom Jr. closed with the memory of the April 1989 celebration of his father's career, which included a parade through downtown Dallas and a ceremony at Texas Stadium. The son remembered that it was "one of the moments that touched my father the most."

"Dad was afraid no one would show up. He only missed that mark by a few hundred thousand.

"I like to think that, now, one more parade is

Landry with his game face on. (Photo courtesy of the Dallas Cowboys)

being held for Tom Landry, and that parade will line the highway to heaven.

"The presence of Tom Landry on earth made this a much better place and his presence in heaven will make heaven a much better place. He may be gone from our world in life, but he will remain in our hearts forever. He will never be forgotten by those of us whose lives he touched so deeply."

Minister Mark Craig

Mark Craig spoke twice, first to open the service then again after Staubach and Landry Jr. Each time, he shared personal memories and passionately described his feelings for Landry.

He began with by telling of "the greatest gift I ever had on Christmas Day," a visit to Tom Landry's hospital room—No. 616 in the Roberts building of Baylor Hospital—less than two months earlier.

"I walked in, said hello to Alicia and we talked. And for the next 20 minutes—most of it was just a blur—I stood at the end of the bed of Coach Tom Landry. Coach Landry was heavily medicated and couldn't speak, but he knew I was there. And I just stood.

"I can't tell you why it was such a great gift, except I just stood. And I cried. And it wasn't one of those cries where you try to pretend you're not crying. I wasn't embarrassed. I didn't have intense suffering in my life. But I stood at the end of this bed on Christmas Day 1999 and I just cried.

"I started thinking, 'Why am I crying?' I realized it was because I was standing in the presence of greatness. I don't think we often have the opportunity to stand in the presence of greatness. And when we do, if we do, have that opportunity, it is very emotional. It was for me.

"As I stood there on that Christmas Day, looking into his face, I simply said to myself, 'This is a great gift. Tom Landry is a great gift. A great gift to his family. A great gift to our church. A great gift to our city. A great gift to athletics. A great gift to his nation.' And I started thinking what a great gift he is to the boys and girls all over the United States of America who for many years have looked at him as a great hero, a great leader and a great man. And I was thinking what a great gift I had this Christmas morning.

"Then, I realized that if he were here speaking to us today, he'd be very, very modest and say, 'It's not that great a gift.' And he would remind us that there's a greater gift that was talked about in the Gospel of John when God said, 'God so loved the world that he gave his only son. Whoever believes in it should not die but have eternal life.'

"Coach Landry would say that is the greatest of all gifts—God's love. So, on this day, we're here to celebrate two great gifts—the gift of Coach Tom Landry and the gift of God's love. They both are worthy of our praise and worthy of our thanksgiving and indeed worthy of our celebration."

When Craig spoke again later in the service, he further detailed the awe in which he held Landry.

"The most important thing for me in coming to this church was the opportunity to do what I'd always wanted to do: meet Coach Landry.

"But he always sat back over there, so far back that I couldn't make it to him after the service. All the kids were always around him. I never could get through.

"Then we had a dinner in our Fellowship Hall that September after I'd come here. We asked the 200 most prominent families to come and talk to them about money; preachers do that. I saw Coach Landry sitting down with Alicia and I was on my way over—and I froze. I just couldn't do it.

"I said to (fellow minister Kenneth M. Dickson), 'I want to meet Coach, but I have a problem. I don't know what to call him.' He said, 'Well, call him Tom.' I said, 'No, I just can't do that, I don't know what to call him.' He said, 'You have to call him Tom.' I said, 'Why do I have to?' He said, 'Because, you're the preacher and he's a member of the church. You have to call him Tom.' So I said, 'Well, if I have to, I'll do it.'

"So I went over and I said hello to Alicia, and I turned to her husband, and I started stuttering, 'T-t-t-t-t-t—' I'm not a stutterer, but I got into a stuttering block. I remember feeling foolish, just mumbled something, shook his hand and walked away. I thought that would pass.

"But in our communion service, when people come for commune, we generally serve them, and I will say, 'God bless you, Mary,' or 'God bless you, Bill,' or 'God bless you, Jack.' I never was able to say 'God bless you, Tom.'

"I often thought that was a weakness. And then, when I thought back later, after all this had happened, what I realized was there were only two people on the planet I was afraid to call by their first name. I think I could call a bishop or pope or president by their first name, but I couldn't call my father by his first name and I couldn't call Tom Landry by his first name."

Then Craig told of the greatest sermon he ever heard, one given by Landry on Palm Sunday 1996.

The basis of Landry's speech was his relationship with God and how it endured even through the death of his youngest child, Lisa Landry Childress. She was 37 when a four-year battle with liver cancer ended in May 1995.

"Coach Landry came and preached from this pulpit; it was the first time a lay person had ever spoken on a Palm Sunday here. It wasn't complicated. Coach Landry just got up there in a modest way and started saying, 'I don't know why I'm here.'

"Then he started talking and he just listed, chronologically, all the things that had happened in his life. He didn't do it in a bragging way—he did it in a very modest way. It's hard to talking about winning a Super Bowl in a modest way. He said, 'I won the Super Bowl' and then he won another one and he got to the epitome of his sermon—and he just stopped! Just stopped.

"And he said, 'But I still felt Him. I'd won all there was to win, but I still felt Him. It wasn't until I felt God's love come into my life in the person of Jesus Christ until I felt happiness and wholeness in my life.' I remember sitting right here, and I said to myself, 'He's just like me! He feels emptiness in his life too!'

"Then he stopped and started going in another direction with his sermon and started talking about what it was like to lose a daughter to death, the pain and the suffering and the agony of losing a child. I can't even imagine how dysfunctional I'd be.

"He started talking about the pain and the agony of that and simply said, 'But God got me through it. The power of Jesus Christ helped sustain me, and I got through it.' I remember saying, 'I could never be like that. I could never be like that.'

"So there was a feeling of ambivalence. I was saying, 'Well, I can be like that or I can't be like that.' And that's the way Jesus Christ is, actually. He's someone you say, 'I can identify, but I could never be that great.' I think that's the greatness of Coach Landry."

Landry's humility and generosity were part of what made him so beloved. Craig stumbled onto another story the morning of this service.

Here's how he described it:

"I was coming back to my car from a breakfast at 7 a.m. It was probably 8:15. Somebody waved and said, 'Hey, hey, hey. You're doing Coach Landry's service today.'

"Yeah, I am," the minister said.

"That's great. Coach Landry came to my house," the man said.

"What? Coach Landry didn't come to your house. When did Coach Landry come to your house?"

"Well, early in the 1970s, he came to my house."

"Did you invite him?"

"No. He came unannounced to my house."

"You've got to be kidding me!"

"He came with a pledge card."

"A church pledge card?"

"Yes. On Sunday afternoon, all the members of the church got pledge cards and they went out to everyone's home."

Craig paused the dialogue to add: "I thought, 'This is unbelievable.' The coach of the Dallas Cowboys gets this at church, just like everybody else, and goes out house-to-house, knocking on someone's door and saying, 'Will you pledge to our church?'

Then he picked up with the end of the story.

"Did you pledge?"

"Man, what would you do if Coach Landry came to your house? I pledged. I pledged!"

Craig closed with two scriptures, the first of which was coincidentally picked by him and the Landry family, something he said had never happened to him before.

"I was talking with the family in my office two or three days ago, and we were talking about scriptures. Kitty simply said to me, 'There was one scripture, and I don't know what it was, but it was very important to my dad, and I hope I get that scripture right.'

"But I knew at that moment what that scripture was. I don't know why I knew it, but I knew what it was. Of the thousands and thousands and thousands of scriptures, I don't know why it came to my mind, but I just knew.

"I found this scripture that said: 'For God did not give us a spirit of timidity, but the spirit of power and the spirit of understanding.' I think the reason it flashed in my mind is this is Coach Tom Landry. He's a man who knew he had a spirit of power—he had a great spirit of power—and no spirit of timidity. And he had a spirit of power that did great things for many people and a spirit of understanding that nurtured people at their most difficult times.

"One final scripture: Paul said to the enlightened, 'You need to run, and you need to run the race.' He said, 'You need to run the good race, and you need to try to win the race.'

"Coach Tom Landry not only ran the good race, he won the gold medal, the absolute gold medal, and that's eternal life.

"And for that, we celebrate two great gifts: The gift of Coach's life and his power and his understanding, and the gift of God's love, Jesus Christ. Both are worth our praise and thanksgiving. Amen."

PUBLIC SERVICE

Dr. Charles Swindoll, president of the Dallas Theological Seminary, began by welcoming everyone to a tribute in honor of "a man who has touched and impacted all our lives."

TOM LANDRY
1924 – 2000

*And we know that all things
work together for good
to them that love God,
to them who are the called
according to His purpose.*

ROMANS 8:28

MORTON H. MEYERSON SYMPHONY CENTER
DALLAS, TEXAS

FEBRUARY 17, 2000

*Program from public memorial service. An enlarged version of the Landry
photo was on the stage.*

"Tom Landry. No name is better known across the city of Dallas. No head coach in the National Football League has ever been more greatly respected for his mixture of faith, integrity, determination, intensity, discipline and humility. No athlete who ever had the privilege of playing on one of his teams—and there are many in this room today—ever doubted his unswerving commitment to excellence.

"They will tell you he fought cleanly, he felt deeply, he studied passionately. He innovated creatively, he despised mediocrity and he embraced priorities—the right priorities. Those priorities were frequently repeated: God, your family and then your work. For him, work was the game of football.

"As Coach Landry would've put it, the game may be important but not more important than your family. And the family, though very important, is not more important than your God.

"Now, not everybody agreed with Tom Landry. But that never concerned the man. They were his convictions, his priorities and he believed in them with his whole heart, regardless of others' opinions. That became one of the inimitable characteristics of his leadership: secure and confident, but always modest. He was never swayed by the shifting sands of popular opinion."

Paul Tagliabue

NFL commissioner Paul Tagliabue worked for the league long before replacing Pete Rozelle in the top job, giving him a great understanding of Landry's impact on pro football.

"If there were a Mount Rushmore for the NFL, the profile of Tom Landry would have to be there, wearing his trademark hat for all of us to marvel at.

"Each day, when I go to work, I walk past one of Coach Landry's hats in our offices in New York. It's displayed there along with the Vince Lombardi Super Bowl trophy and other marks of the league's history. The display case contains a summary of Coach Landry's extraordinary record. And the final inscription says of the hat: 'Gift of Tom Landry to the National Football League.'

"Well, thank you, coach, but the truth is, Tom Landry himself was one of the greatest gifts ever given to the NFL.

"The spirit and the values of Coach Landry will always be with us in the National Football League, as they should be, because he truly was not just the greatest Dallas Cowboy and a legendary New York Giant. Tom Landry was the genuine article, a legend across the entire history of pro football.

"Coach Landry's presence on the Cowboys sideline for three decades represented the NFL at its best. He will be remembered for many, many special reasons, including the innovations he brought to the game and the great teams he brought to the field . . . .

"Coach Landry's legacy is far greater than the Cowboys' 20 consecutive winning seasons and Super Bowl victories. His legacy is one of towering achievement, of modest demeanor, of discipline, teamwork, straight talk, loyalty, commitment and faith. It is a legacy that has no use for ego, instant gratification, wasted talent, opportunism, shortcuts and, yes, no use for taunting, end zone dances or other on-field shenanigans.

"Coach Landry's legacy is a legacy that my generation and every future generation of NFL leaders will know to pursue because of his example.

"Thank you, Coach, for the gifts you have given all of us in the National Football League. In addition to your sideline hat, your life's work will always be a treasured part of our history."

Tex Schramm

As the first general manager of the Dallas Cowboys, Tex Schramm hired Tom Landry and worked with him to build the franchise into "America's Team."

Landry gave Tex Schramm 270 victories to smile about. (Photo courtesy of the Dallas Cowboys)

"Tom Landry and I started in a restaurant, a little one in Connecticut in 1959, and we talked about him coming to Dallas and coaching a football team, because in those days, we didn't have a franchise. But just showing the character and the confidence and the beliefs that Coach Landry had, we agreed that night that he would come to Dallas and coach the team.

"In January, we got our franchise, and we had a team, and he was probably the center block in making that team go on to the, I think, greatest heights you can imagine during his career.

"Today marks a closure to a very great individual . . . who made the Dallas Cowboys become something special and made the team represent something special to the rest of the country.

"I'm sure Tom will be up there looking. I hope we can all fulfill in our own personal lives now the great things he had in mind during his life here."

Ann Murchison

Ann Murchison, widow of Dallas Cowboys founder Clint Murchison Jr., spoke about Alicia Landry, the great woman behind the great man.

"When I think of the man Tom Landry, believe it or not, I don't first just think of him as one of the greatest football coaches in the history of the NFL, though he was.

"I don't just think of him as a very generous, supportive, kind and thoughtful man, though he was.

"I don't just think of him as a dedicated and Godly Christian man of great integrity, though he was.

"When I think of Tom Landry, I think first of 'them'—Tom and Alicia. For them, one plus one always equaled one. Alicia was the most important of all Tom's teammates. Sorry, guys.

"As busy as he was, I never sensed for one moment that Alicia ever felt that she was second in his life. In the 30 years I have known her, Alicia has consistently exuded a quiet assurance that no one could ever take her place, and, most assuredly, no one will ever take his place in her heart.

"There's an ancient symbol for wife in Chinese that literally means the hidden or inside man. In other words, the Chinese believe that a man's wife was a revelation of his own heart. Know her, you know him; know him, you know her.

"I know a no lovelier, more supportive or loving woman and wife than Alicia Landry. And she is indeed a revelation of Tom Landry's own good and kind heart and he hers. Even after 51 years of marriage, it was 'they' who was the real team. Tom knew he could always find love, peace, rest, laughter with Alicia. She made their home a quiet refuge. She was his devoted partner, his adoring lover, his silent confidante, his ardent defender and his greatest fan. And, let me tell you, when you hurt Tom, you hurt Alicia.

"You were a rare and precious jewel to Tom, Alicia. Tom valued you more than all the Super Bowl rings and all the awards he ever received. Side by side, you loved, you raised children, you enjoyed grandchildren, you dreamed, you shared the heartbreak of burying a beautiful daughter. Together, you cried, you prayed, and you loved and served the Lord with all your heart.

"No one really needs to tell you this, Alicia, but I'm going to say it anyway: You lit up Tom's life. You two lived a great love story that will not end just because he is no longer here. He is not just with you in the many scrapbooks, plaques and trophies on your walls and shelves. He is with you in your children and grandchildren. He is with you in all the wonderful memories you have built together, and he is forever etched upon your heart and your mind.

"You were Tom's hero, Alicia, and you are my hero too.

"I'm sure that the first words Tom heard when he entered heaven were, 'Well done, good and faithful servant.' But I want to say the same thing to you, dearest Alicia: Well done, good and faithful servant."

Sam Huff

Tom Landry created the middle linebacker position when he was an assistant coach on the New York Giants. The first person to have the job was Sam Huff, who blossomed into a Hall of Famer. Though known for his ferociousness on the field, Huff had gentle memories of his former coach.

"I first met Tom Landry in 1956. It sure doesn't seem so long ago, but I know it was. It was at the New York Giants' training camp in Winooski, Vermont. You could get in there, but you couldn't get out of there.

"I was an offensive guard and tackle from West Virginia, a position that just did not fit me. As a matter of fact, I hated it. I couldn't play it, I didn't like it and Coach Landry knew it. He moved me to middle linebacker and inspired me to be his first middle linebacker in the NFL.

"When the regular season started, a majority of the New York Giant players and coaches stayed at the same hotel on the west side of New York. Tom would call me every night to ask what I was doing. And, of course, I would say nothing. So, he'd say, 'I'd like for you to come down to my and Alicia's place and let's discuss football.' Little did I know this was the making of his 4-3 defense.

"I did not know then how blessed I would be, as others who followed me when he came to Dallas—Jerry Tubbs, Lee Roy Jordan, Chuck Howley and every linebacker who played for him from then on.

"The New York Giants at that time had the two best coaches to ever step on a playing field: Vince Lombardi, the offensive coach, and Tom Landry, the defensive coach.

"These two people were completely different. Lombardi was basic, fundamental football: hard, tough, military style, and he made you believe that no one could defeat you if you had the desire, the determination and will to win. Tom, on the other hand . . . football was something that technique-wise you could do, he could teach you to do. He'd always say, 'Play my defense the way it's designed, take your keys off what the other team has done in the past, and react.' Tom made you believe that no one can defeat you if you have that teamwork and tackle hard.

"I remember my first interception in the National Football League. I was really excited. When I came off the field, I was expecting a pat on the back. Not a high five, like they do now, but just a little pat on the back, a nice word from Coach Landry. What I received was a very hard look that only Landry could do. As I tried to explain what I had just done, all he said was, 'Sam, you must play my defense.' I said, 'I intercepted the pass! I read the quarterback's eyes. I went 10 yards deep. I broke on the ball. I intercepted it. It's a turnover.' 'Your pass drop was the wrong way. You cannot do that. You must play my defense.'

"Yes, sir. I never went the wrong way again my whole career.

"People always ask me what was my greatest moment in sports. I always tell them it was the day that Tom Landry inducted me into the Pro Football Hall of Fame. . . . There is no greater thrill in your life than to be inducted into that Hall of Fame, particularly by Tom Landry. He was absolutely fantastic.

"Every player that has ever played for Tom Landry has to be a better person. As you all know, and have heard here, Tom Landry and Vince Lombardi were very religious people and true believers in the almighty God.

"This is a vision that I will always have about those two—Vince Lombardi sitting at one hand of God's and Tom Landry at the other, saying, 'Let the game begin.'"

Don Perkins

Like Landry, Don Perkins was signed before Dallas was even granted an NFL franchise. The running back was Rookie of the Year in 1961 and that same season became the first Cowboy to start a Pro Bowl. The first big offensive star of the Landry era was the second inductee into the team's Ring of Honor.

"Sam, I'm glad you took the opportunity to say that Tom was not the easiest guy to work for because I was going to have to say it.

"Tom, you were certainly an enigma to all of us. We loved you and you scared the hell out of us, simultaneously.

"Many of you have heard about the infamous Landry Mile. Well, I was the first notorious failure of the Landry Mile. I would like to assure you, though, that I wasn't the only one. We had followers in years to come—one of them up here on the dais in the name of Mr. Bob Lilly.

"When I had my first private interview with him, it was probably the first private interview that any Cowboy had because it was in 1960. You people who know Tom Landry can just about imagine how the interview went: He talked, and I listened.

"But he really didn't talk much. Tom didn't need to talk much. Tom could just look at you and give you a look of disappointment, and you knew you had to key it up a notch or two. I think all of us learned that.

"I hear an expression used often times today where they refer to a coach as a 'father figure.' I'm not real high on that phrase, but I think it's applicable with Tom and Don Perkins because he was like a father figure to me. I was scared of my father and I was scared of Tom. I think a lot of you know what I'm talking about when you talk about that fear of your father. It's not as though he has ever laid a hand on you, but you had the fear that he might. It was like that with Tom. One of the things we did not want to do was disappoint him.

"But, Tom, I can tell you, we had a little fun at your expense sometimes before meetings started.

"Now those of you who have labored with Coach Landry remember that if a meeting was scheduled for 9 o'clock and Tom showed up at five to 9, that's when the meeting started. And if you came at three minutes to 9, you were late. So, we were always there early. As a result of this, we had time to play little games and do things and not really own up to it. We knew about Tom's very strict religious beliefs. . . . Somebody had written on the board that the wages of sin were $7.26 an hour, or something to that effect. And, of course, when Tom comes in, he takes one glance on it and sees that nobody is going to show any sign of emotion, so it goes off the board and is erased and the meeting goes on.

"I played with the Cowboys during the '60s when our country was so racially torn and racially divided. One of the things that I can appreciate as a Cowboy and as a player is that we as Cowboys players, we transcended ethnicity and racial differences. I think Tom was a big part of that. In spite of the things going on around the country, it never affected us as players. When I see the old players from the '60s whom I know best, you know we try to pull it off in a manly way and extend a handshake, and it doesn't come off quite close enough because we don't feel that. It ends up in an embrace. I'm grateful for that from my athletic experience with the Cowboys at that time.

"I think the game of football was kind of incidental to Tom. I think what Tom wanted us to be was the best we could be. We would have these caucuses after games and we would review video. We had won the game and, almost to the man, coming out of the viewing of the video we would look at each other with astonishment because of the critiquing of it and say, 'We won, didn't we?' I think Tom lived his life that way, and I'm forever grateful for that because it wasn't about winning and losing—and life is not about winning or losing, whatever that is—it's about being the best you can be. I think I learned that first-hand through practical experiences from Tom Landry.

"We'll miss you, Tom. We love you. It's a word that we males kind of throw around like manhole covers. It's real hard for us to express those kinds of things, but we do love you, and we will miss you."

Bob Lilly

Bob Lilly was the first player ever drafted by the Dallas Cowboys. The defensive tackle went on to become the first member of the Ring of Honor and the first Hall of Famer. Nicknamed "Mr. Cowboy," Lilly played in a team-best 11 Pro Bowls.

"My first recollection of the Cowboys was when I came to Dallas. I was a senior in college in Fort Worth over at TCU. I couldn't believe, not only were the Dallas Cowboys here, but there also were the Dallas Texans—and they both drafted me. So, I knew I was going to stay in Texas. That was quite a thrill for a guy who grew up in Throckmorton, which was 1,000 people—and I barely made the team in Throckmorton. I don't know how in the world I got a scholarship to TCU.

"My senior year in college was an interesting year. That was the year that Roger Maris and Mickey Mantle were shooting for the home run championship. I happened to see them interviewing Mickey Mantle on TV one day. I saw Mickey at his locker. It was about 10 feet wide, had his name in big letters, his pinstriped uniforms on the left. It was carpeted. He had a nice, big chair in his locker and he had a big cigar in his mouth—that's where I got that cigar, Alicia, when we won our first Super Bowl, that was my idea, from Mickey Mantle. Anyway, that was my vision of pro football.

"My vision was I was going to get out of this dressing room at TCU, and I'm going to go over and have my own locker with my name on it with my Cowboy uniform in there with the stars on the side, and I'm going to be big time.

"Mr. Cowboy" Bob Lilly was the team's only player on the NFL's all-century team. (Photo courtesy of the Dallas Cowboys)

"Well, my first meeting was at Burnett Field—which brings up another subject. I always wanted to ask Coach Landry what he felt like when he came from Yankee Stadium to Burnett Field. A lot of you younger guys don't know about Burnett Field, but I'll tell you about it.

"I came to my first meeting, and I kept going around this condemned baseball stadium. I was looking for a door to go in and I went around, and around, and there was no door. There was an opening, but there was no door.

I went in there and they had military style lights with wire and 30-watt bulbs. You could barely see. I went into the room where I heard voices coming out of and I heard Coach Landry's voice.

"The blackboard in there was made of green slate—real old green slate. And when you marked on it with chalk, it squeaked real bad. For those of you that that bothers—and I'm one of them—you know what I mean.

"Well, anyway, I came in, and Coach Landry introduced me. Then, he progressed to put his priorities in life on that blackboard:

No. 1, he put God.

No. 2, he put family.

And No. 3, he put football.

"He never did put money in there anywhere. I don't think in all the years I knew Coach Landry that money ever entered into his mind. He always told us if we did a good job, we had faith in what we were doing, we worked hard at it and we win, all the good things follow—and he was right about that.

"But then, when he finished saying God, family and football, he said, 'Lilly, that'll cost you 50 next time you're late.'

"We did not like hearing his voice because it either meant you were going to get fined or he was displeased.

"The only fear Tex Schramm and Coach Landry had about us as players back then was that we were going to find a better job outside of football, right, Tex? In fact, when I got out of college, I had an offer to go coach for $1,000 less than I got to play for the Cowboys—and after the first year, I almost took it. I only had a broken foot, a torn up knee and a broken thumb that rookie year.

"I wasn't supposed to play in this one game, and Coach Landry came up to me and said, 'We've only got four linemen Bob. It looks like you're going to have to play.' So, they taped my legs stiff and I played. Then, on Monday, he said, 'Boy, that's the worst game I've ever seen any defensive end play in my life.' And I'm thinking, 'You've already forgotten, coach, that my knee was hurt? Remind me to never get hurt again.'

"Anyway, that was the beginning. We limped along and became winners to a certain extent. Bridesmaids, I think they called us. Then we went to Pittsburgh in 1965. We had been picked by *Sports Illustrated* to win the Eastern Division of the NFL. At that time, Pittsburgh and Cleveland were in our division. After the game was over, we had lost. We had now become 2-5, which meant we had seven games to go to win our division. Well, Coach Landry got up and said, 'You have done everything I've asked of you.' He said, 'When I was in New York and Vince Lombardi and I used to spend all this time studying those films, I formulated what I thought would be the offense and defense of the future—the Flex defense and the multiple offense.' And then he said, 'I've let you down.' And then he wept.

"Alicia, he wept for several minutes. And we wept. And that same group of guys, that same nucleus of players—and you know who you are, a lot of you are here—we found out in our gut feeling we weren't giving 100 percent. We weren't giving 110 percent; we weren't even giving 100. And I think he touched all of us on that very day. We came back the next week and we started winning. We won five of the next seven and went to our first little playoff game that year. The Cowboys were winners the next 20 years, and 18 of them in the playoffs."

"So Coach Landry was right. His priorities in life were right, his belief in his system. The only problem he had was with us players—encouraging us and teaching us to have faith in what he was trying to teach us.

"He told me one time, he said, 'Bob, you could play an 11-man line if you had faith in it and win. But you can play the Flex defense with faith and win a lot more often.' That's the truth, and it proved itself out over a long period of time.

"But I think the main thing about Coach Landry . . . and I never could call him Tom. I can occasionally, but I just had to look up to him and call him Coach. Because he was my coach. He was like my second father. I know he was to many of you. He imparted principles and integrity and character in us that we probably lost when we went to college. And he kept doing it. He never stopped. I never saw anything like it.

"I thought when I went to that first meeting and he told me of his priorities, he was kidding. I really did. I couldn't believe that anybody would have their priorities in that order because I was green out of college. But when I quit football and was 35 years old, I realized that his priorities in life were the priorities I wanted in my life. I know many of my peers have done the same.

"If it hadn't been for Coach Landry, I don't know that my son Bob Jr. and my other children would be sitting here today. I don't know what would've happened to them. Because I tried, after I grew up, to impart those same values to my children.

"So, we are the legacy. These guys up here, you fellows out there, all the people that Coach Landry came into contact with—we are the legacy of Coach Landry. And we are going to spread that to our children and to our nation."

Rayfield Wright

Rayfield Wright was among the group of players privileged to play for all five of Tom Landry's Super Bowl teams. Wright joined the Dallas Cowboys as a tight end, then became a six-time Pro Bowl pick at offensive tackle.

"In 1967, when I was drafted by the Cowboys, I really didn't want to play football. I wanted to play basketball. And when I was drafted by the Cowboys, I had this phone call from a gentleman named Gil Brandt. He told me I was going to have the opportunity to play for one of the greatest coaches in the game.

"So he drafted me and I came to Dallas. And I had an opportunity to meet the man—and I knew it when I saw him. There was just something about him.

"I never will forget, after playing tight end for two years, he called me into his office one day and said, 'Rayfield, you're a good blocker at tight end. I want to move you, change your position, and put you in at offensive tackle.' I said, 'Coach, I've never played that position before.'

"But, you know, there was always something about the way he said things to you that kind of lifted your spirits and gave you hope knowing that you could do something, even if you hadn't done it before. And that's what I felt inside of me when he called me into his office. He said, 'You'll make a great offensive tackle.'

"So Coach Landry was a man of great vision to me. He could see things that we couldn't truly see at that particular time. And he saw that within me.

"I remember the first play that I began as an offensive tackle. It was against the Rams and I was facing a guy by the name of Deacon Jones. I'm

listening to my quarterback, Roger, and the ball was going to be snapped on two. As offensive linemen, Jim Myers will tell you, we're taught to stay focused and to listen. And I get in my stance and the ball's going to be snapped on the second hut. And there was a little pause in between there and I lost my focus and my concentration because I heard this voice that asked me if my mother knew I was on the football field. So, when Roger called the second hut, I never heard it.

"After the play was over, I'm laying on my back. I kind of rolled over a little bit, and I rolled over toward our sideline. You know

Landry made "Big Cat" Rayfield Wright a perennial Pro Bowl pick by changing his position. (Photo courtesy of the Dallas Cowboys)

whose eyes I focused into. He didn't have to say a word, but I could feel it. It was almost like you could just feel him saying something to you. And he was saying, 'Get up.' So, I got up.

"And Mr. Jones had a tough day after that play."

Drew Pearson

Drew Pearson went from being undrafted coming out of the University of Tulsa to becoming one of the most reliable receivers the Dallas Cowboys ever had. He also caught the most famous pass in team history, the "Hail Mary" that beat Minnesota in the 1975 playoffs.

When Pearson was involved in a car wreck that killed his younger brother and left himself seriously injured, Tom Landry was there for him. The coach who never got too close to his players spent several days in Pearson's hospital room.

After 11 seasons on the team, Pearson spent one season as an assistant coach, then went into the business world. He credits the principles Landry taught him for making him a success.

"When I got word of Coach Landry's death and passing . . . I felt that, deep within my heart, I needed my own time in my own place, by myself, to grieve over the loss of someone that I loved, someone that I admired and someone that I respected so much.

"Through the course of my grieving, my thoughts ran through the gamut of emotions. I felt shock, I felt denial, I felt anger, I felt confusion, I felt frustration, I felt fear, I felt helplessness, I felt numbness. But eventually, through all that, I felt a sense of acceptance.

Landry turned undrafted rookie Drew Pearson into the Cowboys' best clutch receiver. His most famous catch was the "Hail Mary" against Minnesota in the 1975 playoffs. (Photo courtesy of the Dallas Cowboys)

"I was at a point of not knowing what to do but wanting to do something. Then I realized that there really is no death. There really is no end. There is only transformation. Coach Landry has now made that transformation. He now exists in a new time, in a new place, in a new reality, and because of that, so do we.

"The relationship I had with Coach Landry has now transformed from the physical to the spiritual. But it certainly hasn't ended; it has only changed. And instead of talking to him face-to-face, eyeball-to-eyeball, I now communicate with him through prayers. And by grieving, I was able to release the negative thoughts and negative emotions that make it easier to accept this change.

"I also found out that grief is natural, it's normal, and it's to be expected. I further realized that I owed it to Coach Landry to grieve and to cleanse my soul of those negative thoughts . . . so I could accept this transformation. . . .

"I can't believe I played the game, pro football, in a league, the NFL, for a team, the Dallas Cowboys, for a coach, named Tom Landry. And I don't need any honors like the Ring of Honor or the Hall of Fame to accentuate or punctuate my career. What accents and punctuates my career more than anything is the fact I played 11 years for Coach Tom Landry. You can't get any more respect than that.

"When my children, and recently my grandchildren, ask me about my playing days in the NFL, I won't tell them about my catches or touchdowns, or even the Hail Mary. I'll simply say: 'I played 11 years for Coach Tom Landry.' And because they will know about Coach Landry and about his great success as a coach and about his great success as a person and they will also know about the great legacy that he has left, I suspect my children and grandchildren's response will be: 'Man, you must've been a good player to play for such a man for 11 years.'

"If I know Coach Landry like I think I do, he's probably up there in heaven right now trying to start his own football league. He'll probably call it the GFL—God's Football League. Of course, the team will be called the Dallas Cowboys, and we all know why that hole in the roof is there at Texas Stadium: so God can watch his team.

"He'll probably select Clint Murchison as his owner. He'll probably select Vince Lombardi as his offensive coordinator, George 'Papa Bear' Halas will probably be his defensive coordinator, and we must all believe that one or two Washington Redskins have made it to heaven, so he'll probably pick George Allen as his special teams coach.

"And you can bet that he's already recruited Mark Tuinei, Walter Payton and Derrick Thomas as players. And because he's looking for new recruits all the time, we all better beware and we all better get qualified to play in this new league.

"To qualify for the GFL, you don't have to be big, you don't have to be strong and you don't have to be fast. But what you do have to do is live your life according to God's standards. And you had better put all your faith and trust into the Lord, because if you don't, you'll never get the opportunity to play for Coach Landry and the GFL.

"One final thing. You know, in life, sometimes we don't get the opportunity to tell a loved one how we really feel about them. And I really feel blessed that I had the opportunity to tell Coach Landry before he passed on how I felt about him. Face-to-face, eyeball-to-eyeball, I told him simply what he meant to my life, how he's changed my life—through all the good times, through all the bad times—how he always seemed to have been there for Drew Pearson. I feel blessed that I had the opportunity to tell him those things.

"We're all going to miss Tom Landry, but we all know that if we do the right thing and live our lives the way he did, we'll have that opportunity to meet him again."

Randy White

Randy White was the star of the 1975 rookie crop known as "the Dirty Dozen," that helped lead the Dallas Cowboys to their third Super Bowl. When they returned two years later, White was the co-MVP.

The defensive tackle nicknamed "Manster" because he was supposedly half-man, half-monster went to nine Pro Bowls in 14 seasons. He was inducted into the Hall of Fame and Ring of Honor in 1994.

"I'll tell you my first memory of Coach Landry. I came to training camp as a rookie from the college all-star game along with Burton Lawless and a guy named Kyle Davis. We got there and there was Coach Landry. We had to run

Randy White was known as the "Manster"—half man, half monster. (Photo courtesy of the Dallas Cowboys)

this mountain out there in Thousand Oaks, California, and the coach was going to run it with us.

"We're thinking that we're going to outrun this guy. Well, we ran the mile and when we got finished, Coach Landry was down there, had caught his breath and was standing there waiting on us. When we got finished, I said, 'Man, the coach is in better shape than I am. I don't know if I'll ever be able to play football at the professional level.'

"Then Coach Landry moved me from defensive tackle to middle linebacker. Boy, I studied that middle linebacker. Man, I mean, I studied it! Bob Breunig and I would sit there and study it. Lee Roy [Jordan] would help me and I knew every answer to every question he could possibly ask me.

"But I was so intimidated by him, we'd get in those meetings and he'd ask me a question, and all I could do was grab the side of the table and go, 'Aaaaarrrrrrrggggggghhhhhh.' He did this time and time again, and I just, 'Aaaaarrrrrrrggggggghhhhhh.' So, he finally quit asking me the questions.

"They did an article on me one time for the *Game Day* magazine. I like to bass fish and they did an article about the Cowboys' fishing tackle. All the groups had gone out and just the offensive and defensive linemen were still in the locker room. I'm sitting in my locker by myself, getting fired up — I was always pretty intense at that time—and Coach Landry walked by my locker. He looked at me and he goes, 'Randy, that was really a nice article they had on you in that Game Day magazine today.' And I grabbed that side of the desk and said, 'Aaaaarrrrrrrggggggghhhhhh.'

"So, for the longest time, I don't think he thought I could make a whole sentence.

"He moved me to defensive tackle after my linebacker stint didn't work. When I was covering Tony Dorsett one-on-one out of the backfield, ooh, I knew I wasn't going to be a linebacker anymore. So he moved me to defensive tackle.

"Well, I weighed about 245 pounds. He made me go from 260 to 245. And I got to play against this guy from St. Louis. They had [Dan] Dierdorf, [Conrad] Dobler and all these guys, but I played against a guy named Bob Young. I tell you what, Bob Young was 300 pounds before these 300-pound guys got popular. . . . Well, they had a big old 245-pound running back, too. He'd get four, five yards on first down. Well, you know, that wasn't acceptable. You'd have to go into that meeting in front of all your teammates, everybody was up there. You could always tell if you played a good game because he'd go, 'Randy did this,' or 'Randy did that.' But every time we played these guys, it'd be, 'White, you got to stop them on the line of scrimmage.' Then, he'd show you getting knocked back five, six yards. 'White, you got to stop them on the line of scrimmage.' I always wanted to say, 'Coach, you stop them on the line of scrimmage. I can't!'

"My dad died the night before a football game. I didn't tell anybody but Bob Breunig and Bob had told Coach Landry. That next day, I shared a moment with Coach Landry that I'll never forget in my whole life.

"I was getting introduced before the game. The defense was getting introduced, and I shook his hand, and I had tears in my eyes. It was a pretty emotional time. I looked in his eyes, and he said, 'Sorry to see that he's gone.' And he had a tear in his eyes. He shook my hand and . . . I tell you what, when I think of Tom Landry, that's what I think about.

"Tom Landry is one of the finest people I have ever had the opportunity to be associated with. He's somebody I look up to, somebody I respect, somebody that taught me and somebody that I love and will always love. He'll always have a special place in my heart. I'll never, ever forget him.

"The thing I remember and respect most about Tom Landry is that he didn't just talk the talk, he walked the walk. And that's more than anybody could ever do."

Dan Reeves

Dan Reeves was one of Tom Landry's favorites. Signed as a free agent quarterback, Landry turned Reeves into a halfback who lasted eight years, his last three as a player-coach.

Reeves remained an assistant seven more years then went on to become a successful head coach with the Denver Broncos, New York Giants and Atlanta Falcons. He's coached four Super Bowl teams and is a member of the Pro Football Hall of Fame.

"I'm Dan Reeves, a free agent running back for the Dallas Cowboys. You've been listening to all the Pro Bowl players and All-Pros. I was a free agent back when 'free' really was free.

"I can't tell you how much it means to me to sit up here and talk about a man who has meant so much to me and my family. And I'm honored because when I look out, I see so many people who played and coached

Landry gave Dan Reeves a shot to play in the NFL, then helped him become a successful head coach. (Photo courtesy of the Dallas Cowboys)

for Coach Landry who certainly deserve to be up here and would give anything to be able to tell you how much Coach Landry has meant to them. So, I appreciate you giving me this opportunity.

"And, Ann, I just say Amen to all you said. You know, Coach Landry was certainly the person that gave us our character and gave us our integrity and gave us our competitiveness, but Alicia, you were the one that gave us class. I can't tell how nice it was to get off that plane or get off that bus and go into a hotel and have the greatest looking couple in the world leading us. And coming after a game, regardless of whether we won or lost, for you to be there for Coach Landry showed so much class.

"I gotta say, Green Bay at 17 degrees below zero is a little easier than this, to really put into words exactly how you feel.

"You know, a lot of players have talked about Coach Landry, but I'd like to say there's a lot of coaches out here, too. Each of us who had the pleasure of coaching with Coach Landry, we always gave suggestions. A lot of times, they weren't used by Coach Landry because he was the guy who had to live with the decisions. I never really knew what that meant until I became the head coach. When you make those decisions, you have to live with them and sleep with them. Those suggestions are easy to make.

"I thought Coach Landry did it better than anyone because it meant something to him. He was always fair in everything that he said. He was always there talking about what was fair in every situation.

Reeves and Landry going over game plans. (Photo courtesy of Denne H. Freeman)

"I just want to kind of share a little bit about a side that people haven't talked about and that's the humorous side of Coach Landry. He did have a sense of humor. I always remember that.

"My first experience as a player-coach in 1970, one of the first jobs I had was putting in an off-season program for our players for the first time. I remember calling the players . . . for example, the phone would ring and I would say, 'Is Roger there?' And they'd say 'No, he's not.' So I'd say, 'Mrs. Staubach, would you please have Roger call me.'

"I thought that was terrible that I couldn't remember all the players' wives names. So I came into the staff meeting the next morning and Ray Renfro was on our staff at the time. You always knew when Ray didn't know somebody; he'd say, 'How you doing, partner?' So I told Coach Landry it'd be a good idea if we came up with a list where we had the players' names and address and phone numbers and we put their wives names on there so we could call them by their names. And Ray Renfro said, 'Boy, that's a great idea, coach. I come out of the dressing room after a game and all the players are standing around and all their wives are there and I never know what to call them.'

"And Coach Landry looked at him and said, 'So what do you call them? Mrs. Partner?'

"Coach Landry also kind of had a way where you didn't know sometimes whether he was sticking the needle to you, joking with you.

"I remember the first time I played quarterback in professional football. We were playing the Philadelphia Eagles, and Roger threw an interception early in the game. Bill Bradley intercepted it and when the play was over, the tackle was made, Roger was still lying down on the field. He was knocked out cold. Craig Morton went in and did a great job. We were ahead about 35-7 with about eight minutes to go in the fourth quarter. Coach Landry walked up to me—I was a player-coach—and he said, 'Dan, I don't think we need to take a chance on getting Craig hurt. Why don't you go in and finish up at quarterback.' So I knew real quick which was more important, the coach or the player. But he was already thinking about next week.

"Pat Toomay used to keep track of all the little things Coach Landry did. One of them was when he would go over a scouting report or a game plan with us, he'd always use the term 'this particular situation.' So we used to have a little contest trying to guess how many times Coach Landry would say, 'this particular situation.' I remember, coming out of meetings, guys would get together and say, 'How many did you get, Pat?' And Pat would say, 'I don't know. I quit at 45.'

"I'd just like to finish with this. About two months ago, I was fortunate enough to speak to Coach Landry on the telephone. I certainly didn't know at that time that that would be the last time that I would ever get a chance to talk to him. In this particular situation, Coach, I wish I had thought what probably a lot of the people wish they'd have thought the last time that they saw you, that we'd have used the three words that are the most beautiful in the English language and told you, 'I love you.'"

Chapter Three

BUILDING A
DYNASTY

Tom Landry had a choice.

It was 1959 and he was in his sixth year of coaching the New York Giants' defense. He'd done such a good job for so long that he'd become in hot demand to be a head coach.

The Houston Oilers wanted him to coach their AFL startup team and the Dallas Texans were interested, too. Another expansion team was headed to Dallas from the NFL, which hadn't added a team since the All-American Football Conference was absorbed in 1950. And, if he wanted the NFL but not an expansion team, he could always stick with the Giants another year when his boss, Jim Lee Howell, was going to retire.

Dallas was where Landry wanted to be. His family already was living there and he knew the NFL. The Cowboys just seemed like the perfect fit for him.

Besides, he didn't actually consider coaching a long-term job. To Landry, who had a business degree from Texas and an industrial engineering degree from Houston, football was still just something he was doing until going into the real world.

Cowboys founder Clint Murchison Jr., who had been a 130-pound halfback at MIT back in his college days, gave Landry a five-year contract for $34,500 per year. Landry supplemented his income by selling insurance in the off-season. One of his clients was CBS sportscaster Frank Glieber; after selling him a life insurance policy, Landry helped Glieber write his will.

Team founder Clint Murchison Jr. never wavered in his support of Landry. (Photo courtesy of the Dallas Cowboys)

Dallas came into the league too late to be part of the 1960 draft, so the roster was strictly stocked with other teams' leftovers. Some prearranged deals, most of them of the under-the-table variety, helped land a few decent players. Also, George Halas had helped arrange for Murchison to acquire college stars Don Meredith of SMU and Don Perkins of New Mexico.

The Cowboys didn't win a game the first year and through 1963 still hadn't won more than five games in a season. With only a year left on Landry's initial contract, Murchison gave his coach a 10-year extension. At the time, his record was 18-46-4.

"I do not offer suggestions to Landry," Murchison once said. "Furthermore, Landry never makes suggestions as to how I conduct my sixth-grade football team—which, incidentally, is undefeated. We have a professional standoff."

Dallas started to turn the corner in '65, going 7-7 and playing in "the playoff bowl." Then came the big leap.

The next two seasons, the Cowboys and the Green Bay Packers played for the NFL championship. Both were heartbreaking losses for Dallas, while Green Bay—which was coached by Vince Lombardi, Landry's fellow assistant for five years in New York—went on to win the first two Super Bowls.

In the first meeting, the Packers held off a late Cowboys rally to win, 34-27 at the Cotton Bowl on January 1, 1967. They closed the calendar year against each other too, playing December 31, 1967, one of the coldest days in Green Bay's chilly history. The Packers won what's remembered as the "Ice Bowl" on a last-second quarterback sneak from Bart Starr.

Playoff losses in '68 and '69 prevented the Cowboys from shedding their unwanted label: "Next Year's Champions." The worst part was that it fit. Dallas always seemed to be on the verge of breaking through, while Landry struggled to pick a starting quarterback—from Don Meredith and Craig Morton to Morton and Roger Staubach.

The Cowboys reached their first Super Bowl following the 1970 season, only to lose to Baltimore on a last-second field goal.

The following year, Dallas beat Miami, and the burden was lifted. The Cowboys were Super Bowl champions—and the glory days were just getting started.

Tex Schramm

Tom Landry and Tex Schramm were never what you would call buddy-buddy.

But together they forged one of the most formidable teams in the history of the NFL when it came to winning championships and marketing a product.

"Tom and I were never really close personally," Schramm said. "Ours was a business relationship."

Schramm remembers that when he worked for CBS in the late 1950s, Landry's name came up often.

"I kept hearing amazing things about Landry, who was the defensive coordinator of the New York Giants," Schramm said. "When Clint [Murchison] put the money up for an expansion franchise and hired me to be general manager, the first name I brought up was Tom's."

From 1954-58, the Giants had the best of two worlds. Vince Lombardi was offensive coordinator and Landry ran the defense. Head coach Jim Lee Howell handled the press and decided when to punt.

"The Giants had a great team," Schramm said. "I kept hearing what players thought of Tom. They talked about him like he was a god or something.

"He had invented the 4-3 defense. From my days as general manager of the Los Angeles Rams, I thought a head coach should come out of the defensive ranks. You talk to any good defensive coach and they always knew what the hell the offense was doing. I thought this would be the guy we would want."

Schramm, who attended the University of Texas, set up an evening with his wife and the Landrys as the Giants' 1959 season wound down.

"Marty and I had dinner in late December with Tom and Alicia," Schramm said. "He mentioned that [Houston Oilers owner] Bud Adams had called, but Tom said he would like to return to Dallas to either coach or sell insurance. He had in his contract with the Giants that he could sell insurance in the offseason. I told him we wouldn't likely have any offseason."

Landry struck a strong chord with Schramm.

"I liked the way he talked," Schramm said. "He was determined. He wasn't cracking any jokes. He was all business and that's what I was looking

Schramm celebrates the team's first Super Bowl victory. (Photo courtesy of the Dallas Cowboys)

for. He said OK, he'd come to Dallas."

Schramm said he made airline reservations for Landry to come to Dallas after the Giants' last game.

"It was with a commercial carrier," Schramm said. "We didn't have private planes in those days."

Schramm was scratching his head over where to make the announcement of Landry's hiring.

"Back in those days, they had some big Cotton Bowl press conferences," Schramm said. "So we went over to the Baker Hotel with Landry and announced his hiring. There were a lot of press guys there from all over the country."

On December 28, 1959, the day after the Giants lost the NFL championship to Baltimore, Schramm introduced Landry as the new head coach . . . of the Dallas Rangers. It wasn't until after the NFL formally approved the franchise on January 27, 1960, that the name was changed to the Cowboys.

On the field, things didn't start out too great. Dallas went 0-11-1 the first year and 4-9-1 the next. Landry came under media sniper fire by 1964.

"There was all this stuff in the media about getting a new coach and things weren't helped a lot when Tex Maule of Sports Illustrated predicted before the '63 season that we would win our conference," Schramm said. "To me, personally, I knew we were on a good track and it would be a matter of time.

"I went to Clint and told him I had a strong feeling about putting a coach in jeopardy and we needed to do something. I said, 'The players need to know that Tom is going to be there. I think we should do something like giving him a new contract.'

"Clint said, 'Give him a 10-year deal.'"

Schramm said the contract gave Landry the confidence he needed.

"Tom didn't change the way he did business, but you could tell he appreciated it," Schramm said.

Even when the Cowboys lost two close NFL championship games to Green Bay in the late 1960s and Super Bowl V to Baltimore, Landry kept his charted course.

"When we beat Miami in Super Bowl VI, Tom may have put on the field the most prepared team in the history of the game," Schramm said. "In all my years I never saw a team so mentally prepared. We finally got the monkey off our back and it was a big load off of Tom. You could see it in his face. No more were we 'Next Year's Champions,' like Steve Perkins had written."

The only time Landry and Schramm came close to clashing was over the Dallas Cowboys cheerleaders, those twisting beauties in short-short shorts and revealing blouses.

Landry didn't like the idea of their sideline gyrations stirring up the fans

"Tom was very cold to it, saying it was something he didn't approve of," Schramm said. "Then one time he referred to them as 'porno queens.'"

Schramm asked Landry to come to his office, where he had an X-rated surprise.

"I told Tom that we had a difference of philosophy, and I knew how he felt, but to call the cheerleaders 'porn queens' was a bad thing. I showed him a few moments of the real thing on tape," Schramm said. "I said, 'This is what your name for them meant. Here is a girl without clothes. This is a real porn movie. Do you know what you were saying? There is a big difference.'

"Tom got up and walked out the door and never said anything about cheerleaders again."

Despite five Super Bowl teams, the big slide eventually came for Landry, prompting thoughts of retiring.

Schramm said Landry came to him in 1985 and said, "I could retire soon. I think you ought to have somebody ready for a smooth transition. You ought to start now."

Starting in 1986, Schramm began making contingency plans, hiring Paul Hackett to help with the offense.

Schramm also interviewed Marty Schottenheimer, who had made a good mark at Cleveland.

"Marty and I even looked at houses in North Dallas," Schramm said. "Our plan was he would become defensive coach then would become head coach."

Then Landry changed his mind.

"I recall Tom saying at a press conference, 'I'm going to coach as long as Tex Schramm wants me,'" Schramm said. "Getting rid of Tom was something I didn't want to do. I was loaded with letters about getting a new coach.

"All the time Bum Bright was the owner, he was adamant about firing Tom. I said, 'If you want him fired, you fire him. I'm not going to do it.' I defended him all the time against Bum Bright.'"

Then Bright sold the team to Jerry Jones, who didn't mind firing Landry because he had Jimmy Johnson waiting in the wings. Two months later came the retirement of Schramm, who entered the Hall of Fame in 1991, a year after Landry.

Schramm was with Jones when he broke the bad news to Landry on a golf course in Austin.

"Tom was emotional and I was emotional," Schramm said. "I could tell by Tom's eyes that he was very upset."

Schramm said Jones might have done Landry a big favor in the unceremonious way he dumped the legendary coach of America's Team.

"It turned out to be the greatest thing in the world for Tom because he got the sympathy of the world," Schramm said. "All I know is we had a very special relationship. We were a team if there ever was one."

Gil Brandt

For 29 years, Gil Brandt worked closely with Tom Landry to find the talent that brought the Cowboys 20 consecutive winning seasons and five Super Bowl appearances.

"It was amazing to me how Tom comprehended things," Brandt said. "He understood computers and understood the vision you had to have to be successful.

"He was the first to bring in free agents and the first to have computer printouts of the opponent. He was the first to have an off-season program. All this stuff required additional time and work. There was never a period he wanted to stand still. I guess he would have sold papers on the corner if he had to."

Brandt, a former baby photographer who had a flair for discovering players, said, "I had a great relationship with Tom, and he was extremely easy to work for. If you made a bad draft choice, it wasn't some-

Former baby photographer Gil Brandt was Landry's top talent scout. (Photo courtesy of the Dallas Cowboys)

thing you heard about for weeks and years. It was, 'How can we make it not happen again?'

"He was always looking for ways to do things better. He was always trying to make a better mousetrap."

Landry went with Brandt once on a "Kicking Karavan" in search of placekickers. They traveled across the United States and even crossed the Atlantic, where European soccer players were given a chance.

"We'd be in an airport and he would be reading one of his western books while we waited for a plane," Brandt recalled. "People would crowd around for autographs and he would be very patient with them. 'Now, who did you want that to?' he would say. People would be astounded that he would take time to do that."

Brandt said Landry's daily discipline was amazing.

"If he said a meeting was at 8 a.m., he would walk into the meeting at five minutes til with a cup of tea," Brandt said. "He was methodical. There was never any idle time."

That included studying long and hard before the draft.

"We took Tony Dorsett No. 1 over Ricky Bell, who was being boosted by (assistant) Red Hickey," Brandt said. "Tom told him, 'Well, Red, do you realize that only four percent of the players with Bell's quickness make it to the Pro Bowl? Players with Dorsett's quickness make it to the Pro Bowl 100 percent of the time.'"

Case closed.

Dorsett also helped the Cowboys to a Super Bowl victory and became one of the most successful backs in NFL history. Bell had second-tier success.

Brandt said it was Landry's machine-like system that made him successful.

"Have you ever seen a boarded up McDonald's?" Brandt asked. "We had a great system and that's why we never got boarded up. Tom was always scouting himself and had an answer for teams trying to stop what he did."

Brandt disclosed that, every week, Landry set aside a little time for the fans.

"To this day, I don't think many people realized that it was Tom who answered their letters," Brandt said. "On Friday afternoon, he would close the door and answer those letters with secretary Marge Kelley, no matter who we were playing. That's one reason why he was so popular. There are a lot of fans out there with personal letters from Tom."

Brandt said it was a ritual that Landry would pick him up on game day for the drive to the Cotton Bowl and, later, Texas Stadium.

"He was the loosest when we had a tough game," Brandt said. "When it was an easy game, he was the tightest. He realized you couldn't falter against the weak teams. They scared him."

Brandt said Landry was the kind who could forgive and forget—even Jerry Jones.

"Tom didn't hold a grudge against anybody," Brandt said. "He didn't have that big an ego. I don't think even to his death he had any idea of his popularity."

The big names and the small names among the former players were at Landry's funeral.

"I saw only one guy there who I didn't know. I introduced myself, and it turned out to be Charlie Granger of Southern University, who only played half of one season," Brandt said.

Granger told Brandt: "I wanted to come back. I had to be there for Coach Landry."

Eddie LeBaron

Eddie LeBaron answered an urgent call from Tom Landry to be the first quarterback the Cowboys ever had.

LeBaron had retired and was practicing law when Landry tracked him down before the 1960 season.

"We had played against each other for many years," LeBaron recalled. "I was with the Washington Redskins and Tom was a defensive back with the New York Giants. I had always admired him. Tom said he really needed me, so I came aboard."

Landry wanted the 5-foot-9 LeBaron so badly, the Cowboys gave up their first pick in their first draft.

"We didn't win a lot, but I treasure my days in Dallas with Tom," LeBaron said. "I thought he would make a great coach, and he did. We had a good player-coach relationship. I thought he was brilliant.

"Of course, we were handicapped and didn't have many good people. It seems like the good guys we did have were always hurt. It was an interesting time."

LeBaron said Landry wasn't looking at wins and losses but preparing the team for business down the road when the personnel would be better.

"I remember one time, I went up to him and told him I thought we needed to simplify the game plan, and that if we did, we could beat the team we were going to play that week," LeBaron said. "Tom said the teams the Cowboys needed to learn how to beat were the Giants and the Cleveland Browns."

Landry told LeBaron, "We have to get our program and offense down so we can beat those teams in four or five years, when we have better personnel."

"That was an example of how Tom was always talking championships," LeBaron said. "Maybe we could have beaten a weaker team by pulling back on the offense, but Tom wanted to train the team in the multiple offense it needed to learn."

Don Meredith was a rookie in 1960, the team's rookie season, and it was LeBaron's job to teach him the best he could.

"Don and I were roommates on the road," LeBaron said. "He was a free spirit and didn't always agree with Tom on the way things should be run.

"I tried to help Don. I remember Tom asked me to work with him. Don turned out to be one of my favorite people. I told Don he had to learn not to argue with Tom because he had his way of doing things and that was it."

Dallas went 0-11-1 in 1960. Meredith started the 1961 opener against Pittsburgh, then was replaced by LeBaron in the second half. The Cowboys scored 10 points in the final 56 seconds to pull out a 27-24 victory—their first in a regular season game.

LeBaron remained the top quarterback through 1962. The torch was passed to Meredith in '63 and LeBaron went back into retirement after that season.

"Don was a great competitor. He was smart and had a real gun for an arm," said LeBaron, who later was the general manager of the Atlanta Falcons. "He would stand in there and take some big hits. The offensive linemen were still learning the system and Meredith paid the price. I remember Tom admired Meredith's toughness."

LeBaron had some disagreements with Landry, but not many. He remembers one argument he won every year.

"Tom had trouble with the time change every year," LeBaron said. "We would be on the road and Tom would say curfew was going to be at a certain time.

"I'd correct Tom, saying he hadn't figured the time change correctly. He usually thought it was fall forward instead of fall back. We would laugh about it, and he said, 'I guess I'll never get that right.'"

LeBaron later became a broadcaster for CBS and covered the Cowboys one season.

"Tom could dissect a team and tell you what would work better than anybody I ever saw," LeBaron said. "His theory was that he was going to give you a winning plan, and if you worked hard and followed the plan, you were going to win. He convinced the players that his plan would work.

"And it did very well."

Mel Renfro

Tom Landry sized up Mel Renfro during his rookie year and learned everything he needed to know.

"He said, 'Mel, I want to see you move,'" Renfro said. "So, I started backing up, cutting and covering guys, and he said, 'That's all I want to see.' And then he walked away.

"He knew I had what it took and as long as I'd learn the system and give what I could as far as my energy on the field, then he didn't have to worry about me. He said, 'Mel can do it and he does it well, so I'm not going to coach where I don't need to. I'll coach where I need to coach.'"

Landry was right. Renfro made the Pro Bowl as a defensive back the first 10 years of his 14-year career and was just as dynamic on kickoff returns.

Renfro, a second-round pick in 1964, was so good with the ball in his hands that he wanted to get a shot at offense. After all, he had been an All-American halfback and world-class sprinter while in college at Oregon.

In the 1966 training camp, Landry gave Renfro a shot at halfback. He was as elusive as hoped, but when he was caught, he got hurt.

"In one of the first league games, I broke my foot and sat for a few weeks," Renfro said. "When I came back, I was still hobbling a little bit, so Coach put me back at safety. It kind of shored up the defense when they were having some problems. He just felt it would be best if I stayed on defense because I was too injury prone carrying the ball and getting hit all the time."

The time Landry didn't spend coaching Renfro, he used to give other players attention. Renfro remembers one time when Landry tried a little too hard.

"He was trying to tell a linebacker how to do his drop, to run to a certain area on the field," Renfro said. "He was demonstrating a movement and he said,

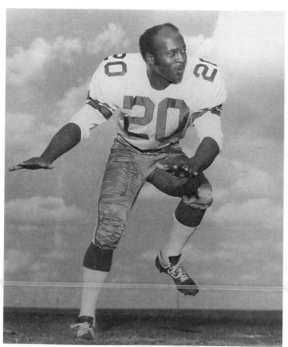

Landry knew Mel Renfro's fast feet were best suited for defense. (Photo courtesy of the Dallas Cowboys)

'Now, this is how I want it done.' And he turns and starts running, then trips and falls flat on his face.

"Everybody was just about to die with laughter, but nobody said a word. Then he got up and all he said was, 'Doggone it.' None of us could believe how he kept his cool."

Renfro went through some tough times after his career. What pulled him through was a devotion to God that he believes he gained by being around Landry for so long.

"He was never threatening with religion," Renfro said. "He was threatening with football and with you doing your job properly. He'd call you out and call it what it was if you made mistakes on the field. But as far as us thinking he was trying to lead us to Christ, we never felt that."

Renfro realized Landry's inadvertent impact years later.

"I knew he was a strong Christian, but I didn't know he was really using all those good things out of the Bible because I didn't go to the Bible all that much," he said. "As I study the Bible now as a strong believer, I see Coach Landry's name and face written all over the scriptures.

"I've said many times that there's no wonder we became perennial winners and America's Team because it was coming straight from the Gospel, straight from the Bible."

Renfro said Landry left a legacy that will never be forgotten.

"Whenever you think about pro football, the Cowboys, the state of Texas—Landry has got to be in the forefront. It will always be that way," Renfro said. "He made such a great contribution, not only to the game and to the city and to the state and the country, but to a lot of players' personal lives.

"Because of him, we have all become better people and we will make our children better people and hopefully, their children. His legacy was very dramatic and significant. We're all very thankful for it."

Lee Roy Jordan

Other than wearing hats, what do Tom Landry and Paul 'Bear' Bryant have in common? Each coached a championship team that featured Lee Roy Jordan.

"The highlight of my life, behind my family, is having had the opportunity to play for Coach Landry and Coach Bryant," Jordan said. "They were both excellent planners. Both didn't want to leave anything to chance. Both would go back and study films that were five, six or even 10 years old just in case they might bring something out. They were very thorough in their preparation."

Their personalities, though, were very different.

"Coach Bryant was much more verbal and an animated kind of guy," Jordan said. "Coach Landry was much quieter, calmer. I think Coach Landry felt like you were in a business."

Jordan came to Dallas in 1963 as a first-round pick. He became the starting middle linebacker in 1966 and started 154 consecutive games, through 1976. He made the Pro Bowl five times and played in three Super Bowls, winning one.

"I think we had a real respect for each other," Jordan said. "Coach Landry knew that I was a gung-ho, hard-charging kind of guy who loved football. I was really a cheerleader for the other guys on the team, screaming and yelling. Tom didn't get on the emotional side, but he recognized that I did, and I think he appreciated it."

What Landry appreciated most was Jordan's ability to understand the complex middle linebacker position that was the heart of his defense. Sam Huff was the first to grasp it, then Jerry Tubbs inherited the role when the Cowboys were born. Jordan was next. He was so good at it that in 1989, he was added to the Cowboys' Ring of Honor.

Landry, who had been fired months earlier, missed the ceremony and was sorry he wasn't there. But Jordan didn't need Landry there to know how his coach felt about him.

"Deep down, Tom loved and cared for each of us," Jordan said. "He didn't have a way of expressing it real easily, but you knew it was there. That level of confidence he had in you and the faith in you as people and players was so important."

Chuck Howley

George Halas didn't know what to do with Chuck Howley. Tom Landry did.

Landry put Howley at right linebacker, taught him the Flex defense and turned him into a six-time Pro Bowler over a 13-year career.

"His system made me a great player," Howley said. "I had to have the ability to perform, but he gave us many advantages through his coaching expertise that put us at the point of attack. All the honors that came to me were a direct tribute to his coaching."

Howley, an All-American center at West Virginia, was drafted by Halas' Chicago Bears in the first round of the 1958 draft. Then he hurt his knee three games into the 1959 season and figured his career was over.

He spent 1960 running a gas station in his hometown, Wheeling, West Virginia, then decided to give football a try again in 1961. The Cowboys acquired his rights by giving the Bears their picks from the second and ninth rounds of the 1963 draft.

Howley was a perfect fit in Landry's system. He knew exactly what had to be done and how to do it. In Super Bowl V, he became the first—and still only—player to be named MVP of the big game while on the losing team, then was on the championship team the following year. In 1977, he became the fourth member of the team's Ring of Honor at Texas Stadium.

After football, Howley became a successful businessman. He again credits Landry for putting him in position to succeed.

"It was all strictly football when we played for Tom. We did what we had to do to play in a game," Howley said. "I think we all realized that football is no different from business. They're both a challenge, and you have to prepare to meet the challenge to be

Chuck Howley is the only Super MVP from a losing team. (Photo courtesy of the Dallas Cowboys)

successful. You have to be dedicated and enthusiastic to play football, and the same is needed in business."

In his brief time in Chicago, Howley had a minor run-in with Halas. The linebacker was walking off the field after a loss and made two mistakes: First, he smiled at a friend on the winning team, the Baltimore Colts; second, he did it with Halas right behind him.

"He chased me off the field," Howley said. "He said, 'I'll teach you not to smile.' He didn't catch up to me, though."

In his long time in Dallas, Howley never saw Landry get that upset— or, at least, he didn't express his anger the way Halas did.

"Tom felt like you had a job to do, and it was up to you to do it," Howley said. "If you weren't measuring up, you would get one of his looks. He'd project that somber stare toward you, and you knew that it meant you weren't doing your job. That was his way of conveying the message that he was very dissatisfied with you."

Like so many other ex-Cowboys, Howley wishes his relationship with Landry had gone beyond football.

"I would've loved to have been closer to Tom Landry than I was," Howley said. "I think he had his own way of wanting to say, 'Hey, that guy is a friend of mine.' But he didn't say that, so we didn't know it. I was honored to have played for him the number of years I did. I admired the man greatly."

Howley believes that Landry faced death with dignity because he saw him do it once before.

"We were having plane problems coming back from a game one time, and we thought we were going down," Howley said. "Later in the flight, he came back in the plane and someone said, 'Hey Tom, were you scared?' And he said, 'When it's my time, it's my time.' So I think Tom was prepared. How much he suffered, I don't think he let anyone know."

Allen Green

Allen Green's claim to fame is simple but significant: He kicked the field goal that gave Tom Landry and the Dallas Cowboys their first-ever regular-season victory.

It was September 17, 1961. There were 23,500 fans and 52,000 empty seats at the Cotton Bowl when Bobby Layne and the Pittsburgh Steelers took a 24-17 lead in the fourth quarter. Then Eddie LeBaron, who had replaced Don Meredith, threw a 17-yard touchdown pass to tight end Dick Bielski with 56 seconds left to tie the game at 24.

With 19 seconds left, linebacker Jerry Tubbs intercepted a pass at the Dallas 38. LeBaron hit Bill Howton on a 41-yard bomb and he went out of bounds with barely any time left. After struggling to find a good spot to kick from, Green drilled a 27-yard field goal as time expired.

"I was having a miserable day," said Green, who had made a 15-yarder just before halftime but also missed from 41 and 35 yards and had a punt blocked. "I had a chance to redeem myself with a last-minute field goal."

The Cowboys ended up winning four games that year. Green still can't believe they did so well.

"He won with a combination of youngsters who didn't know what the heck they were doing and veterans who other teams didn't want," Green said. "We all made a whole bunch of mistakes. Tom did, too.

"But he was so doggone smart that we actually performed way above what we probably would have under just the average coach in the league at that time."

Green put up some unremarkable statistics is his lone NFL season.

Although he made all 15 of his extra-point attempts, he hit only 5-of-15 field goals. Bielski made 6-of-9 to end up the team leader in that category. Green's team-leading punting average of 37.3 yards remains the lowest by a Cowboys' season leader.

Back then, there was no such thing as a special teams coach, much less a kicking coach, like the Cowboys now have. In fact, Green barely even had a place to practice kicking field goals at their training grounds, Burnett Field.

"We had to put up some two-by-fours to make goal posts at the old baseball field," he said. "I got run off the field one night because I was kicking into the screen over the baseball backstop. I was doing that so the ball would roll back to me and I wouldn't have to run so much to go get it.

"Coach Landry must've gotten the word about it because after that he started staying out there with me. He'd kick the balls back to me, working with me. He enjoyed it."

Green lost touch with most of his teammates, but he never stopped rooting for the Cowboys.

"It was fun to watch them grow," he said. "You just knew Landry was going to make them be a success."

Craig Morton

Craig Morton started at quarterback in two Super Bowls and lost them both, once for Tom Landry and once against him.

"I was never on the right side of the scoreboard in those Super Bowls," he said. "At least I made Tom happy once."

That would be on January 15, 1978, when the Cowboys whipped the Morton-led Denver Broncos 27-10 in New Orleans for their second Super Bowl title. Randy White and Harvey Martin sacked Morton so many times in that game, they shared co-MVP honors.

"Tom had a great team that year," Morton recalled. "We could have played them 10 times and lost 10 times. I never got a chance to look up to find a receiver in that game. It was an incredible pass rush that our offensive line didn't handle well."

Craig Morton started Super Bowls for and against Landry. He lost both. (Photo courtesy of the Dallas Cowboys)

Morton started at quarterback for the Cowboys in Super Bowl V on January 17, 1971, and lost 16-13 to Baltimore on a last-second field goal. Had Morton carried Dallas to its first championship, he might have never lost the job to a guy named Roger Staubach.

"Tom was just devastated after that loss to Baltimore," Morton said. "We should have won but got every bad break you can imagine. It was hard to swallow, losing a game you clearly should have won."

Morton, the Cowboys' No. 1 draft pick in 1965, said he was probably a little too carefree for Landry.

"I can remember my wild and rebellious spirit," Morton said. "I think Tom always thought I was going to be another Don Meredith. I don't think he wanted another one of those.

"You never really understood where you stood with Tom. In those days, he kept you off guard all the time."

Landry kept his quarterbacks on a wild merry-go-round. First it was Morton vs. Meredith, then Staubach came along and made it Roger vs. Craig. Once the crowd was shouting, "We want Morton;" later it was "We want Staubach."

Morton said he found out Staubach was replacing him as starter in the darndest way.

"Tom called me over to his house at 10 o'clock one night," Morton said. "He first made a little joke saying, 'What are you doing home at this hour?' Then he asked that I come over."

Landry wanted to tell Morton in person that he was being demoted.

"Tom said he had a 'feeling' and was going to go with Roger," Morton said. "I never found out what that 'feeling' was. As it turned out, Roger became a Hall of Fame quarterback, so Tom had the right feeling."

Morton said he felt like he had to move along once Landry settled on Staubach at his starter.

"I had no bitterness about it," Morton said. "It was a hard decision to make. I know Coach hated to see me go, but he understood. He knew I wanted to be a starter."

Morton went to the New York Giants in the middle of the 1974 for a first-round pick in '75 and a second-rounder in '76. The first-round pick wound up being White.

Morton said he had a fondness for Landry, even though they didn't always agree.

"He taught me everything I knew about football," Morton said. "He also taught me how to be a gentleman and handle myself.

"He was the most consistent person I've ever been around. He had a good sense of humor and was a very shy man. Most people don't realize how shy he was. You kind of had to bring him out to get him to talk about anything."

Morton still laughs about how Landry butchered his name.

"He always called me 'Martin' instead of Morton," he said. "He did that with everybody, of course. He had trouble getting names straight."

Morton said he still remembers Landry taking charge at training camp in Thousand Oaks, California.

Each day, the team had to run the "Landry Mile," trudging up a nearby mountain and back before breakfast.

Landry ran with the team, using the military dictum that he wouldn't ask anyone to do something he wasn't willing to do himself.

"Everybody better make sure they can beat me," Tom told the team.

Several players didn't, huffing and puffing behind their coach.

"You really better make sure you beat me when we do it again tomorrow," Landry warned.

They did.

"Those guys knew they were gone if they lost to Tom two days in a row," Morton said. "Tom was a competitor."

Morton added: "I love him dearly. I miss and cherish the time I had to spend with him. When you're around great people, sometimes you never realize how great they were until they're gone."

Bob Hayes

Although Tom Landry didn't create the zone defense, he deserves an assist for making it necessary.

Landry's contribution was turning world-champion sprinter and long jumper Bob Hayes into a wide receiver then sending "Bullet Bob" on deep fly patterns. Three of his first four catches went for touchdowns and he became only the second rookie to have more than 1,000 yards receiving.

Hayes came to the NFL a year after winning the Olympic gold medal in the 100, earning him the title of "World's Fastest Human." No defensive back could keep up with him one-on-one, so defenses had to find another way to get their job done. Eventually, the answer was the zone, a scheme still used today.

"Coach Landry put it the best when he said Bobby Hayes revolutionized the passing game of pro football," Hayes said.

A conviction for selling cocaine to undercover officers after his career is likely what's keeping Hayes out of the Hall of Fame because his impact on the game and his career numbers make him worthy. But Hayes received another honor in February when he was one of the pallbearers at Landry's funeral.

"Bob Lilly looked over at me and said, 'Bobby, isn't this wonderful?' Being at a funeral, you'd think it's sad. But the Bible tells you to rejoice and we rejoiced," Hayes said. "We were all standing around the coffin, and it wasn't like Tom was dead. It was like he was staring at us. It was such a wonderful feeling seeing all his boys there, all his Hall of Famers, all of us were there. It was such a great thrill for me just to be a part of it. Just knowing what he had done for all of us."

Hayes admires the way Landry treated the family as a team, with the coach taking over the role of father.

"Coach Landry coached a lot of egotistical, emotional players," Hayes said. "He went through a lot, but he controlled it and we won. We won with dignity, pride and respect.

"He wasn't a prejudiced man. He was a man with balance—spiritually, emotionally and physically. All of us in the Cowboys family, we didn't like Coach Landry—we loved Coach Landry. And we continue to love his family today."

Hayes, who made No. 22 a jersey that defenses feared before Emmitt Smith was even born, gives Landry an assist for another important achievement in his life: earning his college degree in the 1990s.

"I decided to come back and get my degree because I always heard him say, 'How are you going to speak to kids about the importance of education when you haven't finished yours?' I had to go back and get it. I couldn't let everyone down," Hayes said. "That family has given me a lot of strength in my success on and off the field."

In early 2001, Hayes learned that he'd need their emotional support. He underwent treatment for prostate cancer and also was fighting heart, liver and kidney ailments.

Tommy McDonald

Statistically, the year Tommy McDonald spent in Dallas did little for his Hall of Fame career.

Spiritually, the season McDonald spent around Tom Landry was the best thing that ever happened to him.

"Tom Landry taught me what life was really all about," McDonald said. "When we had away games, if we didn't have a church to go to, he'd actually bring a minister into the hotel and have him have a service in the hotel. That really impressed me. I thought, 'If this guy is so really dedicated to God, maybe I should be, too.'

"When I got to the Cowboys, all I was ever thought about was football, football, football. Watching him made me realize it's not just a game that you're here on Earth for. We're not here for ourselves. We're here for God. I've been more dedicated to God ever since then. I try to let people know He's my coach and my quarterback in life."

McDonald thanked Landry during an NFL alumni banquet before the January 1989 Super Bowl, Landry's final one as coach of the Cowboys.

"As we were waiting backstage to be introduced," McDonald said, "I told Tom that he helped me realize I had to be more dedicated to God through Jesus Christ. He said, 'You know what? That makes me feel so good. Even though you didn't have a great year with the Cowboys, you're having better years in your life.'"

McDonald was a speedy receiver who twice made All-America at Oklahoma, then starred for the Philadelphia Eagles for seven years.

One of his greatest performances came in 1959 against a New York defense coached by Tom Landry. Although the Giants allowed only 170 points that entire season, they were pasted 49-21 by Philadelphia behind McDonald's big effort. Two weeks later, Landry devised a scheme to contain McDonald and the Giants won 24-7.

The 5-foot-9, 175-pound McDonald became so popular in Philadelphia that he had his own television show. When McDonald was traded to Dallas, it was front-page news.

"Now, guys hope to get traded to the Cowboys," McDonald said. "Not back then."

It was especially bad for McDonald because Landry's offense didn't emphasize passing.

McDonald caught 46 passes for 612 yards and two touchdowns for the Cowboys in 1964. His average of 13.3 yards per catch and his touchdowns were the lowest to that point in his career.

"I went in to see Landry the very next day after the season was over and said, 'Tom, I love the conditions here, and you're really a super, awesome coach, but I want to be on a passing team.' He tried talking me out of it for three or four months—'Tommy, we'll get you the ball'—but I said no," McDonald said.

"It wasn't just that I wanted to catch more passes. Their whole offense didn't suit me. With the Eagles, we threw downfield a lot and I could get away from guys. But in Dallas they mostly threw little short stuff.

"Of course, they changed a lot when I left and Bob Hayes came in."

McDonald went on to play two years for the Los Angeles Rams and one each in Atlanta and Cleveland. When he retired after the '68 season, he was second all-time in touchdown catches (84), fourth in receiving yards (8,410) and sixth in receptions (495).

McDonald didn't make the Hall of Fame until 1998. His induction ended up being one of the most memorable because of how much fun he had throwing his $15,000 bust in the air—twice!—and jumping up to bump chests and hips and exchange high-fives with fellow inductees Anthony Muñoz and Mike Singletary.

"I always thought God had a plan for me," McDonald said. "I guess God made that trade to Dallas to get me with somebody who would make me get a lot closer to Him. And it did. So I think that is one of the blessings in my life."

Pettis Norman

Tom Landry respected Pettis Norman so much that in many of the coach's speeches to youth groups, he used the tight end's rise from poverty to bank executive as an example of hard work paying off.

So when Landry traded Norman to the San Diego Chargers in the summer of 1971, he couldn't bring himself to deliver the news on the telephone.

Pettis Norman remains Alicia Landry's favorite player. (Photo courtesy of the Dallas Cowboys)

"He called at 4:45 and said, 'I need to talk to you. Can you wait at your office?' Then he drove from North Dallas to the southern part of town in rush-hour traffic," Norman said.

"He said, 'Pettis, I had to do the most difficult thing I've ever done in my coaching career: I've had to involve you in a trade.' Then he said, 'Now, the second-most difficult thing is I've got to go home and explain it to my wife. She's going to kill me.'"

Alicia Landry was rather fond of Norman, too.

"She always said I was her favorite player," Norman said. "She said it at the funeral as well."

Norman said that story typifies the way Landry treated the team like a family, with the coach serving as the patriarch.

"He was such a large player in the whole scenario," Norman said. "Management came to him, players came to him and coaches came to him.

He was like the magnet that brought it together and the glue that held it together.

"When he said something, everyone understood that was the way it was. We dressed a certain way because we were professionals. We were expected to act a certain way. We were expected to be together like a team."

"It's interesting because even at that time he was rather unassuming standing on the sidelines wearing his hat. But what was happening is he was forming this image in everyone's mind of dignity and class and all those things that everyone aspires to. It became part of what the star on the helmet represented."

Norman recalled another moment that helped establish the Landry image.

"We were in a Southern city for an exhibition game and there was a policy that blacks and whites couldn't eat together," Norman said. "He just simply said, 'Well, we don't play where we can't eat and sleep together as a team.'

"Somehow, those arrangements were changed and we did play the game."

Norman's respect for Landry is obvious. Landry also made no secret of his admiration for Norman, saying: "I wish I had 22 players like Pettis and Lee Roy (Jordan). All I'd have to do is blow up the football and throw it on the field."

"I worked hard from Day 1, made the team and just did the things I think Coach Landry wanted to see in a player," said Norman, who worked his way from a fourth-string player his junior year in high school to a starter in the NFL. "I think he respected my work ethic."

Norman was so in awe of Landry that he had trouble believing the coach was dead.

"I kept thinking he would pull it out in the last quarter with one last play before time ran out," Norman said. "I was like a child, refusing to believe it really happened."

Norman believes that if Landry was still coaching, he could have the same impact today as he had four decades ago.

"What he would do now is what he did back then, which is to simply say, 'If you're going to play here, then this is what it's going to require,'" Norman said. "I'm convinced he would've had those same principles—and probably some of those same results."

And what would Landry's Xs and Os look like in the 21st century?

"To think what about he would do today is kind of awe-inspiring," he said. "He would probably be out of the Space Age with his defense."

Jim Boeke

Before the Dallas Cowboys were "America's Team," they were "Next Year's Champions." They got that label with narrow losses in big games like the 1966 and '67 NFL championships against the Green Bay Packers.

In the first major clash with the Packers, the Cowboys rallied from a 14-0 deficit and were driving for a potential game-tying touchdown in the final minute. They were facing second-and-goal from the one-yard line when tackle Jim Boeke jumped offsides.

After being shoved back five yards, Dallas didn't recover. Two straight passes fell incomplete, then a fourth-down try was intercepted in the end zone.

The penalty remains Boeke's lasting memory to many Cowboys fans. It's even been called "the most agonizing penalty in Cowboys' history."

Landry, though, never said a word about it.

"He never brought it up," Boeke said. "The only time it was ever brought up was about 20 years after that. We had a reunion and [Clint] Murchison walked over with a smirk on his face, pointed to the picture of the game, grinned and walked away.

Jim Boeke committed one of the most infamous penalties in Cowboys history. (Photo courtesy of the Dallas Cowboys)

I'd never ever spoken to him before. It was just bizarre behavior on his part."

Boeke always did have a way of avoiding Landry's wrath.

"At the Monday film meetings, I'd try to sit next to Jim Myers, our line coach," Boeke said. "That way, instead of Landry yelling across the room, 'Hey Boeke, why didn't you get the block on this guy? All you've got to do is get in front of him and stay there,' Jim would whisper the same thing to me."

Boeke remembers Landry's versatility as a coach. Wherever a problem was, Landry knew how to fix it.

"If the defense was not rated in the top four or five one year, then the next year, Landry would run the defensive meetings and concentrate all his efforts towards the defense. You could count on the defense being No. 1 or 2 in the NFL that year," Boeke said. "But then, the offense might drop a little, so he'd switch over and bring them up.

"If there had been two of him, both sides of the ball would've been ranked No. 1 or 2 in the league—he was that good.

"People thought he should've been more personable on the field, but I don't think I ever felt that was missing. He was always business, and we expected that. We all had fun performing the jobs we had, but we realized he was the taskmaster, and he had a goal in mind, and he was out there to achieve that goal."

After Boeke retired, he remained close to the game in an ususual way: as an actor. Among his many screen credits are roles in the movie version of former Cowboy Pete Gent's book *North Dallas Forty* and on an episode of the television show "Coach."

Cornell Green

Cornell Green knew so little about football that when he tried out for the Cowboys in 1962, he put his hip pads on backwards.

Assistant coach Dick Nolan saw Green squirming and said, "It might be more comfortable if you turned those pads around."

The All-American basketball player from Utah State figured that by the time he learned how to wear his equipment, he would be cut.

"I didn't think I'd make it," said Green, a free-agent discovery on one of Gil Brandt's secret scouting missions.

But he survived his lack of football experience and blossomed under the tutelage of a former All-Pro cornerback by the name of Tom Landry.

Landry turned basketball star Cornell Green into an All-Pro defensive back. (Photo courtesy of the Dallas Cowboys)

"I started getting my confidence, and before long, I figured out nobody else was better than I was," Green said. "Coach Landry could teach you the better parts of the game because he played the position for the New York Giants.

"If he told you what the receiver was going to do, you could guarantee that he was going to do it. There were hardly any surprises."

The 6-foot-4, 200-pound Green became one of the most physical corners in the NFL and was an integral part of the Cowboys' Super Bowl teams. He made five Pro Bowls and was named All-Pro four times in his 13-year career, then worked for the team as a scout.

"I was very fortunate to go as far as I did and it was all to the patience and knowledge of Tom," Green said.

Green said playing for Landry required long, long hours in the film room.

"You had to do a lot of homework because playing in the Landry system meant you had to get your keys down," Green said. "It was all keys, and once you figured it, out the defense was easy.

"It only took you about three years. Sometimes, you didn't get to spend much time in bed. When you did, you had to learn to sleep fast."

Green said Landry never had a lot to say to him while he was a player. He saved his praise for when Green retired following the 1975 season.

"He told me I was one of the best defensive backs he had ever coached or had ever seen," Green said. "That really made me feel good."

George Andrie

When Tom Landry said his priorities were faith, family and then football, George Andrie could relate.

"I came from a very strong family," Andrie said. "All he did was reiterate things I knew.

"He was a very strong individual. He had a great influence on most of our lives, his players. I think we were pretty lucky to be around a person like him getting out of college.

"He never let anything get him down. He felt like he could control just about anything bad happening in his life. I think that had a lot to do with the success we had as a team."

Although Andrie didn't need Landry to be a father figure, he had many teammates who did.

"Tom was probably the first person in their lives to have a profound effect, to give them direction in life," Andrie said. "He kind of put things in perspective for a lot of people."

Andrie came to Dallas in 1962 as a sixth-round pick from Marquette, which didn't even have a team his senior year. The Cowboys were coming off a four-win season.

Andrie started every game for 11 seasons at defensive end, playing in two Super Bowls and winning one. He made the Pro Bowl five times and was once an All-Pro.

"I was lucky that most of the guys I played with, I played with them my whole career," Andrie said. "Very few people came and were traded through the Cowboys. Most of the players they drafted, they developed and kept them through their careers, and I was one of them."

Andrie was saddened by Landry's death because he knew how much the coach still meant to so many people. But he also took solace in knowing that Landry was going to a better place.

"Death is really nothing to me but going to a new life, the real spiritual life of why you're here—and he always talked that way, too," Andrie said. "People here on Earth are the ones who cry because they're losing something, but the person who is dead is better off than all of us, most of the time.

"Deep down, Tom had that same moral approach, that there's more to life than just what we're doing here. We might be 40 guys and we're world champions, but who really cares? There's more to life than football."

Mike Connelly

When Mike Connelly went to his ninth training camp with the Dallas Cowboys, the offensive lineman made the mistake of telling Tom Landry he was retiring after the season.

"I figured, well, I've played for him all these years, he's not going to cut me just because I tell him I'm going to retire," said Connelly, whose career began in the franchise's first game and ended in the "Ice Bowl." "So one day I said, 'Uh, incidentally, Tom, I want to let you know this is my last year.' He said, 'Oh, OK. Thanks for telling me.'

"And a week later, I was in Pittsburgh."

The Cowboys didn't actually peddle Connelly. They merely included him on a list of players Pittsburgh could choose from to complete a deal for kicker Mark Clark.

Another story Connelly likes to tell is about the time fellow lineman Dave Manders tried beating the heat of an afternoon game at the Cotton Bowl by talking someone into bringing him a beer.

"He drank it real fast and got sick as a dog," Connelly said. "But all Tom saw was him throwing up. We ended up losing the game pretty bad, and the next week, we're all hearing about it. Then Landry said, 'Guys like Manders were out there giving it their all.'

"I always wondered if he found out Manders had the beer or if he really thought he went all out."

In the early days, the Cowboys were desperate for positive publicity. Connelly remembers being paid $50 to make public speaking appearances at high schools.

During those trips, Connelly heard coaches swearing and yelling at their students. The former Marine didn't think anything of it until a few years later when he noticed the same coaches had cleaned up their act.

Connelly quickly figured out why.

"The Cowboys hired the local high school coaches to come and grade films and so forth, so they got to know Tom," he said. "And you saw a big change. You didn't have all the cussing and swearing going on. They were emulating Tom. So there's a quiet influence he had over many, many high school kids."

Connelly believes his Marine background made it easier to handle Landry's strict, no-nonsense style.

"You knew where you stood, you knew what was expected, and if you strayed from the lines, you knew you'd be out of there," Connelly said. "It wasn't necessarily that you had to perform. But if you stepped out of his bounds about being a good person on and off the field, you were gone.

"You had to really respect him for that. I think more people will remember him for what he did for society and for being the person he was than for his football coaching ability, because that affects more people."

Dave Manders

Ask Dave Manders for his favorite story about Tom Landry and he gives you a choice.

"True or not true?"

Hmm.

"I like the non-true one," he volunteers with a laugh, then tells the tale that probably started with a few facts and turned into fiction through the years. "Sam Baker was the kicker and it was well after curfew. But Sam never did pay attention to curfew.

"So, he gets on the elevator and pushes the button. Before the door could close, Tom got on the elevator with him. Tom looked at him and said, 'Drunk again, Sam.'

"And Sam said, 'Me, too, Coach.'"

As for true stories, Manders has plenty. Most end with a moral, not a punch line.

"In 1965, Pittsburgh had a sorry, sorry team and we lost," Manders said, recalling an incident that made a lasting impression on many players. "He was talking to the guys and just broke down in tears. When we met again the following Monday or Tuesday, he came back with some readings from the scriptures. It was something on faith, a reading from Paul about 'the race.'

"His faith always seemed to pull him through and he shared it with us.

Landry wasn't always soft. Sometimes, he was so strict that it was funny.

"After a game up in Minnesota where we got trounced, his comments to the whole team were, 'We weren't prepared for that game. I could tell we weren't prepared by the way the captains came off the field after the coin toss. I knew that was going to be a terrible day for us.'

"The team captains were Cornell, Lee Roy and myself. So right away, we bear the brunt of the loss; it's all our fault because we came off the field slow!

Dave Manders learned to better appreciate Landry after his playing days were over. (Photo courtesy of the Dallas Cowboys)

"So after that, we'd flip the coin, then say, 'Ready?!' get down into a sprinter's stance and sprint to the sidelines. He never said a word about it."

Many of Manders' impressions of Landry resurfaced following the coach's death, especially at the funeral and a gathering afterward at the Landry home that was meant to be a celebration of his life.

"It was a happy occasion," he said. "It was good to be together and see each other.

"I think we all knew that's how Tom would've wanted it."

John Niland

When John Niland's life took a bizarre turn, Tom Landry was there to help straighten him out.

In 1973, Niland had what he described as a religious experience. During it, he ran wildly through his neighborhood until police forcibly restrained him and took him to a hospital for psychiatric evaluation.

When he got out, Niland went to visit Landry. They walked around the practice field and Landry listened to Niland's story.

"People were making fun of it, and in a real way, I didn't know which way to turn," Niland said. "I certainly was embarrassed from a secular standpoint. It sounds kind of hokey when people read about it, but it's as real today as it was back then. And Landry listened to me, didn't judge me, didn't question me. He accepted it. I think it was only through God's grace that he understood it.

"He shared with me Bible stories, particularly about Paul being knocked off his horse and blinded by the Lord. I didn't know anything about Paul or the Bible. But he shared that story with me and said, 'Paul didn't know anything either.' Then, he said, 'You're not unique, Niland. That's the way the Lord touches people. Sometimes, he punches people in the mouth to get their attention.'"

Niland then helped start the team Bible study that continues to this day. He also was helpful in starting a golf tournament in Landry's honor.

"My Dad was not the adult male in my life that I looked up to, outside of the fact that he was my father," Niland said. "I grew up in New York in the '50s and '60s and it was an alcoholic environment. My whole family was alcoholics. So to me, Coach Landry was a breath of fresh air.

"He was bigger than life to me because I was looking for the flaws and he didn't have many. That had a tremendous impact on me."

Niland felt Landry's warmth shortly after he retired.

The two were together at a Fellowship of Christian Athletes camp in Estes Park, Colorado. Niland had just finished a speech when he and Landry went for a walk.

"We sat on a log in the woods and we just talked. Not about football, only about spiritual things," Niland said. "We just talked as two men who need God's grace and were thankful for it. It was the first time in my life I felt close to the man.

"I always respected him—he was a great tactician, a great coach, all those things—but I never knew him. And I didn't particularly like him when I played for him. He didn't do anything wrong, but I was used to getting a pat on the back or a kick in the butt."

During his playing days, Niland tried to get to know Landry outside football by inviting him and Alicia for dinner at his house.

John Niland and Landry became close through their shared faith. (Photo courtesy of the Dallas Cowboys)

"For some crazy reason, after I got converted, I invited him over in the off season," Niland said. "I don't think it had ever been done. And I didn't do it for that reason. I did it because, I guess, part of me was always reaching out to him as a father figure.

"He and his sweetheart wife came over. We just sat around the table and had terrific conversation. I don't think we talked about football. . . .

"Talking to Coach Landry was a delight. He was a quiet man, so you almost had to draw him out. And you had to be prepared for some canned answers. But if you asked him about his kids or what he thought about America or some offbeat topic, he loved to talk about it."

A few months later, Landry called Niland into his office. It wasn't to ask for his wife's recipes.

"I got traded to Philadelphia. Maybe he didn't like the dinner," Niland said, laughing. "Nah, that had nothing to do with it."

After Landry left the Cowboys, the two occasionally saw each other at various functions. Niland sensed that Landry's second career was more enjoyable than his first.

"I think he had more impact after he got out of the game," Niland said. "He probably had the opportunity to speak every night if he wanted to.

"He coached thousands of men, but he was a spiritual mentor to millions. I think a great number of the people who admired him did so not for the winning and losing but for the character he projected. I think that's a refreshing indictment on society."

Tony Liscio

Tony Liscio retired from football in the summer of 1971. At least, that's what he thought.

Tom Landry called Liscio a few months into his second career in real estate and said he needed an offensive tackle.

"Do you think you can play?" Landry said.

Liscio asked how much time he had to answer the question. Landry gave him 30 minutes.

"That's how he was," Liscio said. "He wanted to know so he could get on one way or the other."

Liscio decided to give it a shot. If he lasted three games, he'd get a full year added to his pension.

He ended up getting a Super Bowl ring.

"It was probably the best ball I ever played," Liscio said. "We never lost a game."

Liscio had played seven seasons for Dallas, then was traded to San Diego. He tried going through training camp with the Chargers, but pain in his back, hamstring and knee told him he'd had enough.

When he and a friend heard on the radio that the Cowboys had lost Ralph Neely and Forrest Gregg to injuries, the friend told Liscio he'd be getting a call soon.

"You gotta be nuts," Liscio said.

Sure enough, Liscio ended up working out for the coaches a few days later.

"They put me through some maneuvers and said I looked to be in pretty decent shape," he said. "I wasn't working out and I was about 10 pounds lighter than I had played at."

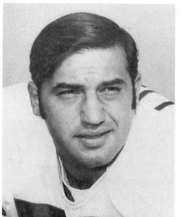

Landry needed Tony Liscio even after the lineman retired. (Photo courtesy of the Dallas Cowboys)

Liscio wasn't allowed to practice with the team until they secured his rights from San Diego. After just two days of practice, "I was sore as hell," he said.

"We played that Sunday in Washington and when that whistle blew, all my pain went away," Liscio said. "All of a sudden I didn't feel nothing. I felt great.

"But after the game, when I cooled down, I paid for it. And that second game was a real killer."

Liscio was in such agony that he decided to make up his own rules, something unheard of on Landry's teams.

"When everybody would line up to do conditioning and sprints, I'd just go to the locker room. I wasn't about to leave it out there on the practice field," Liscio said. "One time, Landry came up to me and said, 'You know, you sure are going to make it tough on me. How am I going to convince my team they have to go to training camp if you come out here and start playing like this.' That was his way."

Liscio actually got Landry to bend his rules once before.

"In 1964, I came to training camp at 264, about four pounds over his weight limit for a guard," Liscio said. "But before they moved me to the fat man's table, I had to run the Landry Mile. I finished with a burst and made it with six seconds to spare, and they never said nothing. That's how I became probably the biggest tackle who'd ever played for him at that point."

Liscio thought he'd lost his speed when a knee injury that season was followed by complications that required several operations. He missed all of '65 and went into the '66 season hoping to win a job as a backup tackle.

"And what does he do? He moves me to offensive guard, a position I'd never played before and one that has twice as much running and tackling," Liscio said. "That also was when he moved Dan Reeves to halfback.

"And, for some reason, the team really started moving."

Through all their quirky episodes, Liscio grew to appreciate Landry.

"He didn't waver much," Liscio said. "He'd make funny faces when something bad would happen in the game, but I never saw him scream at anybody. He was real direct, though. He told you what he wanted, and he had very little patience. If he asked for something, he wanted it done right then. If you couldn't or wouldn't do it, the next season would roll around and you weren't there anymore.

"You had to know the system, and the system was very complicated. It took about three years to be really comfortable in the system. I really studied it. I'd take my playbook everywhere."

One person who felt confined by the system was Don Meredith. Liscio remembers the clashes that ensued.

"Landry would tell you what was going to happen and what you have to do. And Meredith was one to ad-lib," Liscio said. "One time, Landry went over a situation in practice and said, 'The linebacker will stand right here and this is what you have to audible to.'

"Well, we got into that situation in the game and the guy wasn't there — he was out of position. So Meredith stopped the game and told the linebacker, 'Hey, you're not supposed to be there. You're supposed to be over there.'

"Boy, Meredith was loose, a great guy. But those two people didn't understand each other. They weren't cut from the same mold, that's for sure."

Pete Gent

Pete Gent was one of the NFL's original rebels, writing a fictional book after his playing days with the Dallas Cowboys that described the greedy, wild and seedy sides of the sport.

It caused a sensation both pro and con.

North Dallas Forty had a lot of fictional coaches and players who bore somewhat of a resemblance to players on the Cowboys. It was a big success and was made into a movie. But at no time was it meant to have disrespect for Tom Landry.

In fact, Gent thanked his lucky stars he got to play five seasons for him.

"I really admired Tom, although we had our differences," Gent said. "He was an amazing and brilliant man.

"Sometimes, you look back over your life and see how many great men you met. Tom was certainly one of them."

Gent, who only played basketball at Michigan State, came to the Cowboys in 1964 as one of Gil Brandt's free agent discoveries after turning down an NBA contract with the Baltimore Bullets. Cornell Green, a basketball player out of Utah State, had paved the way for such thinking after becoming a brilliant defensive back.

"I think when I came to the team, Tom was still deep in the throes of trying to deal with this business of violence," said the deep-thinking Gent. "It was a great conflict for him because he had to fly bombers in the big war and he had to deal with the loss of his brother. Not many guys survived that exclusive club called the 8th Air Force, and then he was dealing with young men in another form of violence. I think that's one of the big reasons he kept to himself and his own counsel."

Gent's career was marred by injury, but he still had some good seasons, splitting time with Buddy Dial.

Gent said Landry's offense was perfect for cerebral players such as himself.

"I'll tell you this: The game never passed him by like a lot of people thought during his later years," Gent said. "All that happened in Dallas was that Murchison died. He would have coached a long time if Clint hadn't died. Tom could still X and O with the best of them until the day he died.

"There was nothing new out there. They talk about the West Coast offense, but we were running all those timing patterns in the 1960s. Dick Nolan brought it to the 49ers when he left as Tom's assistant to become head coach."

Gent said he thought the pressure was starting to get to Landry in the mid-'60s before Dallas became a championship club. One of the enlightening moments was following a loss to a bad Pittsburgh team.

"Tom came into the dressing room and broke down and cried, saying he was sorry he had let us down," Gent said. "I said to myself, 'OK, I get this. He is human. He's still struggling for an identity and a purpose.'"

Gent knew Landry liked him. Why?

"Because I knew the offense better than anybody. Sometimes, we would run seven different plays off the same formation, and I would know everyone's route," Gent recalled. "Tom understood I would do anything to play or do what he told me. He knew I would play hurt, and he liked that."

Gent had two knee operations and constant back problems with the Cowboys but seldom missed playing time.

"Tom and I would have fights and it would usually be over playing time," Gent said. "He hoped Buddy would be a game-breaker, but if he had left me in more, I could have played at another level. I never got a deep route. Oh, I can remember one, and it went 84 yards for a touchdown. I usually got the ones short and over the middle. That's how I broke my back."

Gent added, "Tom should have let Don Meredith call the plays. It was insane that he didn't. We had more information on the field than he did 30 yards away on the sidelines.

"Once, he called a flare pass to Danny Reeves in the title game to Green Bay. Reeves just had his bell rung, but Don was afraid not to get him the ball. It was a critical play. Danny saw three balls coming his way. He missed the real one."

Gent said he was glad he had his arguments with Landry.

"It taught me a lot about life," Gent said. "And I'll tell you, I had a certain physical fear of that man. Sometimes he looked like he might rip your throat out if you didn't do good."

Gent said there were humorous times, too.

"They had a gal by the name of Bubbles Cash who used to come to games to put herself on display. She was going up and down the aisles, doing her walk during a game, driving the crowd crazy.

"It was a timeout, and me and Meredith were talking to Landry, and he was facing the crowd, which was still buzzing. Suddenly, Tom saw Bubbles, and his jaw just dropped. He just shook his head and called a play."

Gent will never forget what happened after his book came out in 1973.

"There was a Super Bowl press conference and it was the first question asked of Tom," Gent said. "Tom said 'I don't know anything about it. I don't read trash like that.'"

The next question was, "How do you know it's trash?"

From there, the press conference went downhill.

Then came the kicker.

"Years later, after Tom was out of football, I was at a Dallas Mavericks game doing a halftime promo and Tom was down on the floor to get an award," Gent said. "We were waiting in the tunnel with Charlie Waters and I asked Tom what life was like without football."

"Not too bad," Landry replied.

"Tom, I could have told you that," Gent said.

"I think you tried to tell me already with that book," Landry responded with a smile.

Pat Toomay

Pat Toomay seemed to have the perfect background to get along with Tom Landry.

Toomay's father was a military general who looked like Landry and was a big fan of the drama and story lines played up by NFL Films. Toomay's grandfather had been a minister.

Yet, Toomay found himself constantly analyzing Landry and his role within an organization that was somewhat exposed in Pete Gent's thinly veiled novel *North Dallas Forty*.

"I was confused by the extent to which his sort of image and born-again Christianity was, I felt, exploited by the organization," Toomay said. "In other words, the organization itself wasn't very pious."

Toomay said the best example of the contradiction was on the team plane. Booze flowed and soap opera-like relationships played out, yet Tom remained oblivious to it while wrapped up reading a Louis L'Amour novel.

Another example he uses occurred after the Cowboys made him a sixth-round pick in 1970. Players were starting to use agents to negotiate contracts and Toomay was considering it. So he asked his defensive coordinator at Vanderbilt whether he should look for one.

"He said, 'No, the Cowboys are good people. Tom Landry is a man of God. They will treat you right in these financial dealings.' So, I said fine. I didn't get an agent. But as I'm leaving my coach's office, he says to me, 'By the way, when you see Gil Brandt, ask him where is that new suit he promised me. I was supposed to get it last week.' So there you have it. There the whole thing is in adjacent sentences: You can trust these people, Tom Landry is a man of God . . . Where is my new suit? They were exploiting his image."

Toomay, a defensive end from 1970-74, realized that Landry was only accountable for his own behavior, yet he still had trouble understanding how the coach put up with it.

"I wondered a lot about the responsibilities of a man in that situation," Toomay said. "His watchwords were, 'I don't worry about what I can't control.'

"My point is, to somebody like me, who is sensitive to these kinds of issues, it was confusing. You look to a coach for leadership on these things, and he's putting forth this one ethic, but all around him is something else.

"Most people could care less about this kind of stuff. But I was attuned to them. Do I blame him? No. It just makes me wonder."

Toomay said he was afraid to discuss his issues with Landry. Toomay was still searching for answers when Landry died, so he traveled to Dallas for the funeral and memorial services, hoping to sort out his own emotions.

"He was a very powerful figure. There's no doubt about it," Toomay said. "He affected everybody he came into contact with in some way. A lot of people are affected positively; some people are staggered by his impact. I think I was the latter."

Toomay went back home with his emotions still swirling through his mind.

"My own emotional reaction was such that I needed to investigate it," he said. "Even if it was negative, that means there's something going on."

So, what's the bottom line?

"He led me to myself."

Players always knew Landry was the boss. (Photo courtesy of Denne H. Freeman)

Southwestern Bell |  *SBC global network*

Greater Dallas Residence
White Pages

♻ June 2000/2001 • Area Codes 214/972

Tom Landry
1924-2000

Southwestern Bell honored Landry's memory by placing him on the cover of their Dallas phone book.

Chapter Four

AMERICA'S TEAM

Maybe it was the Doomsday Defense or the All-American boy playing quarterback. Maybe it was the quiet, confident guy in the hat who seldom smiled but always won.

Whatever it was, people seemed to love the Dallas Cowboys.

Sure, folks were gaga in Dallas and around the Lone Star State. But even when the Cowboys would go on the road, fans cheered for them.

They were, as NFL Films first dubbed them, "America's Team."

From 1970-78, the Cowboys played in five Super Bowls. They won two and lost the other three by a combined 11 points. That's even more amazing when you consider that two of those losses were to the ferocious Pittsburgh Steelers of the "Steel Curtain" era, considered by many the greatest team ever.

Dallas' peak period, which included two seasons that ended a game shy of the Super Bowl, was part of the greatest sustained success that pro football has ever seen. For 20 years, the Cowboys had a winning record, and they made the playoffs 18 of those seasons. They won the division title 13 times.

The only comparable stretches of dominance come from other sports. Baseball's New York Yankees had 39 straight winning seasons and hockey's Montreal Canadiens did it for 32 years.

Landry wasn't the first coach to win two Super Bowls, but he was the first to do it with virtually different rosters. Roger Staubach, Jethro Pugh and Cliff Harris were the only starters January 16, 1972, against Miami and January 15, 1978, against Denver.

Another incredible feat is the 13 division titles. The first and last were bookends to the 20-year streak: the first in 1966 with Don Meredith at quarterback, the last in 1985 with Danny White calling signals.

Landry, who was named Coach of the Year in '66, '75 and '78, considered '85 among his best seasons because he got that group to overachieve. He thought about retiring then and going out on top.

He remained four more seasons, hurting his career record but not his reputation. His 29 years with one team tied Curly Lambeau for the longest one-team tenure in NFL history and he's fourth on the overall longevity list behind George Halas, Don Shula and Lambeau. Landry's record of 270-178-6 makes him the third-winningest coach of all-time, behind Shula and Halas.

In addition to helping make the star on the Cowboys' helmets among the most recognizable symbols in the world, Landry also has been credited for reshaping the image of the city of Dallas.

For many years, when people thought of Dallas, they flashed back to the November 1963 assassination of John F. Kennedy. Yet Landry, through his victories and values, gave the city a new face and a new reputation.

Dallas residents continue to pay homage to him. In the summer of 2000, a few months after Landry's death, his picture graced the cover of the local phone book.

Tony Dorsett

After 11 record-shattering years in Dallas, Tony Dorsett didn't exactly leave under the best of circumstances.

But he never let it affect his respect for Tom Landry, enabling them to renew their relationship after both were out of football.

"We were together one time at a function in Austin and he said, 'I know you're mad at me. You don't like me,'" Dorsett said. "I said, 'Coach, I have no animosity whatsoever towards you. I went to Denver because I pretty much forced your hand. I wanted it to happen and I was doing things and saying things to make it happen.'

"From then on, I was invited to his golf tournaments and he came to my wife's baby shower."

Tom Landry? At a baby shower?

"We sent him and Alicia an invitation, but I really wasn't expecting them to show up," Dorsett said. "It was a big thrill and he had a good time. Some of my friends weren't involved in the sports arena and they got a big kick out of it. Coach took pictures with them and signed autographs, sat down and carried on conversations."

Dorsett gave the Cowboys the weapon they needed: a breakaway threat in the backfield, the kind defenses knew could score every time he touched the ball.

Dorsett won the Heisman Trophy in 1976 while leading the University of Pittsburgh to the national championship. The following summer, Dallas traded a first-round pick and three seconds to Seattle to draft him.

"The only thing I know about me being drafted was that Alicia Landry had something to do with it," Dorsett said. "In front of Tom, she once said to me, 'You know, I'm the reason that you're here. I told Tommy, 'I like that little Tony Dorsett. You better draft him.'" I said, 'Thank you very much! I'm glad you did that because I surely wouldn't have wanted to be anywhere else.'"

The Cowboys won their second Super Bowl in Dorsett's rookie year, then made it back the next season.

Over 11 seasons, Dorsett set every rushing record in team history. When he retired after a season with the Broncos, Dorsett had the second-most rushing yards in NFL history. In 1994, he was inducted into both the Hall of Fame and the Ring of Honor.

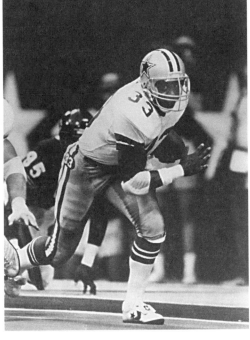

Tony Dorsett wanted to carry the ball more, but he got it enough to make the Hall of Fame. (Photo courtesy of the Dallas Cowboys)

A major point of contention throughout Dorsett's Dallas days was the number of carries he had.

Landry wanted his 5-foot-11, 191-pound star to be hit as little as possible, so he kept his average below 20 carries per game. Dorsett, though, still thinks he could've handled more.

"He was trying to prolong my career because of my size," Dorsett said. "I understood his logic, but I didn't totally accept it.

"My running style was to avoid defenders. I knew that with my size and physical stature, if I tried punishing people, I'd probably ended up being punished more.

"The nature of the business is that your next play could always be your last play, regardless of whether there's a big hit. I tore up my knee without anyone touching me.

"But that was the way he wanted it to be and that's the way it was."

Whether more carries would've led to more yards or more injuries will never be known. Rather than wasting time pondering that, Dorsett's better off savoring the great success he had.

"Coach Landry had a lot to do with it," he said. "He kept driving me. You had to always give your best because he expected it. I was one of the guys who didn't think I needed it pounded into my head.

"But him being around sure helped keep me at that level of concentration."

Dorsett learned how strict Landry's principles were when he violated a rule and wound up in tears—and on the bench.

Early in his career, Dorsett's parents were in town and he missed a Saturday morning practice. His mother told him to call the coaches and tell them what happened, but he didn't know any of their phone numbers.

"My mom was very worried," he recalled. "I told her, 'Don't worry, Mom, other players have missed a Saturday morning practice before. It's no big deal. All we do is just watch the films from Friday, do a little walk-through and that's it.'"

When Dorsett arrived at Texas Stadium on Sunday, a note told him he was wanted in Coach Landry's office.

"What happened?" Landry asked.

"Coach, I overslept," Dorsett said.

"Well, why didn't you call?"

"I didn't know any numbers to call."

Then Landry broke the news: "You're not going to start today and you probably won't play."

"Coach, wait a minute," Dorsett protested. "I've seen other players miss a Saturday practice and not have to come off the bench."

"Well, those other players happened to make a telephone call and explain their whereabouts," Landry said.

His mom was right. And now she and his father were going to be in the stands and their son was going to be on the bench. Dorsett's eyes filled with tears as he explained that his parents had come nearly 3,000 miles to see him perform.

"I gotta play," Dorsett begged.

"You're not going to start and you're probably not going to play—OK?" Landry said.

That last word was the clincher.

"When he says, 'OK' that pretty much ended a conversation," Dorsett said. "So when he threw that OK on there, I knew that was it.

"My eyes were so full of water and I was so mad. I didn't know what to do. It crossed my mind to get aggressive, but fortunately, I knew better."

Dorsett—who ended up getting only "scrub time" at the end of the game—remembers the details so well because it made a big impression on his life. He uses that story in speeches to children to help them avoid making the same mistake.

"It's about holding yourself accountable," Dorsett said. "If the coach couldn't count on me to do little things like showing up for a practice, then how could he count on me in the heat of battle?

"So, right then and there, that taught me a lesson, a very valuable lesson. I never missed another meeting, practice or anything else after that point."

There were other things he took from football into his post-playing days.

"It's unbelievable how many things have lasted with me, things that to this day are a part of my life," he said. "Things like setting reasonable goals and outstanding goals, then coming up with methods on how to accomplish those goals. Another thing is preparation.

"The way Coach Landry handled himself, on and off the field, was something I really watched and paid attention to. Now that my career is over and I'm seeing things from a different vantage point, I've found that those are important things I try to emulate at times.

"But he did it in a way that can't be duplicated."

Harvey Martin

Harvey Martin was a four-time Pro Bowler, an All-Pro and even a co-Super Bowl MVP in his 11 years as a defensive end for the Dallas Cowboys.

But some fans still remember him for an incident against the Washington Redskins on December 19, 1979, that got him in trouble with the boss man, Tom Landry.

In Roger Staubach's last regular-season game as a Cowboy, he threw two touchdown passes, including the game-winner with 1:14 play for a 35-34 victory that gave Dallas the NFC East title. Time ran out on Washington as Coach Jack Pardee tried rushing in Mark Moseley to try kicking a long field goal.

Prior to the game, Martin had been sent a funeral wreath that bore the inscription "From the Redskins." So, afterward, Martin charged to the visiting locker room at Texas Stadium and hurled the wreath inside the door, hitting Moseley in the head.

It gave the Cowboys a big laugh but meant a day in the Landry whipping shed for Martin.

"I remember Tom sending for me the next day," Martin said. "I wasn't sure what it was all about, but I thought I knew. I walked through the door and Tom was waiting without a smile."

Martin said he recalled Landry telling him he shouldn't have retaliated and that it made the organization look bad.

"But Coach, they sent it to me," Martin protested.

"Now Harvey, you know we don't do things that way," Landry replied. "Harvey, I want you to apologize to them."

"To the Redskins?" Martin asked.

"To the Redskins," Landry replied.

So, Martin said, "I went home and sent telegrams to the Redskins organization and to the newspapers apologizing just like Tom wanted. It sure hurt to do it."

"That was the kind of guy Tom was," Martin said. "He was first class. Although they were the enemy, we weren't allowed to act like that."

The 6-foot-5, 250-pound Martin was a third-round pick out of East Texas State in 1973. He had tremendous raw potential, but there were questions about him. His scouting report read, "Exceptional quickness for a big man, but inexperienced and undisciplined at times."

Landry, however, decided he needed someone who could put heat on the passer and inserted Martin into the lineup on third downs.

Martin progressed to the point that in 1977, he had 23 sacks and 85 tackles, an unheard of number for a defensive lineman.

"I was a little undisciplined, but I was gifted, and Tom saw that in me," Martin said. "I perfected Tom's defense later on and it was a defense I grew to love.

"However, you had to do things Tom's way. I can remember one game when I made several great plays, but they weren't within the structure of how I was supposed to be playing the defense. I thought I was going to get a big pat on the back when we ran the films the next day.

"But Tom just went on by them without saying a word. I got the point."

Martin was at Landry's 75th birthday party and said several meaningful things to the coach.

"I got an opportunity to thank him for all he meant in my life and how fortunate I was to get to play for him," Martin said. "I thanked him for sticking with me in the early part of my career. I told him that I wished I had listened to him a little more than I did. I told him, 'I heard you later in life.'"

Landry's response: "All that matters, Harvey, is that you finally heard me."

Jethro Pugh

Jethro Pugh knew plenty of football coaches and plenty of devout Christians.

But he'd never been around a football coach who was a devout Christian—until he met Tom Landry.

Pugh came to the Dallas Cowboys in 1965 as an 11th round pick from Elizabeth City State. He had read about Landry's faith but was skeptical.

"As a football player, you visualize coaches as raging, throwing around chairs, swearing, being intimidators—all those things," Pugh said. "It was so different seeing someone who had such a totally different approach to football.

"At first, I said, 'There ain't no way this guy can coach football. This guy is more of a preacher than a football coach. How can you be a Christian and a football coach?'

"But once I got to training camp and talked to veteran players like Pettis Norman, Bob Lilly, Don Perkins and Chuck Howley, they basically said, 'You've just got to believe him. For some reason, whatever he says is true. We don't know why, but it is.'"

Pugh became a believer, too. The longshot draftee made the team that summer and remained a Cowboy through 1978.

Pugh played in all five Super Bowls of the Landry era as well as the two NFL championship games against the Green Bay Packers. The second one was the "Ice Bowl," when Bart Starr dove over Pugh for the game-winning touchdown.

It wasn't completely Pugh's fault. The frozen field refused to allow him to plant his foot, causing him to fall instead of filling the hole Starr dove through.

Jethro Pugh played in all five of Landry's Super Bowls. (Photo courtesy of the Dallas Cowboys)

Pugh was having trouble getting over the disappointment of the play, so he went to talk to Landry about it. The response wasn't what he expected— or anything he wanted to hear.

"There's nothing you can do about it," Landry said. "That play will be a part of NFL history."

Landry was right. The proof came eight months later when the Cowboys played the Chicago Bears in Canton, Ohio, in the annual Hall of Fame Game. Defensive line coach Ernie Stautner already was an enshrinee and Pugh talked him into going to the museum.

"As soon as we walked in, the first action shot I saw was that quarterback sneak," Pugh said, laughing. "I thought, 'Well, Jethro, now you're in the Hall of Fame. I'm not sure you want to be here this way, but you're here.'"

Landry's no-nonsense advice was among many things Pugh learned from his coach.

"He sort of reiterated the values I was taught when I was a young man, things like going to church, how to conduct myself, how to take care of myself, have a good work ethic, doing a good job at whatever you do, finish what you start," Pugh said. "They're a lot of the same things that parents try teaching their children."

When Pugh and his former teammates look back on their glory days, one of the things they marvel at is how Landry maintained his 1950s-era wholesomeness despite being in the thick of the turbulent 1960s and early '70s.

"We talk about how he managed that situation and kept everyone together and made us a winner on the football field. That's not an easy thing to do," Pugh said. "The racial issues and all those other distractions could've been a problem, but we all just wanted to win, and Coach Landry kept us together like a family."

Pugh fondly remembers that Alicia Landry was the matriarch of that family.

"She was like a member of the team," he said. "She never missed a road game. We were accustomed to her presence. She was there when we'd walk out of the locker room after the game, standing there waiting for him. We couldn't wait for her to show up at training camp."

Since his playing career ended, Pugh has become a successful businessman. He owns five stores at the Dallas-Fort Worth airport, one in Columbus, Ohio, and a bookstore at LaGuardia Airport in New York.

It's only fitting then that one of his favorite stories about Landry involves an airplane flight.

"We had gone through this thing about wearing ties when we travel. Guys wanted to dress according to what the fashion was, but he was firm that you had to wear a tie when you traveled," Pugh said. "Well, we were all sitting on the plane when Thomas Henderson walked on wearing a tuxedo.

"Landry said, 'Hollywood! You going to play in the band?' It cracked us up because you didn't expect that from Coach Landry."

Cliff Harris

Cliff Harris was one of Tom Landry's favorite players because of an all-out, gung-ho attitude mixed with football smarts.

A free agent from tiny Ouachita Baptist College in Arkadelphia, Arkansas, Harris earned a job with the Cowboys in 1970 as a fearless free safety who hit anything that moved.

Landry immediately put "Captain Crash," as he was to be nicknamed, into the starting lineup of what proved to be a Super Bowl team.

"It was Tom's system that made players great," said Harris, who was All-Pro four times and played in six Pro Bowls over his 10 seasons. "It's a testimony to Tom that he could take a player like me and be successful."

Landry saw in Harris intelligence and a no-fear attitude. It was just the way Landry played defensive back with the New York Giants.

"His system allowed you to think," Harris said. "He would come up with some great game plans, and if you questioned it, you had better know what you were doing. You had to understand that he had already been there as a player, and what he was telling you had worked for him.

"When he sat down with you about a possible change, he would literally grill you about what you were thinking. You had better have a valid reasons for questioning the game plan."

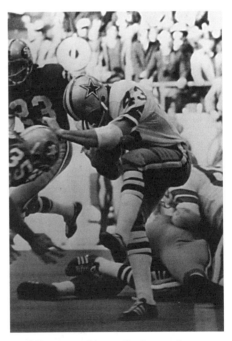

Cliff Harris shows why he was known as "Captain Crash." (Photo courtesy of Denne Freeman)

Harris said if Landry told you something was going to happen, it usually did.

"To him, it was a big chess game as much as it was brute, gladiator force," Harris said. "He wasn't wrong very often."

Woe be unto any player who busted assignments.

"You are not a pro," Landry would tell the rule-breaker. "You are just an amateur drawing pay."

Harris said that kind of criticism really stung.

"It sure motivated me to be better," Harris said. "It was an insult no pro wanted to hear. Tom was great at getting players motivated with a little psychology."

Landry could get mad if things didn't go well.

"It impressed me my rookie year how he chewed us out in the locker room at halftime of a game against the New York Giants," Harris said. "Of all the teams he wanted to beat, the Giants were No. 1. I guess it was because of his history with them. That's where his roots were.

"He told us during that game that of all places to play well was New York because that's where the media was. He said we couldn't make All-Pro if we didn't play well in New York. He loved winning there."

Harris said that all the players viewed Landry as an indestructible force who never missed a day of practice or a game because he was sick.

"When he got leukemia, we all felt like he would whip it," Harris said. "We knew it would be a battle, but we thought he would win."

That why the news of Landry's passing hit him so hard.

"It was a real traumatic moment when I heard he had died," Harris said. "We knew he was undergoing chemotherapy, but every player thought he was going to make it. It was a shock when he didn't."

Harris is left with the wonderful memory of helping host Landry's 75th birthday on September 15, 1999. It was the coach's last social function.

"His family and players were there," Harris said. "It was great hearing the guys get up and tell stories about their feelings for the coach. It was an unbelievable event. A lot of the guys had tears. It was real touching, but it was fun. You could tell he really enjoyed it."

Charlie Waters

Tom Landry saw himself in Charlie Waters.

Like Landry, Waters was a former quarterback trying to make a name for himself as a defensive back despite limited speed.

Like Landry, Waters had an instinct for the game and used his head to survive.

Like Landry, Waters played with a never-give-up attitude.

"I was exactly like him," Waters said. "I played with my mind and I think that's why he had the patience to wait on me to mature."

Waters was a third-round pick out of Clemson in 1970. Although he played quarterback and wide receiver in college, Dallas tried him on defense during training camp.

"I was scared because I had never backpedaled," Waters said.

Waters remembers that at one point, he thought Landry had given up on him.

"I got a call from coach [Jim] Myers during training camp to report with my playbook," Waters said. "I knew what that meant. I was a goner.

"Then, Coach Landry had them call me back to say there had been a mistake. They forgot I had played in the college all-star game and I didn't count on the roster until the regular season began. I was so bad, they didn't think I had played in the game."

Waters recalls catching Landry's attention before the ax could fall.

"I made some plays on special teams and caught Tom's eye and made the team," Waters said.

Before he knew it, Waters was a starter at free safety because good buddy Cliff Harris was called into the military.

Charlie Waters, an overachieving defensive back, reminded Landry of himself. (Photo courtesy of the Dallas Cowboys)

"Coach Landry was great to me through those times because he saw I could pick up his complicated defense," Waters said. "I ended up being the only rookie on our team starting in the Super Bowl."

Waters went back to the bench when Harris returned.

"He had to bench me, but told me I had a great future. That made me feel good," Waters said. "He was a genius. He developed schemes at cornerback that are still being used today. He was amazing at what he did."

Waters was moved to cornerback and had one very forgettable day when he was beaten for three touchdown passes by the Los Angeles Rams.

"I knew it was going to be brutal at the Monday meeting when we went over the films," Waters said. "He got up in front of the team and said things I'll never forget.

"He said, 'Charlie had a rough game, but I've got to say, if we had 45 guys who play as hard as he does, we'd never lose a game.'

"You think I wouldn't run through walls for him after that?" Waters said. "Bless his heart. After that, I went from almost being run out of the league to All-Pro."

Waters, who made All-Pro in the Super Bowl seasons of '77 and '78, said the Cowboys were always prepared.

"He was a great salesman," Waters said. "He always sold us a bill of goods about nobody else in the league doing what we were doing and he was right. He had an engineering degree; everything was so precise and perfect.

"Sometimes, you would see him put something on the board and wonder how that would work, but it always did."

It stunned Waters that Landry could coach the offense, defense and the kickers.

"I held for extra points and field goals and it amazed me how he could get into the heads of the kickers," Waters said. "He told them it was like a golf game with a rhythmic swing. To him, kicking was just a head game."

Waters said the team sometimes became amused by the way Landry could botch names.

"He finally got to the point where he wouldn't even try to correct it," Waters said "He figured it was your job to know he was talking about you. We would laugh about it, but I can tell you we would never tease him to his face."

Waters remembers the most animated he ever saw Landry.

"I was the emergency quarterback for a game because Roger (Staubach) was hurt, as was our third-team quarterback. That just left Danny White at quarterback.

"It was the Friday before the Sunday game and we were on a bus going to practice. I asked Tom if he thought I should take some snaps because I was going to be it if Danny went down.

"Tom starts telling me a story," Waters said. "He said when he was with the Giants and playing cornerback, the club lost both quarterbacks and they put him in a game although he hadn't practiced a down."

It was 1952, and New York was playing Pittsburgh. The Steelers had taken a 38-0 lead and knocked out the Giants' top quarterbacks, forcing Landry to take his first snaps since college. He got his nose broken while absorbing a 63-7 loss, which is still the worst in Giants history.

"Tom said the next week he got to practice all week because he knew he was going to start—and the Giants got whipped," Waters said.

Then, Landry turned to Waters and said: "The moral of this story is, *'Don't practice!'"*

Larry Cole

Larry Cole was about as unheralded as a rookie could be in 1968.

But Tom Landry saw something in the 16th-round pick out of Hawaii that made him take a chance on the big, raw-boned blond lineman.

Maybe it was because Cole was a Bob Lilly look-alike.

"It didn't hurt that I looked a little bit like Bob," Cole said. "I was the Cowboys' prototype for a successful defensive lineman. I didn't have Bob's quick feet, but I had a quick mind to go with my slow feet."

Also, Cole kept making plays that got his name in the newspaper.

"I had unbelievably good fortune," he said. "In one preseason game, I fell on a fumble. Against Green Bay, I got two sacks on Bart Starr when all the pressure was coming from the other side."

Something kept happening to the other contenders.

"Coach Landry cut Larry Stephens, then Willie Townes got hurt and an eighth-round pick didn't produce. All of a sudden, I made the team," said Cole. "But Coach Landry made sure I knew I was still a rookie. He would call the other guys like Jethro, Ed and Harvey by their first names. I was just 'Cole,' and I took a great deal of humor in it.

"Then, good things kept happening. I tipped a Joe Kapp pass, which Cornell Green intercepted against Minnesota; I threw a block and got two guys, and he scored. It was all over national television and I was the NFL player of the week. Then I scored against Washington."

Cole later scored three more touchdowns against the Redskins, prompting a rare Landry accolade one Monday: "I don't know what you're doing, Larry, but just keep on doing it."

"For Tom, that was a stand-up comic routine," Cole said.

Notice that, by then, Cole had worked his way up to "Larry."

Cole was the humor czar for the Cowboys, even coming up with the Zero Club for players who didn't get much recognition. He also was kidded by teammates for wearing sloppy clothes, so he once showed up for a team flight wearing a brand new suit with the price tags still on.

The funny man was to play in five Super Bowls and 26 playoff games before he retired.

The biggest play of Cole's career was a tackle of Washington's John Riggins that gave Dallas a chance for a 35-34 victory that put the Cowboys in the 1979 playoffs.

"I remember Tom calling that the play of a 'real pro,' and it was the nicest thing he said about me," Cole said. "Until then, he would always say that I 'got the most out of my ability.'

"Finally, I decided to retire and went into his office one day and told him I had made up my mind. He said 'Sure, if that's what you want to do.' He asked if I would like a news conference and I said I would. So, we had a little luncheon.

"It wasn't quite as big as Roger's farewell at Texas Stadium."

But it wasn't bad for the chairman of the Zero Club.

D.D. Lewis

Dwight David Lewis keeps finding out about things Tom Landry did for him.

For example, Lewis only recently learned of a kind act Landry made 14 years ago, when Lewis was working to control his alcohol problem.

"He called my daughter to comfort her and ask if there was anything he could do," Lewis said. "She never told me about it until the week he died. On his death, I found another example of just how great he was. Every time I asked him for something, he was always there."

Lewis, a third-round pick out of Mississippi State in 1968, started at linebacker in three Super Bowls for Landry, using his speed and savvy to offset a size differential. He was an unheralded but gritty player—the kind Landry always liked.

"He worked us hard, but it paid off," Lewis said. "He was always so technical. Sometimes, I felt like I had to fight being too mechanical. He was a great football coach, a genius. We just never knew what he was thinking. He kept pretty well within himself. Small talk wasn't one of his deals. That didn't make him a bad person."

However, Landry could take a minute or two for a laugh, like the time Walt Garrison wore a Richard Nixon mask to a meeting.

"All the players and coaches had a good laugh and we were waiting to see what the coach was going to do," Lewis recalled. "The coach came in all serious, then he broke up. It really relaxed us.

"Then, there was the time Don Meredith threw an interception in practice and Cornell Green picked off the ball. Don chased him down and threw his helmet at Cornell. Tom wasn't too amused this time. He said, 'Nothing funny ever happens on a football field.'"

Another time, two cute girls checked in at the hotel just across from the Cowboys' old practice field on Forest Lane. They then went to a top-floor balcony wearing nothing but their birthday suits and towels.

Lewis recalled the scene:

"The next thing we knew, they had towels wrapped around themselves and were sort of wriggling their tails at us. All the players were elbowing each other and pointing and laughing. Tom just looked straight ahead and didn't even acknowledge they were there. That was some concentration."

Lewis recalled the time Lee Roy Jordan was stunned by a Landry question during a bus ride.

"It rained and the practice field was wet, so we boarded a bus to go to another field. Lee Roy got a seat next to Coach Landry's. We were riding along when Tom turned to Lee Roy and asked, 'Back when we played Green Bay, why did you go right?'

"Lee Roy said, 'Pardon me?'"

Landry was referring to a critical play in a championship game against Green Bay several years earlier in which Jordan was out of position.

"Lee Roy couldn't believe that, after all those years, Coach Landry finally got around to asking him the question," Lewis said. "His answer was, 'I don't know, Coach.'"

Lewis felt Landry knew he was struggling with alcohol.

"I thought Tom could always see through me," Lewis said. "Somehow, he knew I was staying at bars and drinking at night. Still, it was hard for me to bring myself to go see him.

"I felt eventually I would need help. Somebody told me once, 'Your mind is like a bad neighborhood. You don't need to go in there alone.' Coach Landry was a help and was proud of me recovering from alcoholism."

Lewis said that in addition to being a solid coach, Landry also was a great psychologist.

A good example was when the Cowboys lost a Monday Night Football game 38-0 to St. Louis. Don Meredith was broadcasting the game and the fans began chanting "We want Meredith! We want Meredith!"

The game didn't sit well with Landry, who felt the team had mailed it in.

Lewis remembers Landry's wrath.

"The following Monday, Tom came in briefly and announced, 'I don't care what you guys do today. You can go play touch football if you want, for all I care.' Then, he walked out the door," Lewis said.

"After Tom left, several players got up, including Lilly and Lee Roy. They said Tom could take us only so far and give us the technical help we needed, but we are the ones who have to go out and play.

"And play we did—right into the Super Bowl.

"Tom wouldn't give you any rah-rah speeches because he figured we were pros and should figure it out ourselves. Eventually we did, and were all the better for the way Tom handled the situation."

Bob Breunig

Bob Breunig was the kind of middle linebacker Tom Landry liked for the complex Flex defense. Breunig used his brain instead of his brawn.

"His system fit my style," said Breunig, who carried on the middle linebacker tradition of Sam Huff, Jerry Tubbs and Lee Roy Jordan. "It required a lot of thinking and study. I loved the cerebral part. I wasn't an overly physical player, so I had to survive by strategy."

Breunig said Landry taught "a form of football chess."

Bob Breunig got by on his brains more than on his brawn. (Photo courtesy of the Dallas Cowboys)

"You still had to play with force and aggressiveness, but the defense was designed to always put you in the correct position," Breunig said.

Wednesdays were when Landry would give the defense its marching orders.

"It was always an eloquent game plan," Breunig said. "He had it framed in his mind how we would attack the offense. He would have the stats Ermal Allen would give him and all the computer printouts. It was something.

"He would go to the chalkboard and he was very artistic. He was an unusually gifted drawer. The lines were clear and direct. It was like a piece of art. He would tell us not to get distracted and execute. If we did, we would ultimately break the offense down."

Breunig said the front seven all had gaps to cover. It worked against most teams.

"Joe Gibbs of the Washington Redskins was the best at figuring out what Tom was trying to do, and we had trouble with them sometimes," Breunig said.

Breunig, a third-round pick out of Arizona State, was a member of Dallas' famed "Dirty Dozen" draft class in 1975. He'll never forget what that first training camp was like.

"I can remember him walking in the room for the first time to talk to us," Breunig said. "He was an imposing figure. It wasn't hard to be a little intimidated because he was such a great man. The Cowboys had been to a couple of Super Bowls and I had seen them on television. Now, here he was."

Landry was always strictly business, but Breunig can remember a time the team loosened him up during an outing at Royal Oaks Country Club in 1980.

"We all had our wives there and were watching the sun go down when someone got the harebrained idea to throw the coach in the pool," Breunig said. "There were about 12 of us, with Charlie [Waters] and Roger [Staubach]. I was thinking we had strength in numbers.

"We threw him in the pool and everybody went in with him. He laughed about it. I think he took it as a gesture of affection."

Maybe. But the Cowboys never had another pool party.

Thomas Henderson

Thomas Henderson hadn't had an all-out, shoulders-heaving, soul-cleansing cry since going through drug rehabilitation in 1983.

Then he went to Tom Landry's funeral.

"I felt like an estranged stepson who had come back home a little late, the funeral is going on and all of a sudden, you realize that you really did love your dad," Henderson said. "It really hit me for the first time. I had to walk 70, 80 yards away and I just sobbed. And sobbed. Then those old airplanes came over and I had to sob again.

"When men cry, they normally cry about all the things they should have. So some of that was Landry and some of it was tears I should've let go a while ago."

Those are the opinions of an older, wiser, sober Henderson. In his days with the Cowboys, he was all about being "Hollywood," a guy who partied even harder than he played and who epitomized everything Landry didn't.

He dressed flashy, loved to draw attention to himself and, when he was in the spotlight, that's when he seemed to shine the brightest.

At one training camp, he got around Landry's rule against facial hair by getting a note from a dermatologist. Another year, he arrived in a limousine.

Calling Landry and Henderson oil and water doesn't do justice to how far apart their personalities were.

"I can honestly say I didn't like Tom Landry," Henderson said. "But I always respected him.

"I thought he missed the emotional piece, the congratulatory piece, the nurturing, the touching. I don't think Landry ever touched me. I don't think he never hit me on the butt and said, 'Good job.' I don't think he ever grabbed me and taught me anything. He was just so distant. So, some of his tactics I didn't agree with and still don't agree with. But I've never not respected him."

There were days when Henderson didn't show that respect.

"I would give him a hard time in practice sometimes," he said. "He'd come over and start trying to give us linebacking drills, and I'd say, 'Did you ever play linebacker?' It was a fair question. But everybody would just about drop dead when I would ask him stuff like that. 'You never played linebacker, did you? What do you know about this?' He would just ignore me. He never answered."

Thomas Henderson flashes his "Hollywood" smile. (Photo courtesy of the Dallas Cowboys)

Landry's formula was all about sticking to his system. Henderson's game was all about unleashing his raw ability. That separated them as much as their off-field differences.

"He taught morality through the Flex," Henderson said, laughing. "I fought the idea you could teach me to play football. I'm a sandlot player. The more technical you get with me, the worse I get. I could either play conservative and score big on Landry's Monday test or take that step and freelance.

"Finally, when Landry saw I could play his Flex and my game, too, he let me improvise. In my fourth year, he said, 'OK, Thomas, you're getting away with it because of your speed.' That was sort of a moment of respect."

Henderson's abusive, drug-addicted lifestyle caught up with him in his fifth season. Landry felt the linebacker was out of control, so he did the only thing he could to get his attention: release him.

Henderson was angry and immediately announced his retirement. Then he tried coming back, but his addiction left him powerless. His career fizzled and his life did, too, until finally bottoming out while he was behind bars in California. Only then did he start to put the pieces of his life back together.

Once his drug-induced haze lifted, Henderson started seeing and thinking clearly again. And he started to realize that his old coach wasn't so bad after all.

"I never listened to Landry, but I heard everything he said," Henderson said. "I appreciated it. I just didn't know it. I got a chance to be in the presence of a man who no matter what you thought of him, as a husband, father and grandfather, you knew he was a man of God and Christianity.

"I'm never going to be Tom Landry, but I can look at the principled life he led and see that he was everything he said he was."

Henderson's life is in great shape these days. About five weeks after attending Landry's funeral, Henderson won a $28 million Texas Lottery jackpot.

"I was on a radio show right after I won," Henderson said, "and a guy called in and said, 'Hollywood, I believe a man in a hat had a talk with God about you.'"

John Fitzgerald

John Fitzgerald said he loved playing 11 seasons for Tom Landry, but he sure dreaded the Monday film sessions when the coach would broil those who had less-than-perfect Sundays in his own unique way.

"Monday meetings were miserable, brutal," said Fitzgerald, the starting center in three Super Bowls. "If you played a bad game, Tom would get you. Unless you were perfect, you knew you were going to get it.

"Tom didn't let anybody off the hook. It didn't matter if it was Roger [Staubach] or some rookie. He never played favorites.

"There was never any cussing. Tom had his own way of doing stuff to make you feel like dogmeat. We'd all feel bad for the one getting chewed out.

"Some guys couldn't sleep and some would get physically sick knowing what was coming. That's how bad it was. I knew because sometimes it was Fitz's day in the tub."

Fitzgerald said Landry operated on the theory that there was a fine line between a winner and a loser.

"He was a perfectionist," Fitzgerald said. "He had a tight tolerance between his level of excellence and his level of acceptance. Even the assistant coaches felt sorry for us."

John Fitzgerald was among many who dreaded Monday film sessions. (Photo courtesy of the Dallas Cowboys)

Fitzgerald said players got pumped up when the coach praised them.

"He didn't throw compliments around, so you felt good when he said you did good," he said.

Fitzgerald said game films took longer to watch than Gone With The Wind.

"It would take three or four hours to show both the offense and defense and there weren't any commercials," Fitzgerald said. "It was kind of funny. If we beat a team bad, say by 20 or 30 points, we knew we would get killed by Tom in the film room because he didn't want us to get overconfident. If we played close, he wasn't nearly as bad."

Fitzgerald recalls one time when he considered teasing the coach, but thought better of it.

"I recall he was a very good golfer and a tough opponent," Fitzgerald said. "He carried around about a 15-handicap. Well, he once played in a tournament at Denton Country Club and shot a 1-over-par 73.

"I wasn't about to kid him about being a sandbagger. I wasn't that brave."

Robert Newhouse

Tom Landry never got over wanting to be a quarterback, even though he played halfback in college and defensive back and punter in college and the pros.

Maybe that's why he called for the pass that became the greatest memory of Robert Newhouse's 12-year career as a running back.

In the fourth quarter of Super Bowl XII against Denver in January 1978, with Dallas ahead 20-10, Landry had Newhouse take a handoff to the left then throw deep to Golden Richards on the right side of the field. The throw and pass were perfectly executed for a 29-yard touchdown that was the knockout blow of the game.

"Never in my wildest dreams did I expect him to call that," said Newhouse, smiling at the memory and still laughing about it.

What made the play as surprising to Newhouse as it was to the Broncos was the fact the right-handed running back was moving to his left while throwing. That's an awkward play for quarterbacks, so you can imagine how difficult it is for a running back.

Landry had added it to the list of possible plays for the Super Bowl, so that week, the team tried it at the end of practice along with other so-called gadget plays. This one wasn't met with much success.

"I don't think I ever threw it more than two yards," Newhouse said. "But then, after practice one day, I asked Danny White how to do it. He taught me how to move my feet and shift my weight."

Still, Newhouse was shocked when the play was called. He didn't have time to think about his footwork. He just reacted—and it worked. In fact, it was the second TD pass of his career. He had a 46-yarder in 1975.

Newhouse had an interesting career. A second-round pick out of Houston in 1972, he began as a backup to Calvin Hill and Walt Garrison then became the featured back in 1975, rushing for a career-best and team-high 940 yards. When Tony Dorsett arrived in 1977, Newhouse became primarily a blocker.

After the 1983 season, Newhouse's 12th, he wasn't sure whether he'd go for a 13th year. In January, he requested a meeting with Landry to discuss it. As of March, they had yet to talk.

"I was at Valley Ranch one day doing something and I bumped into him," Newhouse said. "He said, 'I heard you wanted to see me.' So we went into his office and I told him I was thinking about coming back for another year, but I wasn't sure. He told me that he had a lot of good players at running back, but if I came back, I'd definitely be given a chance to win a spot. That was all I needed to know. I left there knowing I was done."

Danny White

When Danny White thinks about Tom Landry, he flashes back to a speech the coach gave before the last of his 454 games with the Dallas Cowboys.

"You know, we've had a rough year," Landry told the team. "I just want all of you to know that I know we never quit. We played hard. This has been a crisis year for us, but you've got to understand that when you face a crisis, the way that you handle the crisis is more important than the result of the crisis."

Said White: "I've never forgotten that because with all the wins and the great record he had, I think we learned more about him when he lost than we did when he won because the man could lose with dignity and character."

White had the misfortune of seeing Landry suffer more lows than highs.

After being the punter on the Super Bowl champion squad in 1977 and the team that went

Danny White learned how to become a coach by watching one of the best. (Photo courtesy of the Dallas Cowboys)

back to the Super Bowl in '78, White took over quarterback when Roger Staubach retired following the 1979 season.

Dallas reached the NFC championship game the first three years White was at the helm but lost to Philadelphia, San Francisco and Washington. In his last three years as the starter, the Cowboys suffered their first home play-off loss in seven years, missed the playoffs for the first time in 10 years and then lost another home playoff game. White lingered through three more disappointing seasons filled with injuries and quarterback battles.

White later got into coaching with the Arizona Rattlers of the Arena Football League. As he guided his team to a championship, White gained a better insight on his years with Landry.

"When I played, there was kind of an unspoken relationship, but I think there was a lot of mutual respect. I know I certainly had a lot of respect for him," White said. "As a coach now, I find myself continually asking, 'What would Coach Landry do in this situation?'

"It's not so much probably on the field as off the field, which I think speaks a little bit to the influence he had, being able to deal with players when they had problems and things like that. Coach Landry was always there for you."

Mike Renfro

"I was a lucky kid."

That's the way Mike Renfro saw his life with the Dallas Cowboys and Tom Landry.

Renfro's father, Ray, was an assistant coach for the Cowboys from 1968-72. Young Mike got to hang out with the players and even went to training camp in California with the team.

After a college career at TCU, Mike played six seasons for the Houston Oilers. Then, in 1984, the former Cowboys ballboy came home when Tex Schramm traded Butch Johnson to the Oilers.

"I had a great relationship with Coach Landry," said Renfro, whose best season in Dallas was 1985, when an overachieving bunch won Landry his last division title. "He had a wonderful sense of humor."

Landry also helped Renfro on a financial matter at the close of the receiver's career.

"My playing days were just about over," Renfro said. "Tom called me in during the season for those famous last words.

"I asked him to stay one more week because it would complete my 11th year in the NFL and help me financially with my pension. Tom let me stay. The decision meant thousands of dollars to me.

"That's how gracious and generous he was."

Preston Pearson

Preston Pearson spent his 14-year career playing for three of the greatest coaches of his era: Don Shula, Chuck Noll and Tom Landry. He enjoyed his greatest success under Landry.

Landry claimed Pearson in 1975 after he was cut by Noll and the Pittsburgh Steelers. As a runner-receiver out of the backfield, Pearson was the perfect fit in the Dallas offense and a key reason why the Cowboys reached the Super Bowl that season and two of the next three.

"I've been around some guys who know football, and that's the bottom line about them—they all know football and they all know how to judge talent," Pearson said. "In my opinion, 90 percent of your job as a coach is to recognize talent and put them in the right spots."

Pearson said the biggest difference in the coaches was demeanor.

For example, Shula got his points across by screaming, while Landry used his stare.

"I never heard Landry say a curse word, never really heard him raise his voice," Pearson said. "He didn't have to because he had that stare. If you were a player for Tom and you'd basically done the wrong thing, he could give you a look that just ate you apart without him having said a word."

Pearson is still eaten up by a stare he received late in his career. He believes the incident that prompted it soured his relationship with Landry.

"I had become a part of a management group that was interested in negotiating contracts and Butch Johnson was one of those guys," Pearson said. "One way or another, word got out that I was negotiating Butch's contract. Well, I was part of the team, but as a player you could not represent another player in contract negotiations.

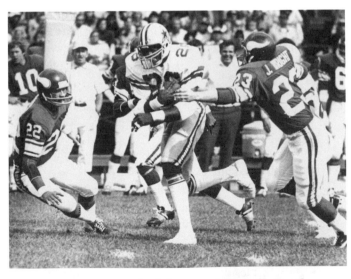

Preston Pearson was a third-down specialist and a catalyst on Landry's first Super Bowl champion. (Photo courtesy of the Dallas Cowboys)

"Tom didn't take too well to that thought.

"I came off the practice field one day and I knew there was a problem, so I immediately went to the man, and explained my side of it, like a respectful businessman. During the process of explaining my side of it, he was giving me those daggers, those swords. They were ripping me apart.

"That kind of hurt my feelings, hurt me deeply, because I thought Tom might understand—and he didn't. After that, I thought my relationship with him never really got back to where it should have been."

Ironically, it was Landry's rare involvement in a contract matter that helped Pearson become a Cowboy.

"We were going back and forth over what I consider to be a minuscule amount of money—$5,000," Pearson said. "I wanted $5,000 over and above my contract with the Steelers simply because I was going to be making a move to Dallas, having to take my kids out of school. I felt that would cover basically my moving expenses.

"Well, Gil Brandt and the Cowboys, they didn't think that was the route they wanted to take. I told them if they can't do that, then I need to move on and check out these other teams that were interested in me, San Diego and Green Bay.

"So Gil Brandt basically said, let's go see Coach Landry. We walked in, he sat me down and the first thing he said was, 'What are your concerns?' I told him and he immediately said, 'Give it to him.' I'll always be grateful to him for that."

Pearson's role was greatly reduced when Tony Dorsett arrived in 1978. The way he handled it earned Landry's highest compliment.

"Somebody asked about me after Dorsett took over and Landry said, 'Preston is a pro.' Hey, coming from Landry, that sends chills up and down your spine."

Dennis Thurman

Dennis Thurman never thought about going into coaching until Tom Landry told him that he'd be good at it. Now, Thurman has spent more years in coaching than he did playing in the NFL.

"After my seventh year, he asked me if I've given it any thought," Thurman said. "He said, 'You're a pretty good football player, but I think if you go and do this right, you'll be an even better coach. I think you have the aptitude it takes to be a successful coach.'

"He asked if I'd be opposed to going to training camp early and working with the rookies with Coach Gene Stallings. I said no, but it's why I'm doing what I'm doing today—because he planted the seed.

"I took it as a compliment. I talked to Dan Reeves and Mike Ditka about it later, and they said he'd said those things to them and planted the seeds in them, as well."

Thurman, a defensive back, played one more year in Dallas, then a year in St. Louis for Stallings, who had become coach of the Cardinals. After a year away from football, Thurman spent two seasons working for Stallings, one year in the World League and was at USC, his alma mater, from 1993-2000.

Although Thurman never coached for Landry, the coach still served as a mentor.

"He was so thorough that if you paid attention in meetings, that if you took notes and studied, then you already were picking his brain," Thurman said. "His philosophy was that we had a system and we're going to stick to it. We're going to get the athletes and plug them in, and the system is so good and so structured that it'll keep rolling.

"He looked for people who were disciplined, self-motivated, what he felt to be intelligent football players who could learn his system and get it done the way he wanted things to be done. That was pretty much the way we were—very business-oriented, very structured.

Dennis Thurman credits Landry for Thurman's getting into coaching. (Photo courtesy of the Dallas Cowboys)

"But then he got some players who didn't buy into the system. In the end, I think that cost him."

Thurman said the Xs and Os of football never bypassed Landry, but the changing attitudes of players did.

"I think he still understood the game from a tactical and strategic standpoint, but the type of athlete he was coaching started to ask, 'Why do you want me to do it like this?' rather than just saying, 'Hey, that's Tom Landry. He said do it like this.'

"It was a change in society. I think that was one of the things that bothered him more than anything else because he'd had so much success. It wasn't that he was arrogant. It's just that his attitude was, 'Hey, do it my way, and you'll have more success.'"

Thurman said Landry failed to address the growing gap.

"To me, he had a tendency to ignore it rather than do anything about it," Thurman said. "I think he wanted to believe there were just isolated cases. But, the fact of it was, that's the way things were going."

When Landry had players he could relate to, he had a knack for getting the most out of them.

"Coach Landry was a great teacher," Thurman said. "One thing I took from him was to understand how to get through to your players. You need to correct them, but have an explanation for them. Don't just tell them they can't do it; show them how to do it so they will be successful."

Thurman didn't have much of a relationship with Landry but enough of one to know there was more to the coach than just his cold game face. That point is best illustrated by a scene in a Hawaii hotel prior to the February 1981 Pro Bowl a few weeks after the Cowboys lost to Philadelphia in the NFC championship game.

"He saw me in the lobby and said, 'Dennis, how are you doing?' Then he walked over, gave me a hug and said, 'It's nice to see you,'" Thurman said. "It was a spontaneous reaction by him.

"I knew he was a warm person, but his stance was not to ever get to close to his players. That showed me that he really did care."

From 1998-2000, Thurman's boss at USC was Paul Hackett, who spent three years working with Landry. Although their Dallas tenures did not overlap, their ties to Landry give them a common ground they both cherish.

"I think anybody who ever worked for the man or was around the man had a little bit rub off on him," he said. "One way or another, you'll see the influence on the people who were around him."

Something that rubbed off on Thurman was a respect for Landry's game-day attire.

"If I ever become a head coach, I'd dress like he like did on the sidelines," Thurman said. "It says something about you as a man.

"As players, one of the things that made us feel like we were different and stood above the others was not only that we played well most of the time, but we always dressed well and classy as a group. We'd go to hotels in different cities and people would say, 'Hey, it's never like this with teams from other cities. You guys always dress the best, you look the best and you also know how to go win games.' We had it together and we knew that it all started with the head coach.

"Tom Landry, as far as I'm concerned, will not only be the man under the hat, but also the best-dressed coach in the history of the National Football League."

Bill Bates

Tom Landry picked Bill Bates to make the Dallas Cowboys in 1983 even though the free agent from Tennessee could be timed with an hourglass, as the old joke went.

Landry once said of Bates: "If we had 11 players on the field all of the time who play as hard as he does and do their homework like he does, we'd be almost impossible to beat."

Bates kept working hard and hung around for 15 years, tying Ed Jones and Mark Tuinei for the most seasons in team history. He was a three-year starter at safety and a special teams standout. In his second season, he became the first player ever chosen to the Pro Bowl just for special teams.

Bates, who four times won the Bob Lilly Award as a fan favorite, went into coaching after his career ended. After two seasons as an assistant on special teams and defense, he was promoted to secondary coach in 2000.

He credits Landry with helping set his life's goals.

"I saw the way he set his priorities and that's what I tried to follow," Bates said. "With Coach Landry, it was God first, family second, football third.

"That's the way he was."

Landry wished every player worked as hard as Bill Bates. (Photo courtesy of the Dallas Cowboys)

Everson Walls

Everson Walls has been talking about Tom Landry for about three minutes when he realizes something.

"Right now, you and I have talked about him longer than he ever spoke to me," Walls said. "But that's just the way he was.

"The unique thing about our relationship is, he always respected the way I played. Even though I didn't have the size he liked, he appreciated the fact I always made plays."

Walls' rookie year ended when he reached in vain to try stopping Dwight Clark from "The Catch" in the back of the end zone, putting San Francisco into the Super Bowl.

Landry, himself a former defensive back, never said a word about the play.

Everson Walls led the team in interceptions five times. (Photo courtesy of the Dallas Cowboys)

"Tom had plenty of tough losses," Walls said. "Just like any other coach, he learned from his experiences. He never dwelled on any particular situations. If he had, he wouldn't have been so successful."

Walls grew up in Dallas at the same time the Landry legend was growing. By the time he joined the Cowboys as an undrafted rookie out of Grambling in 1981, Walls felt like there was a distance between the aging coach and his younger players.

"It was a difficult relationship," Walls said. "He'd already established himself as a hands-off coach. The guys in the '60s and '70s, they got closer to him. But for those of us in the '80s generation, we didn't really get to know him at all.

"That generation gap was so wide and it got wider every year. So you were going to have those problems. But his formula was in place. He was depending on older players to make sure there was cohesiveness. He expected them to control the emotions of the team."

In college, Walls had the exact opposite relationship with another legendary figure, Eddie Robinson.

"It was certainly different being with Coach Robinson," Walls said. "What they had in common was that both had their hands on every aspect of running the team. But, for the most part, they were totally different."

Walls has spent enough time around the current Cowboys to have an interesting observation.

"Tom and Troy Aikman are a lot alike: country boys, kind of quiet, unassuming, perfectionists," he said. "He's the next generation Tom Landry."

Tom Rafferty

Beating the Washington Redskins was always sweet for Tom Landry.

But when the Dallas Cowboys beat the dreaded 'Skins 24-17 on December 11, 1988, there were even more reasons than usual to celebrate.

"We weren't very good that year; it was only our third victory," center Tom Rafferty said. "We'd won a couple of games early then had a long dry spell. The media was on him and on us as a team."

Rafferty took center stage in the winning locker room by making a little speech then giving Landry the game ball.

"I remember stumbling through it, kind of spitting the words out," Rafferty said.

Landry was touched. He'd received the game ball after his first victory, on September 17, 1961, and was taking home another for his 270th and, ultimately, final victory.

"I think everybody knew he deserved the game ball because he had hung with us the whole year," Rafferty said. "He got on us, but he never publicly took things out on us. He worked to make us better and never blamed us for his shortcomings.

"I mean, the next year I was there under Jimmy Johnson. Let's just say they were two totally different personalities."

Landry was fired on a Saturday and cleaned out his desk the following day. He returned Monday morning because he wanted to say goodbye to the players, who had to be there for the first day of an off-season minicamp.

"That's as uncomfortable as I can ever remember being in a meeting," Rafferty said. "He couldn't even finish what he was starting to say. We didn't know whether to get up and clap or cheer. We all just sat there. We all felt bad for him. Nobody knew what to do. He just ended it and left.

"When we went outside, they wanted us to lift. I went out to go home and he was still walking around. We said a few words, then I just hoofed it."

Rafferty succinctly compared the feelings Landry evoked in February 1989 and February 2000.

"We buried the coach in '89 when they fired him, but when we buried the person that was a lot harder," Rafferty said. "He had such great beliefs, morals, ethics. He taught

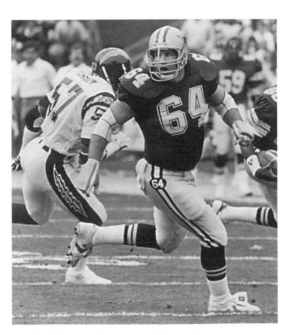

A kind gesture by Tom Rafferty meant a lot to Landry. (Photo courtesy of the Dallas Cowboys)

by example. He was the consummate 'Do as I say and do as I do' person. You don't see too many of those."

Rafferty credits Landry for making him conscious of being on time. He also said his coach taught him "to do the right thing, whether it's good for me or not."

"That's what he was all about," he said.

Rafferty was with the Cowboys from 1976 through '89. He jokes that he saw "the good, the bad and the ugly."

"As a whole, I'd say Tom was pretty much the same guy," said Rafferty, one of four players from the 1977 Super Bowl champion squad that were still there for Landry's final season. "The thing that made Coach Landry so different was that he didn't have the ups and he didn't have the downs. He was pretty steady. He'd be like a wave in the Gulf of Mexico compared to a wave on the north slope of Hawaii."

Michael Irvin

Although Michael Irvin is best remembered for his role in helping coach Jimmy Johnson rebuild the Dallas Cowboys into Super Bowl champions in the 1990s, it was Tom Landry who brought the flamboyant receiver to Dallas.

Coming out of the University of Miami in 1988, Irvin offered tremendous ability and an outrageous personality. Landry saw the substance beyond his style and made Irvin the 11th overall player taken in the draft and the final first-round pick the coach would make.

"He was such a great coach, such a great man. He was in that draft room, he approved drafting me," Irvin said humbly. "We all respect Tom Landry, what he accomplished on the field and the kind of man he was.

It's a great accomplishment that he thought enough to draft me in the first round."

Irvin rewarded Landry's faith from the start. He became the first rookie receiver to start the opener for Dallas since Bob Hayes in 1965—and he caught his first touchdown pass that day.

Then, in the second-to-last game of the year, Irvin caught six passes for a season-best 149 yards and three touchdowns as the Cowboys knocked off the defending Super Bowl champion Redskins 24-17 in Washington. The victory ended up being the last of Landry's career. The three TDs was a feat Irvin would accomplish only once more in his next 11 seasons, but the clutch performance in a big game was only a glimpse of things to come.

Landry was looking forward to using the No. 1 pick in the 1989 draft to take UCLA quarterback Troy Aikman, but was fired before he got the chance. Johnson followed through with the plan and Aikman, Irvin and 1990 draft pick Emmitt Smith led the Cowboys to Super Bowl championships following the 1992, '93 and '95 seasons.

In July 2000, five months after Landry's death, Irvin retired because of a neck injury suffered the previous October. His departure left the Cowboys' roster without a player directly tied to Landry for the first time in the team's 41-year history.

END OF AN ERA

Tom Landry made the cover of *Sports Illustrated* in November 1988, along with Chuck Noll, whom he coached against in two Super Bowls. The cover read: "Under Fire . . . Have NFL coaching legends Tom Landry and Chuck Noll lost their touch?"

The accompanying article noted some numbers that supported their theory, but, in retrospect, the most impressive figure was 197—that's how many other head coaches had come and gone on other teams while Tom Landry remained in charge of the Cowboys.

After deciding to keep coaching in 1985, Landry considered grooming a successor. Then he stunned everyone, especially Tex Schramm, by announcing one day that he planned to stick around 10 more years or as long as it took to get things headed back in the right direction.

He never got the chance.

On February 25, 1989, Schramm called Landry at an Austin golf course and said he was coming to see Landry, along with new Cowboys owner Jerry Jones. Jones already had made it known that University of Miami coach Jimmy Johnson was going to be his head coach. Still, he wanted to break the bad news in person.

Dallas residents and Cowboys fans across the nation were outraged. They didn't like a thing about Jones, and even though many people thought it was time for Landry to go, this wasn't the way it should've been done.

To show Landry how much he was loved and would be missed, the city of Dallas hosted a "Hats Off To Tom Landry" celebration. The day included a parade, a 90-minute program at Dallas City Hall, a rally at Texas Stadium and various concerts and parties.

The event cost nearly $100,000 and drew more than 100,000 people. President George Bush couldn't make it, so he sent a telegram. Bob Hope called and said, "You know, Tom, you've had winning teams for so long that a lot of people thought Tom Landry was the capital of Texas."

Other dignitaries included Mayor Annette Strauss, Gov. Bill Clements and Lt. Ellie Shuler, the commander of the 8th Air Force. Dozens of former players were involved, too.

"I know that I'm not worthy, really, of the things that have been said of me today by any measure," Landry told the crowd. "I've been blessed to be a part of this community and a part of the Dallas Cowboys."

Landry drove through the parade in a 1954 Buick Skylark convertible. He needed an 18-wheeler to take home all the gifts he was given. Among the honors were lifetime passes on several airlines; Braniff named a jet after him.

There wasn't much to smile about in Landry's final seasons. (Photo courtesy of Denne H. Freeman)

"I think the airlines want to get me out of town," Landry said.

Landry pretty much cut his ties to football after that, devoting himself to a business he started with his son and continuing his tireless work for charities and religious organizations. He also was chairman of the Dallas International Sports Commission, which was instrumental in the city becoming a site for soccer's World Cup in 1994.

Landry also spent a lot of time accepting honors.

A few of the highlights include:

- He was inducted into the Hall of Fame in 1990, along with linebackers Jack Lambert and Ted Hendricks, running back Franco Harris, quarterback Bob Griese, defensive tackle Buck Buchanan and offensive tackle Bob St. Clair.

- In 1991, Baylor University Medical Center in Dallas opened the $16 million Tom Landry Center, a sports medicine facility that includes workout facilities as well as treatment and rehabilitation.

- In 1996, the Carrollton-Farmers Branch school district in suburban Dallas opened Tom Landry Elementary. The school doesn't just carry his name. It also teaches the guiding principles of his life. "The Landry Way" is part of the school curriculum, and it uses the letters of his last name to represent loyalty, achievement, (being) neighborly, discipline, respect and you're a leader. Every six weeks, a student in each grade, kindergarten through sixth, is honored for best epitomizing those ideals.

- In 1999, the Fellowship of Christian Athletes, which already had several tributes to Landry, began a new one called the Tom Landry Excellence of Character Award.

Jerry Jones

When Arkansas oilman Jerry Jones was deciding whether to buy the Dallas Cowboys, one of the factors that made him decide to do it was his respect for Tom Landry and the way his image symbolized the franchise.

"I couldn't have made the kind of commitment in time and money and had a career change had I not respected him as one of the great figures of his time," Jones said.

But Jones also had decided Landry's time had come. As part of his plan to buy the team from Dallas businessman Bum Bright, Jones wanted his former college teammate Jimmy Johnson to become the second coach in Cowboys history.

"Mr. Bright offered to make all the changes before I bought the team," Jones said. "But I felt Coach Landry would know that ultimately my buying the team probably prompted the change, so I felt it was important that, out of respect, I visit with him about the change."

Word got out before Jones could deliver it himself. Rumors were flying about the sale and the coaching change; a picture of Jones and Johnson, then a successful coach at the University of Miami, eating together at a Mexican restaurant that was among Landry's favorites fanned the flames.

By the time Jones flew to Austin with Tex Schramm to break the news, Landry was braced for it.

Jones doesn't regret his decision to change coaches. He and Johnson rebuilt the Cowboys into Super Bowl champions in their fourth season, then defended the title. In 1995, Dallas won a third trophy in four years, this time with Barry Switzer the head coach.

Jones, however, deeply regrets how he replaced Landry.

"In hindsight, while we've ultimately had success, I probably would've done it differently," he said. "I probably made an F in that decision-making process; the timing of it. It appeared not to have the sensitivity that I really felt."

If Jones could do it again, he would've spaced out the announcements.

"The proper sequence of things would've been a public digesting of a change from Coach Landry, then probably me buying the team and then ultimately me hiring Jimmy Johnson," he said. "The sequence of events gave the impression of being insensitive and disrespectful, and that was not in my heart."

In 1993, months after Dallas won its first Super Bowl without Landry, Jones had a chance to clear the air with Landry.

"We had a good opportunity to have lunch together, just the two of us, in a very private setting," Jones said. "We had a chance to specifically talk about the events of the prior several years and what that was all about. We reconciled our thoughts as much as we could. He expressed genuine support of what we were doing and basically agreed to go into the Ring of Honor."

Landry and Jones were together several more times over the ensuing years. There was a news conference that summer to announce the Ring of Honor decision, then the celebration-filled weekend that fall. The pair also was involved in charitable functions together and Landry participated in a Cowboys' training-camp golf tournament.

Jones described their relationship as being cordial. He felt at ease enough to attend the memorial services following Landry's death.

"My wife and I were very comfortable being at the funeral to recognize what he meant," Jones said.

Jones wanted to make a grand gesture to recognize Landry this season. He came up with two.

In 2000, the Cowboys wore a fedora-shaped patch on their uniforms, much like the hat logo that hangs next to Landry's name in the Ring of Honor. The hat also appeared on parking passes, and a different Landry photo was featured on the tickets for the 11 home games. In the 2001 football season, the team will unveil a statue of Landry outside Texas Stadium. The 9-foot, 2-inch bronze sculpture is remarkably detailed. The Landry family worked with artist Robert Summers to refine all the nuances. Summers used one of Landry's fedoras, his watch and even an old pair of coaching shoes to make it as authentic as possible.

"Whether it's rationalization or not, I've always thought the best way I could do something for Coach Landry—and his legacy—is to do everything we can to make the Cowboys the top team," Jones said. "Winning teams would serve as a reminder of the franchise that he made singularly the biggest contribution to its success."

Herman Ross Fillingane

Accomplished poet Herman Ross Fillingane is inspired by his emotions. When it hits, he grabs a pen and paper and expresses himself in words and verses.

That's what happened the morning after Tom Landry was fired. Fillingane got choked up seeing a picture of the coach walking off the field following what ended up being his final game. His thoughts, though, came together quickly. Within 15 minutes, this is what he wrote:

> *The greatest men in the world*
> *The world will never know*
> *They lived only for God and Family*
> *So, they passed away unknown*
>
> *Then, sometimes there is a change*
> *When someone everyone knows and loves*
> *Becomes famous in our eyes*
> *And in God's eyes above*
>
> *You became a living legend*
> *Because of what you believed and taught*
> *Your character never questioned*
> *Dignity is what you brought*
>
> *You gave us more than football*
> *You taught the Game of Life*
> *Never selfish with your time*
> *And cherished by family and wife*
>
> *We could always tell our children*
> *No matter what was in the news*
> *When they saw the morals of others fall*
> *They could still look up to you*
>
> *You have given your strength and wisdom*
> *Your talent and most of your life*
> *To a team, a city and the world*
> *Where you are remembered for all things right*

Fillingane showed his work to his friend, Cowboys linebacker Jeff Rohrer, and the two of them took it to Roger Staubach. Staubach decided to have the poem etched in silver by Tiffany's as a gift from Landry's former players and coaches. It would be presented to Landry at an April 1989 event at Texas Stadium in his honor, and Staubach wanted Fillingane to be part of the show.

"The day of the parade, I was lucky enough to be treated like I was one of the Cowboys, even though I never was," Fillingane said. "When we got to Texas Stadium, myself, Roger and Drew Pearson walked up onstage. Roger read the words on the plaque, then we presented it to him. Coach Landry hugged my neck and told me he loved it and it would hang in a special place."

For Fillingane, it was his third personal tribute but by far his most public.

In 1976, he presented his first such poem in a private meeting with the man who inspired it: Elvis Presley. In 1984, a poem he'd written as a tribute to Ronald Reagan was presented to each delegate at the

Landry shows off the plaque given to him by his players that's etched with a poem written by Herman Ross Fillingane (left). (Photo courtesy of Herman Ross Fillingane)

Republican National Convention. Later in 1989, his tribute to Ralph Earnhardt was placed in the National Motorsports Press Association Hall of Fame.

The Landry poem remains a source of pride.

"It was from the heart," he said.

CAL LUTHERAN

Thousand Oaks, California, is an ideal place to spend two months every summer. Temperatures are always in the 80s, with hardly any humidity and always a slight breeze. The beach is nearby and Los Angeles isn't much farther.

From 1963 to 1989, that was the setting surrounding the Dallas Cowboys' training camp on the campus of California Lutheran University.

Playing host to the Cowboys was as rewarding for the school as visiting Thousand Oaks was for the team. Practices drew large crowds, helping create a strong bond between the school, which opened in 1961, and the town. Both Cal Lutheran and Thousand Oaks became known throughout the country as "the summer home of the Dallas Cowboys."

Kids buddied up with players and carried their equipment from the field to the locker room. An annual welcome dinner was the biggest bash of the summer and players sat at different tables so everyone could meet them.

Tom Landry made himself at home in Thousand Oaks, too. He prayed every Sunday at the local Methodist church and was an active speaker throughout the community. He welcomed college and high school coaches who wanted to observe him and his staff, and he reached out to the coaches at Cal Lutheran.

In 1980, the school honored him by creating The Landry Medal. The award honors "those who are an inspiration to America's youth."

"Recipients are individuals who provide leadership through strong

Summers in Thousand Oaks, California, were no vacation for Landry. (Photo courtesy of the Dallas Cowboys)

Christian commitment and who distinguish themselves through the integrity of their personal lives and careers," according to a school brochure.

The medal has been given out annually all but twice since cartoonist Charles M. Schulz received the first one in 1980. Coincidentally, Schulz and Landry both died February 12, 2000.

Recipients have covered a wide range. In addition to an athlete (Roger Staubach), a sportswriter (Jim Murray) and three coaches (Sparky Anderson, Gene Stallings, John Wooden), there also have been many politicians, businessmen and entertainers, including Bob Hope.

The annual presentation banquet is the school's biggest event of the year. The money raised goes toward the school's scholarship fund.

On June 22, 2000, Cal Lutheran held a special tribute dinner in honor of the medal's namesake. Several of Landry's relatives, including his widow Alicia, attended the event.

Bob Shoup

For 26 years, Bob Shoup attended sort of an informal summer school on Cal Lutheran. His professor was Tom Landry.

As the school's head football coach, Shoup (rhymes with "trout") was the de facto host for Landry and the Dallas Cowboys. He spent a lot of time around the team and the coaches, and he paid close attention to Landry in hopes of picking up a few tricks of the trade.

"I think the biggest thing that affected me was his patience with all people, in all circumstances," Shoup said. "I watched him sign autographs after all the other players and coaches had left the practice field. It was late in the afternoon and I knew he was tired, but he just never refused a request. I've tried to emulate that in my personal and coaching life as well."

Shoup understood that summers were an important time for Landry. So although he watched, he tried not to be heard.

"He was busy from early in the morning until late at night. So I did the best to not infringe on what I felt were his few very precious moments where he was not actively coaching," he said.

The Cowboys' scouting department always cast a wide net for talent, which led to an overcrowding at positions during training camp. It was up to Landry to decide who stayed and who went, which created some tense times in the serene setting.

"Not only was he involved in the evaluation process, but at the end, as each of those players were waived or cut or traded, Landry had to be the person who gave the final word. The famous phrase, 'Coach Landry wants to see you, and bring your playbook' meant that you were not going to remain with the Cowboys," Shoup said.

In recent years, the Cowboys' training camps have been marred by players trashing a dormitory in Austin and a bizarre incident in Wichita Falls in which one player cut another's neck with a pair of scissors. Things like that didn't happen during Landry's reign.

"He just ran a really good ship," Shoup said. "I think everybody knew what his rules were and you needed to make sure you remained within those rules."

Each summer, Shoup and Landry put together two major events: a coaching clinic that drew as many as 500 people and a charity function known as the Christian Businessmen's Club Day.

"Youngsters were brought in by various Christian businessmen in the Southwest," Shoup said. "He just never said no. Whatever the situation was, he rose to the occasion. I was always very happy to count on him as a colleague, as well as a friend."

The careers of Shoup and Landry mirrored each other a bit.

Shoup's team won its first national championship in December 1971. A few weeks later, Landry's Cowboys won their first Super Bowl.

Landry was forced out of coaching in 1989; Shoup gave it up in 1990.

In the 1990s, the pair was together almost every year for the presentation ceremony of the Landry Medal, which Shoup helped to create.

CALIFORNIA LUTHERAN UNIVERSITY
Thursday, June 22, 2000 ★ Hyatt Westlake Plaza

A Tribute to
Tom Landry

Instead of giving out the Landry Medal in 2000, California Lutheran held a banquet in honor of the award's namesake. (Photo courtesy of California Lutheran University)

"We were anxious to take advantage of our long-standing relationship," Shoup said. "I'm just real proud the university singled him out for that high honor and bestowed it on other people as well.

"I don't think he ever missed a presentation. Not even in 1999, when he didn't feel well. He and I were going to have lunch with the president of the university. He was in Los Angeles and said he just didn't feel well. But he showed up for the banquet that night and I don't think very many of the people knew he wasn't feeling well."

After Landry's death, Shoup represented the school at the memorial services in Dallas.

"It was an uplifting experience," he said. "I went home feeling very good about the world in general. I was disappointed with the loss of a dynamic person, but I think he would've been very pleased with those events."

George Engdahl

The 2000 recipient of the Landry Medal was chosen early in the year but had not been notified when school officials put things on hold because of the failing health of the honor's namesake.

"We decided it wasn't the right thing to do," said George Engdahl, the school's vice president of advancement and overseer of the award. "Then, after Tom died and things settled down, I thought that because of the love this community has for Tom, Dallas, Alicia and everybody else, it was real important that we do something.

"So, Bob Shoup and I were sitting here thinking about honoring Tom's life and celebrating those wonderful summers. The more we talked about it, the more enthusiastic we got. Then we just started calling around and everybody got excited about it.

"Alicia was a little bit hesitant at first. But she later told me, 'I'm glad we're doing this.'"

Engdahl's relationship with Landry goes back to the first summer the Cowboys were on the campus. He was a student taking classes and working the soda fountain. He remained on the scene a dozen more years as a student and school employee. Among his duties was planning the Community Leaders Club's annual dinner, which brought together the team and the community. Landry spoke at the function every year.

"Through those summers, I developed relationships with Tom and others," Engdahl said. "It wasn't a close personal relationship, but there was always that feeling of 'Welcome back.'"

Engdahl left the school in the mid-70s and returned in the late '90s. Working on the Landry Medal was one of the perks of his new job because it reunited him with Landry.

"Although I was a nobody in the early days, he still remembered me," Engdahl said. "It was like time had stood still.

"He always treated everybody the same and he always had time for people. He never turned down an autograph request. It's easy to see why everybody around here absolutely adored him."

In the fall of 1998, Engdahl traveled to Dallas to personally tell businessman Robert Dedman he'd been chosen to receive the Landry Medal. While he was in town, he met with Landry at his office for help on another project.

"We were getting ready to launch a new capital campaign that would include a new football stadium and a whole new athletic complex at what we call the north campus of our university. I asked Tom if he would serve as our honorary chairperson of the football portion of our project," he said. "We sat in his office for about an hour and went over the plans and he consented to do that."

Landry's willingness to help was no surprise. In the years the Cowboys were on campus, Landry and other team officials very involved in developing the school's athletic facilities.

When it came time for Dedman to receive the award, Landry flew to Los Angeles as usual. The day before the banquet, Engdahl arranged for a golf outing at the Los Angeles Country Club and he ended up sharing a cart with Landry.

"That was my last memory of Tom and my most cherished," Engdahl said. "We just talked about the old days, who was where and so on and so forth. We even talked about the death of his daughter. He was still pretty shaken by it.

"It was such a wonderful day. You know, everything that's written about him—all the adjectives—it's all true."

Chapter Five

THE ASSISTANTS

Tom Landry's knack for judging talent wasn't limited to players. He also had a keen eye when it came to picking assistant coaches.

That ability was displayed best at Super Bowl XX in January 1986 when Mike Ditka of the Chicago Bears coached against Raymond Berry of the New England Patriots. Both were graduates of the Landry School of Coaching, both handpicked by the schoolmaster after successful playing careers.

Dan Reeves is another of the program's success stories, having coached Denver and Atlanta to four Super Bowls after leaving Dallas.

Landry brought Gene Stallings and John Mackovic into his graduate-level program after they'd both worked as college head coaches. Other NFL teams plucked both away and made them head coaches. Former NFL players Dick Nolan and Jim Shofner became head coaches a few years after leaving Landry's staff.

Reeves is the only one still a head coach in the NFL, although Paul Hackett—who was once being groomed to replace Landry in Dallas—is now the offensive coordinator of the New York Jets.

Jim Myers

Jim Myers always knew whether his work was pleasing to his boss of a quarter of a century.

"If he thought I was doing a good job he would call me 'James,'" Myers said. "My wife always got a big kick out of that."

What if things didn't go so well?

"Well, if looks could have killed, Tom would have never coached the Cowboys because he would have been in prison all of his life," Myers said, laughing. "He could make you feel like a sheep-killing dog."

Myers had a unique perspective of his boss and friend who hired Myers in 1962 after Texas A&M let him go.

"My contract had run out at A&M and I went into school president Earl Rudder to look over my new one," Myers said. "I looked at it and said, 'I'd rather be fired than settle for this contract.' Rudder said 'OK, you're fired.'"

Landry quickly put Myers to work as a scout, then made him the offensive line coach. He held that job through 1986, two seasons before Landry finished.

"I'm not sure I ever signed a contract," Myers said. "He just put me to work. Nobody could have ever had a better boss. He let you do your job."

Myers said the early 1960s were a challenge as Landry tried to build a winner.

Jim Myers was Landry's right-hand man for three decades. (Photo courtesy of the Dallas Cowboys)

In fact, Landry made a joke about it to Chicago coach George Halas that still makes Myers smile.

"We were playing the Bears in Soldier Field and Tom walked out on the field with Halas," Myers said. "They stood there talking for a while and then our whole squad came charging out of the tunnel.

"They made a mad sprint for the Cowboys sidelines that impressed Mr. Halas. He asked Tom, 'That's amazing. How do you get your team to do that?'

"Tom laughed and said, 'It's easy. I told them the last 11 players arriving on the bench had to start against your team.'

"You should have seen Mr. Halas laugh."

Landry could even find humor in his fiery special teams coach, Mike Ditka.

"Mike had a big temper," Myers said. "An official made a call against his special teams and Mike walked five yards out on the field and threw his clipboard down.

"The officials started walking toward him, but Tom calmed things down. He smiled and said to the officials and Ditka, 'Just ignore him. You know ol' Mike isn't worth 15 yards.'"

Myers said that before the debut of computers, Landry used a slide rule to figure out team projections.

"He would take our preseason statistics, put a slide rule to them and project our goals for the upcoming year in various categories," Myers said. "He would figure out offensive yardage, defensive stats, everything based on the preseason.

"I started calling him 'Slide Rule Tom.' It was amazing how close he came to the actual performances. Tom had a brilliant mind, but he didn't push it on anybody. I was around a lot of great coaches in my 40 years of coaching, like Red Sanders and Gen. Robert Neyland. But Tom could analyze things quicker than anybody I ever saw.

"We eventually got into computers and made some good draft picks and some bad draft picks. But Tom's mind was almost quicker than any computer."

During training camp at Thousand Oaks, California, Landry depended on Myers to do several things other than coach.

"I roomed across the hall from Tom and did all the breakfast cooking," Myers said. "I was also nominated for the unsavory task of telling players to get their playbooks together and report to Tom because they were about to be cut.

"Walt Garrison called me 'The Turk,' but I was just the messenger. I guess Tom picked me because I was in the Marine Corps. It was tough seeing some 280-pound lineman in tears waiting to be cut, but an old Marine could handle it."

Myers also had the duty of bed check. One night, he discovered Tony Hill missing.

"It was an elaborate scam," Myers said. "He had put stuff in the bed like he was sleeping. He even had the playbook opened up like he had been studying."

"I saw a softer side of Tom that night. The fine was supposed to be $17,000. Tom just fined him $5,000. Discipline was one of Tom's strong points, but I think he had a little favoritism toward Tony."

Myers said Landry was conservative with his compliments.

"I can remember one time when Tom came into a dressing room after a big win and said, 'You guys did a great job,'" Myers said. "Everybody started looking around. They were wondering who he was talking to. You very seldom got a lot of praise. He figured your job was to do your job, and that was it."

The relationship between Myers and Landry was strengthened by their mutual devotion to the Fellowship of Christian Athletes. Landry helped start the Dallas FCA chapter and Myers was the driving force behind the Tom Landry FCA Open golf tournament becoming a gigantic success. It's grown from an event that made $50,000 the first year Myers took over in 1980 to generating $640,000 in 2000.

In return, the Dallas FCA made Myers the first recipient of the Tom Landry Excellence of Character Award. He received the honor, which included a bust of Landry, at a November 1999 ceremony that the namesake was too ill to attend.

Landry died three months later. Myers said it was difficult for him to believe that his strong-hearted friend was gone.

"I thought Tom would live forever because he was always so health-conscious," Myers said. "He was in just great shape.

"But there was no question to me that he was sick when I worked his golf tournament with him the last time. He didn't have that look in his eye. It was hard to see him go. We had some great seasons together."

Jerry Tubbs

There were only two original members of the Dallas Cowboys who were with the organization until the infamous Saturday night massacre in 1989: Landry and Jerry Tubbs.

Tubbs had the unique perspective of observing Landry as both a coach and a player. Tubbs was second in Landry's long line of great middle line-backers, making All-Pro once in nine seasons in Dallas, then taking a job on Landry's staff.

"His integrity was something," Tubbs said. "If he said something, you could believe it.

"Sure, he wasn't perfect. We all have things in our life we messed up some and wished we could do differently.

"Most of us have a dump truck full of stuff. He just had a toy dump truck full of imperfections."

Tubbs recalled that Landry was in the mold of John Wayne.

"He was tough. He had what I call a World War II mentality," Tubbs said. "He believed it was your job to do something right and you didn't get bragged on when you did. He didn't think it was his job to motivate you. He demanded that you do your job and it worked."

Tubbs said Landry softened his attitude in later years.

"At some point, I think he started thinking in his own mind, 'I need to change.' He started understanding players a little more. It was not easy for him. He was used to 'my way or the highway.' He was still tough as the devil, but by 1980, he had a better understanding of people.

"The last few years, he was still tough, but maybe too understanding. He might have hung on to some people a little too long. He liked a player that would give you all he had. He believed in experience. He would go to war for an experienced guy he believed in."

Tubbs said Landry was no party animal, but he did host some gatherings at his house.

"At a party like that, he was always upbeat," Tubbs said. "He would make jokes and had a subtle sense of humor.

"For his 50th anniversary, he had people over and a lot of the coaches were there. He made a good speech. Alicia made a good speech. Everybody was laughing and carrying on."

But the best time of all was after the Cowboys had finally won a championship, Super Bowl VI.

"It was a relief for Tom to win a Super Bowl," Tubbs said. "We were all sick of hearing that 'Next Year's Champions' crud. It really relaxed Tom. It took a lot of strain off of him. Nobody could take that away.

"We were all part of something special and Tom was the one who got us there. He was a great guy, and it was too bad what happened with him being fired.

"But, you know, it might have been the best thing that happened to him. People didn't like the way the new owner handled it and Tom got the nation's sympathy. In the long run, it worked out well for him.

"Tom was a great guy, but he didn't have a scintillating personality."

Tubbs sized up Landry this way: "I'll remember him as being World War II serious."

Ernie Stautner

Tom Landry's face met Ernie Stautner's fist almost a decade before they worked together for the Cowboys.

Stautner was a fire-breathing defensive lineman for the Pittsburgh Steelers and Landry was making his first-ever appearance as a substitute quarterback for the New York Giants.

"That's when we had our first contact," Stautner said.

It was 1952, and the Steelers had run up a 38-0 lead and knocked out the Giants' starting quarterback and his backup by the second quarter. Coach Steve Owen was desperate, so he put in Landry, who hadn't thrown the ball since college.

Pittsburgh wasn't about to let an emergency quarterback beat them, Stautner said.

"I broke free on a play and my fist slipped through his face mask and knocked him on the ground," said Stautner, who had a Hall of Fame career.

"He came up fighting mad with his nose bloodied. He kept pounding on my back as I walked back to the line of scrimmage."

Years later, Stautner got a call from Landry for a job interview. Stautner wondered if Landry had forgiven him for past transgressions.

"After the interview, Tom told me he would let me know if I got the job," Stautner said. "He called me back and I walked into his office. He said, 'Ernie, I'm going to hire you. You want to know why? I'm going to hire you so I can fire you.'

"All I know is it took him 24 years and I went out the door with him after Jerry Jones bought the team."

Stautner, a rugged sort with the physique of a lumberjack, left the team two weeks before Landry was fired.

Early on, Stautner learned that the man he almost knocked out was as tough as a fence post.

"There wasn't much time for sleep during the season, I guarantee you that," Stautner said. "I would get up at 3 a.m. every day and get back to sleep at midnight. I liked road games so we would get some rest.

"We were always very prepared. He would work just as hard as he made us work.

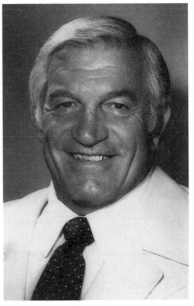

Landry forgave Ernie Stautner for punching him in their playing days, then entrusted Stautner with the Doomsday Defense. (Photo courtesy of the Dallas Cowboys)

He wasn't just the king who told us what to do and took off.

"Training camps were horrible, too, how hard we worked. I guess we got four hours of sleep a night then."

It was ironic that Landry, the stoic and calm one, would hire coaches as explosive and emotional as Stautner and Mike Ditka.

"How he ever tolerated me and Ditka, I'll never know," Stautner said. "He was a great coach. He taught me a lot."

Dick Nolan

Dick Nolan got to know Tom Landry every way you could.

Nolan was Landry's teammate and one of his players on the New York Giants in the 1950s, played for him and coached with him in Dallas in the '60s, then coached the San Francisco 49ers against him in the early '70s.

"I even knew Tom when he had hair" is the way Nolan jokingly describes how far they go back.

Nolan was the left cornerback and Landry the right cornerback on the Giants. Landry also was the defensive coach.

"He was a very smart, detailed, methodical guy," Nolan said. "I remember Tom drew up a play one time and I questioned it. It was a coverage play and I wasn't sure my man would be there like he was supposed to be."

Landry looked at Nolan with sure-fire confidence and said, "He'll be there."

And he was.

Nolan retired as a player after the 1961 season. He came to Dallas the next year.

"I thought I was going to coach the secondary," Nolan said. "Boy, was I wrong."

Landry had other ideas.

"He asked me on a Saturday how I'd like to play again," Nolan said. "I told him I hadn't worked out and I was 25 pounds overweight. Finally, I said, 'When do you want me to start?'"

"Tomorrow!" Landry replied.

A stunned Nolan took the field the next day against the Philadelphia Eagles as starting safety, backing up youngsters Mike Gaechter and Cornell Green at the corners.

Dick Nolan played with, played for, coached under and coached against Landry. (Photo courtesy of Denne Freeman)

"I fought for my life on every play," Nolan recalled. "It was 107 degrees in the Cotton Bowl and I must have lost 25 pounds. Tom was a competitor and he knew I was a competitor."

Nolan had a tough year playing for Landry.

"I dislocated my shoulder three times during the season," Nolan said. "I told Tom, 'You can stick a gun in my back, but I'm not playing anymore.'"

Nolan because a full-time coach after that.

Landry and Nolan ended up being deep defensive schemers and made the Cowboys one of the best defensive teams in football. They would spend hours at Landry's house each Wednesday night during the season, burning the midnight oil.

"We would watch film of the other team 10 times or so," Nolan said. "He would always say, 'You can see something different every time you run the film.'"

Nolan later left to coach the 49ers and, as fate would have it, met the Cowboys twice in NFC championship games. San Francisco lost narrowly on both occasions, sending Dallas to its first two Super Bowls.

"We came so close to beating them," Nolan said "He was a hard guy to get down and I thought I had him whipped twice. As it turned out, I was his victim twice."

One of Nolan's fondest memories was in a game he and Landry played for the Giants against the Los Angeles Rams. They had Deacon Dan Towler, a bruising runner who specialized in short-yardage plays, especially touchdowns.

Towler charged through and crashed into a goal post, which in those days were planted on the goal line. It nearly knocked him out.

"Who hit me?" Towler asked.

"We did," Nolan said, with Landry standing nearby. "And if you come back this way again, we'll give it to you again."

Raymond Berry

Raymond Berry, the son of a successful high school coach, had a reputation for being a student of the game during his Hall of Fame career as a receiver for the Baltimore Colts.

But when his career ended, Berry planned to go into the business world. He even had a job lined up in Baltimore.

Then Tom Landry called.

"He wanted me to be in charge of his pass offense," Berry said. "I told him, 'Tom, I'm not capable of running your offense. Up the road maybe, but not now. I've concentrated on being a player for 13 years. One of my strengths as a player was that I could tune everything else out and concentrate only on my job. In coaching, I'm going to have to learn this game from another angle totally.'"

"After several conversations with him, I decided to go to Dallas and go into coaching."

Berry started in Dallas in 1968. He remained in coaching through 1989. Along the way, he guided the New England Patriots to the Super Bowl in January 1986, losing to fellow Landry disciple Mike Ditka and the Chicago Bears.

"To be able to go from 13 years playing in the Baltimore Colts system to the Cowboys system was great because he was doing things at that time that we weren't even dreaming about doing in Baltimore," Berry said. "I learned so much about coaching from him."

At the time, Landry was pioneering the use of formation changes, motion and shifting. It was all part of an overall philosophy that Berry compared to a military strategy.

"His whole intent was to prevent the defense from recognizing the point of attack until it was too late," Berry said. "He knew if he could neutralize in their heads where we were going to hit then they wouldn't be able to stop it."

Berry and Landry didn't have much of a relationship before they began working together, although their paths had crossed many times.

It started in 1947 when Berry, a teenager, went to the Cotton Bowl and saw Landry and the Texas Longhorns lose 14-13 to Southern Methodist. Next came a 1955 game between the Colts and the New York Giant, when Berry was a rookie receiver and Landry was in his last season as a defensive back. In 1958, the Colts beat the Giants in "The Greatest Game Ever Played," with Landry coaching New York's defense.

After Landry joined the Cowboys in 1960, he lost to Berry's Colts three times, including a so-called "playoff bowl" game in 1965, which was the first postseason game in Cowboys history.

"We were not really aware of Tom when he was with the Giants," Berry said. "We weren't in their division, so we didn't play them twice a year. But we played them enough to know they had a very unusual defense that was difficult to beat.

"I became aware of the caliber of coach he was by watching Dallas in '60, '61, '62. They were very undermanned, yet they were competing right at the top offensively. They were putting up a tremendous amount of points with an expansion group of players.

"They were doing it because of the innovation and application of so many things that Tom, being a defensive coach, knew were difficult to defend so he was installing them in their offense. That caught my eye and a lot of others' too."

Berry remains amazed by Landry's coaching ability.

"I can't think of a coach that's ever come along in pro football who could do what he did in establishing a defensive system then establishing an offensive system. That's just unheard of," he said. "He brought such a rare combination of abilities to his job.

"When I became a coach, I basically carried out my father's advice. He said, 'You don't have to know it all. You've just got to hire the people who do.' That's a totally different approach than Tom Landry had."

But there were similarities between Berry and Landry.

"When I was a head coach, people would watch our games on television and tell me, 'Raymond, you don't smile enough.' People who saw Tom on the day of a ballgame weren't going to see a whole lot of personality either," Berry said.

"The man was able to concentrate totally on what he was doing. So did I. As coaches, we're involved in surgery out there. We've got to focus on our patient."

Berry said Landry's intense focus gave off the impression that he was cold or aloof when he actually was a caring person with a good sense of humor.

"Tom Landry was not perfect by any means. He had the same struggles in life that all the rest of us have. But he had better equipment to deal with it than most of us.

"It's kind of like when he had Bob Hayes, the fastest human in the world, playing wide receiver for him. What Bob brought to the table was that he could just outrun everybody. Well, Tom Landry, what he brought to the table was that he could think better than all the rest of us."

Sid Gillman

When Tom Landry decided to start a "research and development" department, he asked Sid Gillman to help run it.

Gillman, an offensive guru, had been a successful coach with the Los Angeles Rams, where he worked with a general manager named Tex Schramm, and the Chargers, which he coached from their inception in 1960 through 1969 and again in 1971.

Gillman joined the Cowboys in '72, taking on the title "special assistant to the head coach." Ermal Allen, who'd been a Landry assistant since '62, also had the same title.

Neither had on-field duties; instead, Landry wanted them to study the rest of the league, research trends and evaluate players then report back to the rest of the assistant coaches.

"He was a top-notch coach and a top-notch individual, without question," said Gillman, himself a Hall of Famer. "I had so much respect for Tom. He was one of the top coaches I've ever known. He was really great."

Gillman, though, spent only one season with the Cowboys. Oilers owner Bud Adams lured Gillman away by making him the general manager.

Offensive guru Sid Gillman spent only one season as a Landry assistant. (Photo courtesy of the Dallas Cowboys)

"I hated to leave Dallas, but I went to Houston because there weren't that many general manager jobs," Gillman said. "That was the only reason I left."

The years have clouded Gillman's memory of specifics during his year in Dallas. However, there is one thing that still stands out.

"We had dinner together a lot during the season, the whole coaching staff," he said. "That was really a great time."

Gillman's past relationship with Schramm has led to speculation that if Landry wasn't the first coach of the Cowboys, Gillman might have been.

"Probably," he said. "Tex and I knew each other pretty well."

Despite their long coaching careers, Gillman and Landry only went head-to-head one time. In 1974, after Gillman had become Houston's GM and coach, the Cowboys beat the Oilers 10-0 in the Astrodome.

Paul Hackett

Paul Hackett was supposed to be the second coach of the Dallas Cowboys. Problem was, the first coach wasn't ready to leave.

"That was clear from the beginning," said Hackett, who oversaw Landry's pass offense from 1986-88, the coach's final three seasons.

Tex Schramm liked what he'd seen in Hackett, an up-and-coming assistant in Bill Walsh's new-era offense in San Francisco. Schramm's plan was for Landry to groom Hackett then turn the reins over when he was ready. Along the way, Hackett could add some modern ideas to Landry's stagnant playbook.

"At that time, everyone was enamored with Bill Walsh's offense," said Hackett, who was part of the early lineage of Walsh disciples, a group that included Sam Wyche, Mike Holmgren and Dennis Green. "I think Tex Schramm was fascinated by it.

"Coach Landry was interested in it, although I don't think he had the same interest that Tex did."

Landry's system had been so successful for so long, yet by the mid-'80s, things weren't going so great. The Cowboys' combined offensive numbers for the two-year span prior to Hackett's arrival were their worst since 1964-65, the last two seasons before Landry's famed streak of 20 consecutive winning seasons began.

"I think they said to themselves, 'Hey, if we're going to stay on the cutting edge, let's get somebody in here who understands it and can show us about it,'" Hackett said.

"I think Coach Landry was a man of his word and great honor. He did a great job holding up his end of the bargain as far as letting me be involved and do things."

Landry was open-minded enough to accept changes he thought were improvements.

"What caught his eye offensively were things that were going to make it tough for the defense," Hackett said. "He'd say, 'You know, Paul, this looks really good.' Or he'd come into my office after the first practice after game-planning and he would say, 'I like this,' or 'How about that?'

"As far as a wholesale change from what he'd been doing for all those years and had won all those divisions, there was no way you ever could have convinced Tom this was better than what he was doing before."

Hackett estimates that he changed about 30 percent of the playbook his first season.

"We certainly weren't going to change the whole offense," Hackett said. "We took bits and pieces of the Bill Walsh offense and tried to infuse into Tom's offense. That was the whole intention—picking and choosing which things to bring in.

"I think it was a sound, sound theory. And there was evidence early that season that the concept was working and we were heading in the right direction. But by the end of the year, all that had been forgotten."

Dallas started 6-2 in 1986, then quarterback Danny White broke his wrist and Steve Pelluer took his place. The Cowboys lost seven of their last eight, including the last five, to finish 7-9—ending the streak of winning seasons.

That off-season, Hackett turned down a chance to become the head coach at the University of Southern California because he wanted to see things work out in Dallas. But a players strike caused turmoil early in 1987, then the Cowboys went 7-8 with a stretch of seven losses in nine weeks. They won their last two games after Landry went with a back-to-basics playbook for Pelluer.

"That second year, things were tense," Hackett said. "We were trying to do some new things, but not too much so it wouldn't hurt the core of what we had—yet the core was struggling. The end result was that we were a bad team, offense and defense. A lot of the things that went on led us to say, 'Hey, we're going in the wrong direction.'

"He wanted to get back to what he knew and understood and was comfortable with. So he got more and more involved, to the point where, by the end of that year, there were a lot of questions about me and my role."

Still, Landry kept Hackett.

"He agreed to try it one more year, but I think there was some real hesitation on his part that maybe it wasn't working," Hackett said. "I'd be lying to say I wasn't doubting it too."

Dallas went 3-13 the next year, which was the last for Hackett and Landry.

"I will always be the coach I am because of what I learned from watching him handle adversity," said Hackett, who became head coach at the University of Pittsburgh from 1989-92, worked for the Kansas City Chiefs from '93-97 and in '98 got the USC job he'd turned down almost a decade before. He coached the Trojans for three seasons, then was fired in November 2000 after going 19-18.

"Coach Landry was a master of remaining steady when things were exploding around him. He was being hammered mercilessly in the newspapers, but he never blinked, never faltered. He believed in himself, believed in the Cowboys, believed in the system, believed in all of us.

"It was really something to behold. There's no question that was the No. 1 thing I left with. When things go bad, and I've had my share, that's always part of my thinking."

Hackett's fondest memories are of dinners spent with Landry during road trips.

"If you got lucky, he would not have a dinner engagement and you could kind of snuggle up to his table. Inevitably, old stories would come up about the war, the early days of the Cowboys, the Lombardi days with the Giants," Hackett said.

"He loved those Saturday nights. It was the night before a game and he always felt prepared. Of course, I'm sure he left the table, went upstairs and spent another four or five hours watching video in his room, preparing.

"If I had it to do over, that's where I really should've been."

Despite the way things worked out in Dallas, Hackett is glad he tried.

"The experience of being with Tom, Jim Myers and being around the Cowboy organization, it was an absolutely fascinating period of time for someone who was consumed with football like I am," he said. "It was a tremendous learning and growing experience—not as nice as I would've liked, but the growing was what I anticipated.

"It was a thrilling time in my life. I consider it a wonderful experience."

John Mackovic

John Mackovic began absorbing Tom Landry's influence 15 years before he joined the Dallas Cowboys.

"I was so much of a fan that in 1966, when I was an assistant high school coach, we put in shifting patterns just like the Cowboys," Mackovic said. "My head coach, who had been my high school coach, could not understand it. He said, 'How in the world can you do this?' I said, 'It's really neat. Let me show you how it works.'

"We had players shifting and moving, and they loved it. They thought it was fantastic."

Mackovic appreciated the cerebral side of football and looked to Landry as a pioneer long before joining his staff as quarterbacks coach in 1981.

"He made football as much an art as it was a science or anything else," Mackovic said. "He was one of the great thinkers. Genius is a word that gets used so much, it's almost unfair. It suggests he couldn't be that good

"But he really had a brilliant mind.

"He had a discipline of purpose and an uncanny ability to stick with what he believed, even when things weren't great. His whole life was that way. Football was just something he did. That's how he made his living, how he made his career."

Mackovic noted that Landry had a degree in industrial engineering. He's convinced that Landry would've been just as successful in that field or any other he might have chosen.

"He might've been one of those guys up there in space, instead of John Glenn," Mackovic said.

NASA's loss was the NFL's gain. Landry invented revolutionary formations on offense and defense, plus brought in so many wrinkles that are now taken for granted.

"One of the things he taught that every coach in football uses now is situational play-calling," Mackovic said. "For years, coaches just had formations and plays and called them. Tom Landry started the technique of breaking the game plan down to situations like first-and-10, second-and-3-to-5 or second-and-1-to-2, third and short, third-and-medium and third-and-long.

"Then he trained the team in segments of the game plan. Rather than running plays and picking them out of a hat on Sunday, he trained them to be ready for particular plays. Even in 1980, many teams were not doing that yet. And he had been doing it long before that."

Mackovic was preparing for his fourth year as coach of Wake Forest, his alma mater, when Landry hired him to replace Dan Reeves on the Cowboys' staff after Reeves had become head coach at Denver.

Mackovic worked with other assistants to put together parts of the game plan. They would then work with Landry to put the whole thing together.

"He would start, we would start, then he would finish," he said. "There were times he didn't like what we brought, and he'd say, 'Go back to the drawing board. This doesn't fit the way I see it. You're not done. You still don't have this thing put together the way it should be done.' But he was always open to suggestions. He didn't always take them, but no one should."

While getting ready to play Philadelphia one week, Mackovic thought he'd discovered a weakness in the Eagles' defense.

"I told him I had a sure-fire touchdown pass and he stopped the meeting and said, 'Oh. You do? Why don't you tell us about it,'" Mackovic said. "So I went through the whole play—diagrammed it, told him about the cornerback and what he was doing and showed how I thought it would work.

"Then he just kind of looked at me and said, 'John, we tried it on him three years ago. It didn't work then and I doubt it's going to work here.'"

Mackovic made another big pitch that Landry squelched.

"We were getting ready to play the Redskins, and I said, 'Coach, we ran that play against them last year and hit it for a touchdown. Don't you think they're going to know it's coming?' He said, 'I'm not worried about what the Redskins know. I just want to be sure our players know what's coming.'"

After two seasons in Dallas, Mackovic became head coach of the Kansas City Chiefs. He went 30-34 over four seasons, including a 41-21 loss to the Cowboys his first year.

"What happens in sports is that people hire someone from an organization in hopes that that person will bring that organization with them to a certain extent," Mackovic said. "In this particular case, I'm sure Lamar Hunt was very much interested in bringing to the Kansas City Chiefs some of those same things the Cowboys had. And that's what I was trying to do. I wanted to bring the same style of coaching, preparation, good administration.

"The Chiefs were molded much differently, though, and because of that, it wasn't easy to do. As much as people envied the Cowboys, some people resented someone coming from the Cowboys because they felt the Cowboys had everything.

"You come in and say, 'In Dallas, this is the way we did it.' Well, the players say, 'We don't care how you did it in Dallas.'"

Mackovic later coached the University of Illinois for four years and was at the University of Texas from 1992-97. He spent three years as a college football commentator on television, then returned to coaching at the University of Arizona in December 2000.

Being in Austin, where Landry maintained a second home, and coaching at Landry's alma mater gave the two more reasons to visit. They occasionally had dinner together or played golf.

"I played golf with him about two weeks before he found out he had leukemia," Mackovic said. "He was in great spirits. He looked good. We were just out hitting balls, and I said, 'Come on, let's go play.' He birdied the last hole.

"He was a great competitor. He sure loved to beat me."

Neill Armstrong

Tom Landry would've made a great journalism professor, judging by the way he made assistant coach Neill Armstrong perfect the art of self-editing.

"We were working on quality control and there were some stats he wanted me to research," Armstrong said. "I'd work on it awhile, then take it to him. All the figures would be there for him, handwritten, about three pages. He'd say, 'Well, that's real good, but give me a summation of that.'

"So, I'd have to go work on it again to try getting three pages of details and figures down to one page or a half-page. I'd cut out some of the facts and figures I thought weren't as important. But it would take two or three times before he'd be happy."

Quality control, which basically involves evaluating your team the way an opponent would to detect trends in play-calling or formations, was another of Landry's many innovations.

"He'd look at all these reports and he'd say, 'OK, for us to get better at what we're doing, we're going to have to throw away these offensive plays or defensive sets because they're not effective,'" Armstrong said.

Landry's background in industrial engineering spawned that idea. It also led to his use of statistical goals.

"All of us in the league always kept stats to see what was successful and not successful. But Tom would use them to set goals," Armstrong said. "He'd change the goals during the season, about the halfway point. Especially after the Thanksgiving game, we'd have to come up with some new goals for the remainder of the season and playoffs."

Landry hired Neill Armstrong to scout the Cowboys. (Photo courtesy of the Dallas Cowboys)

Armstrong was working in the Canadian Football League when he met Landry at an FCA camp in Colorado in 1966. Armstrong later went to the Vikings and was their defensive coordinator in 1975 when the Cowboys beat Minnesota in the playoffs on Drew Pearson's "Hail Mary" touchdown grab.

"That was probably the best team the Vikings had while I was with them, probably their best of any era," Armstrong said.

Having worked for Landry and Bud Grant, Armstrong saw many similarities.

"Bud always said, 'I don't have time for emotion. I'm trying to do a job,'" Armstrong said. "Tom was that way, too."

Armstrong went 0-2 against the Cowboys as head coach of the Chicago Bears from 1978-81. When he was fired, Mike Ditka left Dallas to take his place and Armstrong wound up joining Landry's staff.

Two games into the 1982 season, the players went on strike. Still, the coaches had to prepare for games just in case a settlement was reached in time for the upcoming Sunday.

"We'd get all our work done and have the game plan in to him by Wednesday," said Armstrong, who remained on Landry's staff through 1988 and even remained one more year with Jimmy Johnson. "Then they'd make the decision Wednesday night or Thursday that there weren't going to be games that week.

"So us coaches would go play golf on Friday. You really saw what type of competitor Tom was playing golf. He was out there trying to win, just like when he was coaching."

A DIFFERENT KIND OF ASSISTANT COACH

Randy Smith

When Tom Landry played golf, he went after the diabolical game with the same zeal he had coaching the Cowboys.

"Tom was a perfectionist on the course," said Randy Smith, a golf pro who often worked with Landry during the summers at Royal Oaks Country Club. "He approached everything like he did football, cool and calm and under control. If he missed a shot, he would get that glint in his eyes that this is not the way it's supposed to be."

Landry was a 14-handicapper who could shoot in the low 70s with some practice in the summers, said Smith, who later honed Justin Leonard's game.

Landry could boom the ball 270 yards off the tee but had trouble controlling it. His short game would range from hot to cold, depending on how much he practiced.

"I guess I would give him eight or nine lessons a year," Smith said. "Alicia would call for Tom and set up practice times.

"He could hit the ball pretty good. His biggest fault was a slice, but with work he could straighten it out. He always needed to turn his knuckles on his left hand a little to the left and that would fix it."

Once, Smith figured he knew Landry well enough that he could suggest a play for the Cowboys. It was something Smith had worked on for months with dreams of making a contribution to the team he loved to watch.

"I had all the Xs and Os and everything," Smith said. "Tom took a look at my drawing while we were on the practice tee."

Landry studied the play for a few minutes, smiled and said, "Randy, this really looks good. But we've already run this play.'"

The red-faced Smith never suggested another play for Landry.

Although Smith wasn't able to help the Cowboys, Landry made sure the team came through when Smith was in need.

After cutting the tips off several fingers with a lawn mower, Smith had them surgically repaired and needed a spot to rehabilitate.

"Tom set it up so I could come to the Cowboys practice field and work with trainer Don Cochren," Smith said. "Can you imagine that? I would show up for the treatments and there would be Bob Lilly and all the guys. It was so thoughtful. I'll never forget him for it."

Just another of the little things Landry did that nobody heard about.

OTHER COWBOYS COLLEAGUES

Don Cochren

Tom Landry was boss of the offense, defense and kicking game for the Dallas Cowboys.

However, when it came to the health of the players, Landry discovered that his opinion didn't amount to much.

Longtime trainer Don Cochren said Landry learned the hard way that he better not mess with the late Dr. Marvin P. Knight of Muenster, Texas.

"The first year of the Cowboys, Dr. Knight told Tom that a certain player shouldn't play because of his injuries," Cochren recalled. "Tom put the player into the game anyway.

"After the game, Dr. Knight approached Tom and told him, 'Coach, I know you have your hands full coaching the team, but I don't think you have time to be the team doctor, too. If you ever put another player into a game after I've ruled him out, you'd better get another doctor because we're parting ways.'

"From that time on, if we told Tom a certain player couldn't play, he would always ask, 'What's Dr. Knight think?' Tom never went against one of Dr. Knight's recommendations after that."

Cochren's relationship with Landry was strictly business.

"I was always a little scared of Coach Landry and didn't joke around too much," Cochren said. "I know he appreciated what we did. If we had a progressive idea, Tom was all for it.

"In the late 1960s, we started developing an off-season program for lifting weights and running. The players cited that as the reason we had an excellent season. From that point on, Tom was sold and we always had a weight program. We were one of the first teams in the NFL to start off-season programs like that."

Cochren said working for Landry did have its humorous days.

A favorite is the tale of the missing buses in Buffalo in the first year of the late Doug Todd's tenure as public relations director.

When Landry's players were wounded, he'd send them to Don Cochren for treatment. (Photo courtesy of the Dallas Cowboys)

"We flew to Buffalo and landed in a cold, misty rain," Cochren said. "Doug was there, but the buses—which were his responsibility—weren't.

"Doug was in a panic. He was on the telephone talking to people, but nobody could find the buses. There we stood on the tarmac with the rain coming down. Finally, after 15 minutes, Alicia, who was along on the trip, sneezed.

"Boy, you should have seen the look Tom gave Doug, who could have crawled into a hole."

Finally, the buses appeared.

"After that trip, the advance PR guy always rode with the buses to the plane," Cochren said.

Cochren recalled a joke he tried on Landry once that fell as flat as a tortilla.

"I always reported to Tom at his dorm room in Thousand Oaks just before training camp got underway to see if he had any questions," Cochren said. "I told him everything was under control and we were ready to roll. Then I wondered if there was anything I could do for him."

Landry said there was some help he needed, much to Cochren's surprise.

"Don, I'm having problems with my knee, and you are going to have to put me on a program," Landry said.

Feeling frisky, Cochren replied, "Coach, what about going on 'The Gong Show'?"

"He looked at me like I had lost my mind," Cochren said. "He didn't crack a smile and gave me that stare."

Cochren, recalling how his stomach was churning, said, "I nervously beat a hasty retreat. I don't know whether he didn't like my joke or didn't know what 'The Gong Show' was. Whatever it was, I got the hell out of there."

Barbara Goodman and Marge Kelley

When Barbara Goodman was being interviewed by Tom Landry to become his personal secretary, she had a confession to make.

"Coach, I have really bad knees, and sometimes it hinders me getting around quickly," she said. "I just thought you ought to know."

Goodman still remembers his reaction.

"Tom looked at me, and said, 'That's all we have around here—bad knees and bad hips. If we eliminated everybody who had those, we might not have any workers.'"

Goodman got the job and kept it for eight great years.

"I was so impressed with him," she said. "He was the ultimate executive, and you certainly knew who was in charge. He was very quiet and very easy to work for.

"He was the kind of boss who was right there for you if you needed anything. He would help you in any way. He never got upset with me for anything."

Not a thing?

"I can remember one time when I double-booked him for the same time. I felt sick," she said. "He said, 'Don't worry about it. I'll just go here, then I'll go there. Everything will be OK.' It wasn't a big deal with him. He was a sweetheart of a guy."

Goodman said she would take a lot of dictation on Friday afternoons.

"He would dictate 35 or 40 letters, answering people," she said. "He had heavy correspondence, but would always try to answer everyone.

"He would work from dawn to dusk. That was the nature of the football business. And he appreciated everything you did for him."

Goodman remembered the dreadful day spent helping Landry clean out his office at Valley Ranch.

"It was hard for him, but he was under such control," Goodman said. "He had his picture made with everyone who came by. He was such a dear man."

Goodman was hired after Marge Kelley left the desk. She worked for Landry for 18 years.

"He was a very good boss," Kelley said. "He came in early and stayed late. We always seemed to have enough to do. We worked hard, I'll tell you that.

"The winning seasons were the best."

Curt Mosher

As the liaison between Tom Landry and the media, Curt Mosher had the NFL's dream job. No coach ever made public relations any easier.

"At most NFL franchises, PR people are beat down and intimidated and not allowed to go about their life's work," Mosher said. "I can't remember—and I've tried—Tom ever letting me down once in the nine years I was with the team.

"I screened some stuff, but if I went to him and told him I believed he needed to do an interview, he would do it. He would wait in his office and take the call. That's pretty incredible. Not many PR guys in the NFL can say that."

Mosher said Landry was available night and day.

"I can remember a couple of times late at night when we were in Thousand Oaks that I really needed him for something," Mosher said. "It would be midnight or something and he would meet me at the door in his shorty pajamas. He never questioned me doing my professional duty. He figured if it was important enough for me to wake him up, then it was something that needed to be handled. He knew I wouldn't knock on his door unless it was necessary."

Mosher said he marveled at how calmly Landry always handled things.

"He had a lot of grace and humor, particularly when things got tough," Mosher said. "He always seemed to be under a lot of pressure, but I think he loosened up a little bit after the Cowboys finally won their first Super Bowl. It let him breathe a little."

Mosher said one of his fondest memories of Landry was sitting next to him on an airplane ride to a playoff game. They both had to go ahead of the team because of media interviews.

"Tom read a Western novel the whole flight to Los Angeles," Mosher remembered. "It was one of those with a lot of shooting and rustling and Indian fighting."

As the plane landed, Landry put down the paperback and said: "We think we have problems. Now, those guys back in those days really had problems."

Greg Aiello

The way Greg Aiello sees it, Tom Landry helped the Dallas Cowboys' rise in popularity through more than his Xs and Os.

"From our end of the business, he was part of the formula of the franchise becoming America's Team," said Aiello, who worked in the team's PR department from 1979-89 and is now vice-president of PR for the entire league. "He was with the program by understanding the role of the media and making himself available.

"He was the ultimate pro. He respected people and their jobs and dealt with them on that basis. He had a good sense of humor and cracked an occasional joke in his own style."

Landry's midweek warmth was in contrast to his Sunday scowl.

"I think reporters were always surprised at how open and accessible Tom could be," Aiello said. "The image he had could be a little intimidating for those who had seen him with his stone face on the sideline.

"The local media knew, but some outsiders were impressed how accommodating he could be and how he tried to answer every question."

Aiello said Landry was a physically imposing person.

"You got no sense of just how big he was watching him in a jacket and a tie besides football players on the sideline," Aiello said. "And a lot of people used to seeing him in his hat didn't even know he was bald until they saw him on TV doing his coaching show.

"Tom commanded great respect with his players and that's why he had such a great control of the team. People looking at him on TV saw strength and character we all wish we had.

"It was ironic that when Tom left the team in 1989 what an outpouring of emotion people had for somebody who supposedly had no emotion. Remember, Duane Thomas called him a 'plastic man.' But Tom was a rock in a lot of people's lives."

Aiello had some humorous moments with Landry.

One came in the mid-1980s after George Allen, the former Washington Redskins coach, had finally hooked a television job. Allen and Landry had gone at it tooth-and-nail for years.

Club president Tex Schramm, who had a broadcast background, thought it would spice up the preseason games to have Allen do the analysis.

It fell to low-man-on-the-totem-pole—Aiello—to tell Landry that not only was Allen going to be an announcer, but that he was on his way to training camp to do some homework.

"I sheepishly tiptoed to the field after practice and told Tom, 'Coach, I want to let you know that George Allen will be visiting later today. He's doing the color on preseason broadcast,'" Aiello said.

"He just looked at me and said 'George Allen?!' Then he made a face and walked away."

"Tom was fine with it, although I got that great stare. Obviously, he didn't like it and didn't agree with the choice, but he didn't worry about things he couldn't control."

Aiello also has a warm memory from Landry's last season as coach, a miserable one in which the team sagged to a 3-13 record.

Dallas stunned defending champion Washington 24-17 in the next to last game of the season, damaging the Redskins' division hopes.

Aiello had a brainstorm in the dressing room.

"I suggested to Tom Rafferty that he give Tom the game ball," Aiello said. "Rafferty did and made a great speech about Tom taking all the heat for the team having a bad season.

"Tom smiled. I was proud of that."

Landry's cooperation with the media made things easy for the team's PR department. (Photo courtesy of the Dallas Cowboys)

Chapter Six

THE NFL VIEW

Tom Landry never had to worry about his playbook falling into enemy hands. Even if it did, they probably wouldn't understand it.

Consider these insider opinions on the Xs and Os handbook from one of the NFL's greatest tacticians:

"I took a page of Landry's playbook to a Chinese laundry and they gave me three shirts and a lace pillowcase."—Don Smith, former New York Giants publicist.

"Don't bother reading it, kid. Everyone dies in the end."—Receiver Pete Gent's advice to a rookie.

Landry changed the way football is played at all levels through his various innovations, which he considered his greatest contribution to the game. His own players often needed three years to understand what they were supposed to do, but it took the rest of the league longer to figure out how to counter them.

Landry's Flex defense was one of his few ideas that was never duplicated. Like the Triangle offense in basketball, it works great for one team but doesn't make any sense to anyone else.

Landry's background as a defensive back helped him understand that side of the ball. Long-ago days as a quarterback and years spent analyzing how to stop offenses taught Landry what not to do and gave him ideas of what worked against his defenses.

There was one peculiarity about his offensive plays. Because Landry always viewed offenses from a defensive perspective, he had even-numbered plays on the left and odds on the right. That was the reverse of the way most

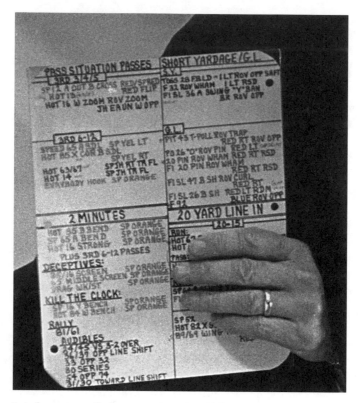

Landry was ready for every situation. (Photo courtesy of Denne H. Freeman)

players learned it in high school and college, but they were the ones who had to change.

Landry, who as a former punter also knew about kicking, had such a well-rounded knowledge of the game and was such a stickler for doing things his way that he oversaw every aspect of his team. He called plays on offense and defense, which is unheard of in today's era—and wasn't too common before, either.

Among the things Landry brought to the NFL or made an intricate part of coaching are the 4-3 defense, the multiple offense, the shotgun, the Spread formation, situational play-calling, shuttling quarterbacks in and out with new plays, off-season weight programs, a quality-control department to essentially scout his own team, color-coded play charts and the chorus-line offensive drill to shield the defense from seeing how players behind them were becoming realigned.

So even though Landry's playbook might have been complex, it was incredibly thorough.

"I opened the defensive playbook and there was everything I'd spent 15 years learning how to play the position. I felt like I was a cheat. The bums ought to find out the hard way like I did."—Hall of Fame defensive lineman Ernie Stautner, a Landry assistant for 23 years.

Don Shula

Don Shula and Tom Landry, two of the winningest coaches in NFL history, didn't get to know each other until they retired.

Their teams collided only six times over their lengthy careers and they bumped into each other infrequently at get-togethers such as league meetings. They respected each other from afar and had mostly a formal, business-as-usual relationship.

Until the time NFL Films got the two coaching legends together in Richmond, Virginia, to film a promotional spot.

"It was the funniest thing," Shula remembered. "You know how stoic and emotionless Tom was. Well, we were supposed to be playing a chess match against each other, one-on-one, like we had done in Super Bowl VI.

"Part of the deal was that every time a chess piece moved, we were supposed to change expressions. Tom couldn't do it. They wanted all these different expressions and Tom just had that one.

Don Shula was the losing coach in Landry's first Super Bowl victory. (Photo courtesy of the Miami Dolphins)

"Later on, we had a big laugh about it. It seemed like it took all day to get that promotional shot done."

Shula said he recalled getting tickled at Landry on another occasion.

"We were playing golf in Palm Springs, California, with Eddie LeBaron and Don Klosterman," Shula said. "After nine holes, we stopped to get some refreshment. Eddie was riding in a cart with Tom.

"Eddie bought a big cigar, lit it up and started blowing the smoke toward Tom. The rest of the day Tom drove the cart with his head leaning out over the cart path like he was a big dog in a car with its head stuck out the window. It was humorous as it could be. We all got a big kick out of it. Tom could be really funny. Probably not a lot of people knew that."

Shula and Landry met just once in a Super Bowl. The Cowboys prevailed 24-3 in Super Bowl VI in New Orleans at old Tulane Stadium.

"It was so difficult going against Tom's teams," Shula said. "We had to overprepare for just about everything. He had such a uniqueness in his coaching style.

"His Flex defense was different, and on offense, he had that crazy shift that camouflaged the movement of his backs. They had so many different motions. Playing the Cowboys was something special. You had to work hard.

"Tom got me that time in the Super Bowl. We had a good team and thought we were ready, but Tom found a way to win."

Shula ended up with a 4-2 record against Landry, one of the few coaches who can say he bested Tom. Then again, not many fared well against Shula, the winningest coach of all-time.

"He was a tough guy to beat," Shula said. "He also was a wonderful man. He'll be missed by everybody."

Bill Walsh

As football rivals, Tom Landry and Bill Walsh squared off in some classic duels.

As tennis teammates, they made a pretty good pair.

"When I would travel to Dallas, we would play tennis," Walsh said. "He and I would be partners at his tennis club."

Although Landry and Walsh are forever linked by the 1982 NFC championship game best remembered for Dwight Clark making "The Catch," their relationship began in the early 1960s when Walsh was the defensive coordinator at the University of California and the Cowboys were just starting.

"I was sent on a trip to Texas to observe spring practices and to visit with the Dallas Cowboys," Walsh said. "Tom Landry gave me an audience and we went over the Flex defense.

"He gave me all the time I wanted—and I was scared to death. I was afraid to even ask a question because I would reveal how little I knew. But he was a true gentleman. He had an interest in those who were interested in the game; he was committed to the fraternal aspect of football, at least with people like myself."

In addition to their tennis outings, Landry and Walsh occasionally spent time together at league meetings.

"I can think of at least two instances where just he and I shared dinner, which was really a thrill to me," said Walsh, a three-time Super Bowl champion. "It sure helped my self-esteem to think he would invite me to dinner. We just talked about our lives and our sport."

Paul Brown had the biggest impact on the Xs and Os in Walsh's life. But Walsh also drew inspiration from Landry and his teams.

"He set a standard for all coaches of his time," Walsh said. "He was a giant in the football world, one of the greatest coaches of all-time. He could very well be considered the greatest coach of all-time because he coached both offense and defense for a world championship team, and this is the only instance I've heard of since the primitive days of football when that was the case."

The Cowboys showed Walsh and the 49ers how much rebuilding they had to do with a 59-14 pounding in October 1980. Dallas tied the franchise scoring record, Danny White threw four touchdown passes and the defense had five interceptions.

Walsh's troops got their revenge the following season with a 45-14 regular-season victory followed by the victory in the league championship. A great rivalry was born between the teams, but there was no bitterness between the coaches as there had been in the heyday of the Cowboys-Redskins wars.

"He didn't come across the field to shake hands; he'd just tip his hat," Walsh said. "We'd make eye contact after the game—he'd tip his hat and I'd salute and we'd go to our locker rooms. I remember that so vividly."

Although their accomplishments and innovations make Landry and Walsh among the highest echelon of coaches, Walsh says he wouldn't put himself in Landry's category.

"I wouldn't say there was mutual respect: I'd say he respected me, and I adulated him."

Chuck Noll

Chuck Noll's great Pittsburgh Steelers teams of the 1970s cost Tom Landry two more Super Bowl rings. The games won by the Steelers couldn't have been much closer or more fiercely fought.

"It was very tough beating a Tom Landry-coached team," Noll said. "When you played his teams, you knew there wasn't going to be any subterfuge or nonsense. They were going to come at you with tough, hard football and no shenanigans. It was the kind of football that commanded a lot of respect. He was a very classy individual."

Dallas lost 21-17 in Super Bowl X and 35-31 in Super Bowl XIII to Pittsburgh teams that featured a "Steel Curtain" defense and an offense powered by such stars as Terry Bradshaw, Franco Harris and Lynn Swann.

"I'm just glad we had two weeks to get ready to play his teams and not one week like they sometimes have now," Noll said. "Getting ready for Tom's team was tough. Their defense was different than anybody in the league. It was difficult to get our people to understand what they were trying to do. Tom taught me a lot of football, I know that."

Noll said he learned from Landry that "everything he did had a purpose, how you have to work at it and study long and hard."

Noll said the second of their two epic clashes was the toughest on his stomach.

"We got a big lead, but then Roger Staubach kept bringing them back," Noll said. "I was scared we were going to blow it."

They might have had Jackie Smith not dropped a wide-open pass in the end zone.

Noll said he and Landry got to be good friends after they both retired. There wasn't time to be civil when they were going head-to-head in 100-yard wars.

"We went to Hilton Head together one time and played some golf," Noll said. "It was great just sitting around with Tom and Alicia and getting to appreciate them. We didn't talk football. We just socialized and tried to get our golf games straightened out."

Noll added that Landry got his revenge on the golf course.

"I never did beat him," Noll said. "He was a good player."

Noll said he and Landry had similar personalities.

"We wanted to make sure we kept our poise so the team wouldn't lose its poise," he said. "We were pretty much straight-faced. Tom's teams never did lose their poise."

Noll concluded that Landry's legacy is "how well he prepared his people."

"There's no question he was the best at tactics and the scheme of the game," Noll said.

Bart Starr

Among the many things Vince Lombardi taught Bart Starr was to have a healthy dose of respect for Tom Landry.

Lombardi got to know Landry when they were assistant coaches for the New York Giants in the 1950s. Lombardi left in 1959 to become head coach at Green Bay; the following year, Landry became head coach of the expansion team in Dallas.

The Packers and Cowboys played an exhibition game in Minneapolis and a regular-season game in Green Bay that inaugural year, 1960.

"From the beginning, Coach Lombardi had immense respect for Coach Landry," Starr said. "He talked about how well prepared Landry's young team would be and he was exactly correct. You could tell as he would chat about him or make references to the team that, from a coaching perspective, he had the greatest respect for Coach Landry."

Lombardi's instincts were right. He and his Packers would go on to face Landry's Cowboys in the NFL championship game following the 1966 and '67 seasons. Green Bay won both games by a total of 11 points, with each decided in the final minutes.

"The biggest single advantage we had over the Cowboys in each of those championship games was maturity, experience," Starr said. "They had great talent—outstanding talent—and they had a quality team.

Bart Starr and Landry were rivals on the field, friends off of it. (Photo courtesy of the Green Bay Packers)

We just had more team maturity and more team experience."

The Packers always considered the Cowboys admirable adversaries.

"We viewed them as a very solid team, well prepared and well organized." Starr said. "They were beautifully coached in every phase of the game.

"I had the greatest respect for him because of how he conducted himself and how well prepared he had his team. Although it takes some time for an expansion team to reach a winning level, when you look at what he did so well, so soon, it was remarkable."

After his playing days ended, Starr became an even bigger Landry fan through time spent together away from football. They had "several very, very meaningful periods" at FCA functions and Landry once invited Starr to speak at his church in Dallas.

"I was obviously thrilled and honored to do it," Starr said. "It was a wonderful experience for me and I was always grateful for the opportunity."

Starr said the FCA gatherings were special because of the atmosphere. Football and coaching were incidental; faith was the top priority.

"That's where I really came to appreciate the depth and the quality of the man," he said.

"I had the greatest respect for Coach Landry. I thought he was the ultimate class individual. I've never known a more consummate gentleman than this man. He was very, very special."

Bud Grant

Over a nine-year stretch in the 1970s, either Tom Landry's Dallas Cowboys or Bud Grant's Minnesota Vikings went to eight Super Bowls. Four of those times, the teams went through each other, resulting in some classic playoff games.

Yet, despite their frequent meetings, there was no off-field relationship between the coaches.

"I never knew Tom," Grant said. "I can't think of one occasion where we ever talked one-on-one. We never had an occasion to be together, not even before a game. We never shook hands before or after a game. I wasn't big on shaking hands and I don't think he was, so we just never did."

Had they gotten together, there would've been plenty to talk about.

Drew Pearson's "Hail Mary" catch knocked one of Bud Grant's best Vikings teams out of the playoffs in 1975. (Photo courtesy of the Dallas Cowboys)

Grant's Vikings played in four Super Bowls, losing all four. Landry's Cowboys made five Super Bowls, losing three. Grant was a head coach for 28 years, including 10 in Canada. Landry led Dallas for 29 years. Both were superb strategic leaders.

"Some people have compared us as being somewhat stoic in nature," Grant said.

Grant said the Vikings were always aware of Landry and the Cowboys.

"That was the path to the Super Bowl. There was the Cowboys and the Rams, and Pittsburgh and Miami," Grant said. "There wasn't free agency, so players played a long time. So you'd go into every year saying, 'Well, Dallas has the same team they had last year, except they've made some improvements. We've got the same players and made some improvements, so we're looking forward to Dallas probably being one of the contending teams again.'"

Grant said the Vikings never went out of their way to target the Cowboys.

"You do the things you do best rather than try to structure what you do based on what Dallas does," he said. "There was nothing we did to prepare against Dallas that was any different than anybody else, even though they were very, very good."

Dick Vermeil

When Dick Vermeil left the Philadelphia Eagles in 1982 because he was "burned out," Tom Landry couldn't have been too surprised.

He saw it coming.

"One day, around my third year, we were playing in Dallas and we were visiting during pregame warmups," Vermeil said. "He said to me—and I'll never forget this—he said, 'Dick, you've got to learn to relax a little bit because you're going to be in this league for a long time.'

"I didn't relax, but I accepted it as a compliment out of respect. He was very sincere, very honest with his statement, and it's something I've held onto for the rest of my life. He was really showing his respect for me by making a very honest statement. You know, he had a great ability to keep things in the proper perspective, which I didn't have. I thought that was really nice."

When Vermeil took over the Eagles in 1976, they were near the bottom of the NFL and the Cowboys were at the top. But because they were both in the NFC East, they would meet twice a year. So Vermeil set beating the Cowboys as his long-term goal.

"This is the honest truth: I prepared for Tom Landry's team on a year-round basis," Vermeil said. "They were sort of our motivational force. In the off-season, we'd study tapes of what every team did against them. I don't think we ever missed a game they played, just to study them. And we learned to steal things from them, too."

Vermeil remembers the night it all paid off.

"Monday night, November 12, 1979," he said. "They scored the first time they had the ball, went up 7-0, and we came back and beat them. We'd finally found a way to beat them!

"It was a big, big, big thrill. Of all the wins in my coaching career, that was probably one of the five biggest."

Vermeil took the long road to becoming an NFL head coach. He had jobs as an assistant and head coach in high school, junior college and college before getting his big break.

"My very first season as head coach of the Philadelphia Eagles, 1976, the very first game of the year, we played Dallas in Dallas. I remember looking across the field and saying, 'Oh, my gosh, that's Tom Landry over there. I can't believe I'm on the same field with this man,'" Vermeil said. "I was sort of in awe of him and nervous around him."

Vermeil got over the nerves. But he remained in awe.

"I think I respect most the dignity and class he always showed and gave to the profession. I think he was the epitome of what a great football coach should be," said Vermeil, who was 4-10 against Landry but won the biggest game of their rivalry, the NFC championship following the 1980 season, which sent the Eagles to their first Super Bowl.

"When I got into broadcasting, I was around some players that he had coached. I heard some cute stories about him. And I never heard a player say a bad word about Tom Landry. That's almost impossible."

One of Landry's trademarks was his stone face. Vermeil's trademark was getting emotional after being wins.

"A critical thing to be is yourself," said Vermeil, who came out of retirement to coach the St. Louis Rams in 1997, led them to a Super Bowl title in the 1999 season, retired again, then came out of retirement again to coach the Kansas City Chiefs in 2001.

"Tom was himself, not influenced by media or fans. And I've always been myself. Sometimes, I've been embarrassed by being myself. But I am what I am.

"Tom wasn't in the business of trying to impress anyone. He was just himself."

Don Coryell

Playing Tom Landry's teams twice a year made George Allen do some weird things. Don Coryell saw it as a challenge.

"We were always fired up to play them because they were one of the top teams in our divisions and we were the upstarts," said Coryell, who coached the St. Louis Cardinals from 1973-77. "It was a real rivalry as far as we were concerned."

Landry's Cowboys went 6-4 against Coryell's Cardinals, which says a lot about Coryell.

You have to go back nine years before Coryell took over to find four St. Louis victories over Dallas. After he left, the Redbirds beat the Cowboys only four times over the next 10 seasons, then moved to Phoenix.

Those Coryell-Landry games were always tight. The teams split the final eight, with all but one decided by seven points or less.

"All of them were close games, very hard-fought games," Coryell said. "We were very, very concerned every time we played them, believe me. We had to change some things because of their defensive players."

Coryell's record against the Cowboys is especially impressive considering Dallas went to two Super Bowls and an NFC championship game in the five years he coached the Cardinals.

"I think they were the standard," Coryell said. "They had great teams, a great organization, great players, a super following. They were called 'America's Team' and they really were."

The Air Coryell offense really took off during his next stop, San Diego. But because the Chargers and Cowboys were in opposite leagues, the coaches battled only twice more. The home team won each time, Dallas in 1980 and San Diego in '83.

"We had a good relationship as far as coach against coach," Coryell said. "Of course, I greatly respected him. He was always a real gentleman. He knew how to contain himself and he was never derogatory about anyone."

Bum Phillips

When Bum Phillips uttered his memorable claim that a rival coach "could beat yours with his or beat his with yours," he was talking about Don Shula.

"But Landry could do the same thing—and did," Phillips said. "He did what he could do and did it better than anyone else. And he was the same kind of guy as he was a coach."

In the late 1970s, Landry and Phillips were cross-state rivals who shared the same nemesis: the Pittsburgh Steelers.

The Steelers and Phillips' Houston Oilers met in the AFC championship game in January 1979 and January 1980, with Pittsburgh winning both. Had the Oilers won the first of those two title games, there would've been an all-Texas Super Bowl.

Although Landry and Phillips were both NFL coaches in Texas who were from Texas, only Phillips looked the part. A big belt buckle held up his jeans and he wore boots and a cowboy hat. He spoke with a thick drawl and uttered folksy sayings.

Phillips got into coaching at Amarillo High in 1960. He went to Texas-El Paso in 1962 and later worked for the San Diego Chargers. Somewhere along the way, Phillips and Landry met and got to talking about defense.

Landry tried explaining the principles of the Flex, but Phillips was among many who didn't grasp it.

"You had to have perfect personnel to run that Flex defense," Phillips said. "I didn't really understand it. He gave me a coaching book, but I just didn't feel like I could use it. We played something we could teach and could handle.

"Nobody else ran it. Nobody! It took some special personnel to run that."

Phillips never knew Landry very well, but he always admired him.

"Everybody respected him. How can you not respect him? He was just one of those guys who always did the right thing. He was a class guy," Phillips said. "He was the same in '79-80 as he probably was in '59-60. He didn't change. There wasn't anything counterfeit about him."

Bud Adams

Imagine going to a job interview and ending up hiding in the bathroom. That's what Tom Landry did when he met with Bud Adams to discuss becoming the first head coach of the Houston Oilers.

Adams got his AFL team in August 1959, giving him a year to stock the club. He'd already gone through the draft and had hired a personnel director. As he asked around about head coaching candidates, Landry's name kept popping up.

So Adams went to New York to meet with Landry, who was then running the Giants' defense. While he was there, Adams also planned to interview potential players.

Landry wanted to keep a low profile, so he agreed to meet in Adams' hotel room. Things were going fine until . . .

"There was a knock on the door," Adams said. "It was one of those players. He had gotten there early.

"Tom said, 'Oh, golly, I can't let him see me in here.' Tom was a real straightforward guy. He didn't want it to look like he was talking behind the Giants' back, looking for another job, because I was the one soliciting him for the job, not him soliciting me.

"So I said, 'Well, we've got two doors here. One's the bathroom and the other's the closet.' So he went into the bathroom. I told the guy at the door he was early, and I had someone else coming up, so I'd appreciate if he'd come back in an hour. Tom came out and he was a little nervous."

Landry, the first coaching candidate Adams interviewed, was leery of the upstart AFL after having been part of the All-American Football Conference when it folded. More importantly, he knew the NFL was planning to expand into Dallas, where Landry lived in the off-season, and that was the job he really wanted.

But Adams had his heart set on Landry. So the oilman sweetened the pot.

"I knew his wife's father was in the insurance business and that he handled commercial insurance for businesses," Adams said. "So I told Tom that I'd already checked it out and arranged for him to be my agent. I'd run all my company's policies through his father-in-law's company and he'd get all the commissions. It would've been pretty sizable. I thought that would really be a plus-plus."

Landry said he'd consider the offer. But he also told the truth about his interest in the Dallas job.

"He said he thought he had a chance to get that job, and if he could get it, he'd want to go there," Adams said. "But if he didn't get it, he'd give me a shot. Well, he got the job there, and the rest is history."

Adams and Landry saw each other throughout the years and were always cordial.

"I'd say, 'Tom, you had a wonderful record.' And he'd say, 'Well, you've had a lot of coaches.' And I said, 'Well, I don't know if I'd have had that many if you'd been with me,'" Adams said.

Adams, whose team finally made the Super Bowl for the first time after the 2000 season, said that every time he's hired a coach, he's looked for someone with Landry-like qualities.

"His moral standards were so high and he wasn't really looking for all that publicity. He just wanted to do his job," Adams said. "He was cut from a different mold. You didn't find many guys like Tom Landry. He was so soft spoken, yet he could stare right through you."

Lamar Hunt

Tom Landry, head coach of the Dallas Texans and Kansas City Chiefs? It's not as far-fetched as it sounds.

Hunt spoke with Landry in 1959 about the American Football League team he was starting in Dallas. At the same time, Tex Schramm was hustling to help form the Cowboys of the National Football League.

"I talked to Tom one time, but I wasn't yet at the stage where I was ready to hire a coach," Hunt said. "It was in the football season of 1959 and Tom was still an assistant with the New York Giants."

Hunt said he was putting together a list of candidates and, "Tom was one of the names suggested to me. We talked one evening."

Landry was in hot demand because of his success as the Giants' defensive coordinator. While Hunt had the team in the city Landry preferred, Schramm had the team in the city and league Landry liked best.

"Tom was just a terrific guy and turned out to be a wonderful coach," Hunt said. "I'm glad he did well."

The Texans and Cowboys were both playing in the Cotton Bowl and were fighting over the same core group of fans. Although the Texans won the

AFL title in '62—while the Cowboys finished fifth in their conference—Hunt ended the battle on February 8, 1963, and moved his team to Kansas City, renaming them the Chiefs. Later, Hunt and Schramm were the driving forces behind the merger of the leagues.

Hunt, who kept a home in Dallas, often saw Landry. He recalls one social gathering of which he is quite proud.

"Tom and I were both given the Leather Helmet Award by the NFL Alumni Association for service to the game," Hunt said. "We had dinner in Ft. Lauderdale, and it was a high point for me to just be on the same podium with him. I told the story about how he almost became a Dallas Texan."

Hunt said he was always impressed with Landry's coolness under fire.

"His professionalism is what impressed me," Hunt said. "He was even-minded and not an up-and-down type of guy. He always had control of his emotions. He was an exceptional person and had great teams."

Hunt also served on the board of the Fellowship of Christian Athletes with Landry.

However, Landry couldn't persuade Hunt to play in the annual charity golf tournament.

"I was so bad, I think they put out a bounty to keep me from playing," Hunt said. "I was always the sponsor who never played. It was great to be associated with Tom and that organization. Tom was class."

Hank Stram

When Tom Landry didn't become the first coach of the Dallas Texans, Hank Stram did.

Both teams started in 1960 and both played in the Cotton Bowl. While the arrangement wasn't exactly ideal, there was no bitterness or envy among the coaches.

"It was a very competitive situation because of the two leagues, but it never had any bearing on the friendship we enjoyed," Stram said. "It wasn't like it normally would've been if we were in the same league.

"I think of Tom as a guy with style, class, grace and dignity. I can't think of anything but positive things about him. I liked him very much."

Still, Stram remembers there being somewhat of a turf battle between the teams.

"We felt that the winning team in Dallas would stay in Dallas and the losing team would leave," Stram said. "I guess it was a lopsided thought because it turned out to be just the opposite. We won a championship in 1962 and the Cowboys were having a hard time. Yet we left and they stayed.

"We had so many people on our team who were from Dallas. We had sold them on the idea we'd be staying in Dallas. So we were all very disappointed when we found out we were going to leave."

Stram was a short, stocky guy who spoke from the hip. Landry was a tall, trim guy who rarely spoke.

"I admired the fact that that's the way he always was," said Stram, who was with the Texans-Chiefs their first 15 years. "I kind of got a kick out of him because he was so quiet. He'd laugh sometimes when you'd tell him a story, and you'd get a kick out of just watching him laugh!

"But when he spoke, you listened because you knew he had great ideas. It was no surprise they went on to have great success."

Stram likes to tell the story about a time in the early 1970s—long after the Texans became the Kansas City Chiefs—when he and longtime Cowboys assistant coach Jim Myers played racquetball against Landry and Mike Ditka.

"Jim says, 'Hey, Coach, I understand you play racquetball a lot and are pretty good. How about you and me play against Landry and Ditka? Every time I play against them at home, I get beat because I never have a good partner.' So we played.

"Well, I'm very talkative in competition. I like to make comments, stuff like, 'Here comes the elevator ball . . . the sausage ball . . . the submarine ball . . .' all those kinds of things. Anyway, Jim and I beat them.

"Mike was chewing his gum and got ticked off because they lost. Jim Myers acted as if he'd just won a million dollars. It was comical.

"Then Tom walked off, and as he went down the hall, all he kept saying was, 'Man, was it noisy in there. Ah, was it noisy! Gee, I never heard so much of a racket in my life playing racquetball.'

"He was serious as can be. I can still see him walking down there and shaking his head saying that."

Red Cashion

Tom Landry always had time to be compassionate. Even for referees.

Former NFL official Red Cashion—remembered best for distinctively declaring "First down!"—remembers Landry going out of his way to console head linesman Eddie Marion after his daughter died in a car wreck.

"Tom is one that we really never talked to very much because he never said very much," Cashion said. "But Eddie showed up in Dallas to work a ballgame and one of the fellows happened to mention to Tom what had happened.

"Tom made a special effort to go see Eddie and tell him how much a daughter meant and how much he regretted Eddie's loss. He really made Eddie feel a little better. I don't know of any other coach who did anything like that."

Cashion said he won the only argument he had with Landry; Landry even said so.

"We were in Pittsburgh," Cashion said. "Right before the half, Staubach threw a long pass, which was completed. As soon as it was completed, he turned to me and called timeout. The only trouble was the guy who caught the ball was still running. So I waited until he was down, which was several seconds, and then signaled timeout.

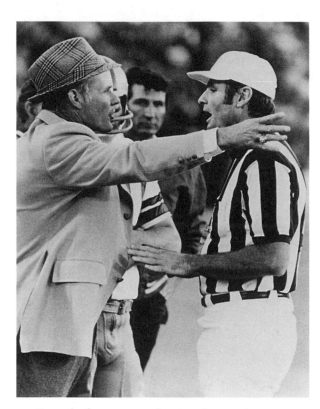

Compared to most coaches, Landry wasn't too tough on officials. (Photo courtesy of the Dallas Cowboys)

"As we walked off at halftime a couple plays later, Tom said to me, 'You sure let that clock run a long time after that long pass.' I said, 'Coach, the receiver down there was still running. I'm not going to blow that whistle until he's down.' He said, 'I'll check with Roger.'

"Well, when he came back after halftime, he said, 'You were right' and kept walking."

For an official, "you were right" are the three sweetest words a coach could ever say.

"It was kind of a rare thing, but that's what he did," Cashion said. "He was a great, great gentleman."

Even though Landry had a soft side, officials didn't exactly fight to work Dallas games.

"I wouldn't say he wouldn't give you any trouble because he would if you were wrong," Cashion said. "But he was always a gentleman about it. Compared to most coaches, he was awful quiet, although I must confess that he had some assistants who could bellow pretty loud."

Steve Sabol

NFL Films began a few years after Landry and the Cowboys got started. Their cameras captured some of the greatest moments in team history, and their productions helped mold Landry's image as their quiet yet assertive leader.

"Cinematically and visually, Tom was an interesting person," said Steve Sabol, the president of the company started by his father. "He wore a suit or a sports jacket. He had the hat. He sort of looked like an FBI man walking around on the sidelines.

"Other coaches would wear windbreakers or sweatshirts, but Tom had a certain dignity and a unique sense of personal style that came through in the way he dressed, the way he walked, his posture."

Many considered his attire and demeanor a bit boring. His offense, though, was so exciting and innovative that NFL Films assigned two cameras to Cowboys games, which was a rarity at the time.

"Landry's personality came out on the field," Sabol said. "You watched the Cowboys with all the double shifting and the shotguns and the Flex defense. He was a brilliant innovator. So much of the game today came from his brains, his philosophy. You saw the Dallas Cowboys and then you realized how all the wheels were turning underneath that hat."

The cameras rarely focused on Landry. There was no need to get much film.

"You knew what you were going to get," Sabol said. "He was totally immersed in what was going on on the field. He was one step ahead. He wasn't reacting to what you're seeing on the field because he's already thinking about the move or countermove to make on the next play."

NFL Films often gets coaches or players to wear microphones during games. Landry never went along and the company never really pushed him too hard.

"He wasn't our first choice because he really wasn't all that talkative," Sabol said. "He didn't speak in the same vernacular like Lombardi or Joe Kuharich. They really addressed effort and will and character; Landry was a coach who stressed systems and strategy and techniques.

"In the beginning, we sort of felt about Landry like Albert Einstein's wife once said about him. She said that when she was having a conversation with him, she understood the words, but not the sentences. Landry was like that—an Einsteinian, towering kind of intellect. But his particular type of coaching wasn't as dynamic on film as Lombardi or Kuharich or Allie Sherman or Don Shula."

NFL Films cameramen were challenged to find creative ways to capture Landry.

A popular technique was filming him from his feet up to his hat, giving him a larger-than-life feel straight out of an old Western movie.

But the best shot was the silhouette. It became the definitive illustration of Landry and one of NFL Films' signature images.

"The sunlight is falling across the stands and the fans in Texas Stadium and all you see is his head and shoulders," Sabol said. "You see the hat and the profile and you know exactly who it is."

Bob Ryan

No person watched as many tapes of Dallas Cowboys games as Tom Landry.

But Bob Ryan came close.

From 1965 through 1993, Ryan was the NFL Films producer in charge of putting together the annual Cowboys highlight film. His 1978 film was entitled "America's Team," giving birth to a nickname that has lasted more than two decades and has been adopted by teams from practically every sport.

"They had lost again in the Super Bowl and we were looking for something different to do," Ryan said. "When you went through all the film, you saw all these kids wearing Cowboys jerseys, rooting for the Cowboys—and not just in Texas Stadium, in away stadiums too.

"So, my thought was, if there's a national team in pro football, it would be the Cowboys—sort of like the Celtics were in basketball, the Yankees are in baseball, Notre Dame in college football. All those teams were so good for so long, they had this rabid following and, of course, they also had that love-hate relationship where fans either loved them or despised them. I think the Cowboys were like that, too."

Landry was not exactly a producer's dream. Although his teams were exciting and had great players making great plays, Landry's rock-like demeanor made for pretty dull video.

The cameras did catch a few memorable moments though.

"Once, when they wrapped up a playoff game against the Detroit Lions, he almost did a pirouette with his hands almost in prayer and a gleeful smile on his face," Ryan said. "Then there was the shot we got when Jackie Smith dropped the touchdown pass in the Super Bowl. There was a moment of dejection there.

"He probably had a big smile twice—once when they carried him off the field after beating the 49ers in San Francisco for the NFC championship and when they carried him off after the first Super Bowl victory.

"Another moment I think was emotional, and he was not the centerpiece, was when Roger Staubach retired and he broke down while talking about the man in the funny hat, Tom Landry, and how much Landry meant to him. That probably said more about Tom than anything that anyone could've ever done."

Landry's sideline stoicism led to some creative cinematography, like the time Ryan put together a montage of slight gestures, each of which seemed magnified because they were coming from someone who rarely moved a muscle.

"I put a whole bunch of shots together where he would shake his head just slightly or crook his mouth. He'd move just a little, but because we had a very long lens, you saw only his face. If the shot was wider, you would've never seen it," Ryan said.

"We thought that was interesting. The analogy was just the slightest tick revealed a torrent of emotion to him because you knew he was angry. It was just the slightest body movement and you could tell he was mad or angry that something didn't work out."

Landry once agreed to wear a microphone during a day of training camp, providing NFL Films with a rare behind-the-scenes glimpse of the master at work.

"It was interesting because you saw that teaching side of him. And, since it was training camp, you saw the lighter side of him," Ryan said.

"They were practicing for the Oakland Raiders. I remember vividly he came up to Staubach and said, 'If you try and run through the middle on one of your scrambles, you know who you're going to meet.'

"Then he pointed to one of the Cowboys who was playing the part of the Raiders and said, 'You know who that is: Jack Tatum. So if you try that, you're going to end up on the sideline and you're not going to be playing.' He didn't say it in an intense manner, he said it in a lighthearted manner."

COWBOYS SUCCESSORS

Only five men have had the keys to the big office in the coaching wing of the Dallas Cowboys' headquarters. Tom Landry held down the fort for 29 years. The team has gone through four successors in the last 12 years.

Any sort of turnover would seem like a turnstile after Landry's tenure, but Dallas' change has been high even by NFL standards.

No matter who else holds the job and regardless of the success they have, every Cowboys coach will always be compared to Landry.

Jimmy Johnson

On January 22, 1989, Tom Landry was in a luxury box at Joe Robbie Stadium in Miami watching the San Francisco 49ers beat the Cincinnati

Bengals in the Super Bowl. Among the visitors to the Cowboys' box that day was Jimmy Johnson, the head coach of the University of Miami.

Johnson had long admired Landry from afar and had gotten to know him a little bit over the years. He'd been among the many up-and-coming college coaches who visited Dallas to try to learn from the master.

"I used to go to the Cowboys' practices, and he was so nice and polite to me," said Johnson, who made trips even when he was the head coach at Miami and Oklahoma State. "He'd always come over and say hello. He was really a class, class individual."

A little over a month after seeing each other at the Super Bowl, Johnson replaced Landry as coach of the Cowboys. And while the changing of the guard was bungled in many ways, the Port Arthur native wound up being a worthy successor to the man from Mission.

At first, they couldn't have seemed more different.

Johnson was demonstrative on the sidelines, waving his warms while his cheeks turned bright red. He didn't wear a hat, although some called his heavily sprayed hair a "helmet."

But there were similarities, too.

Johnson came to coaching with a defensive background and became a winner through a keen eye for evaluating talent. His first team went 1-15, but by the fourth year they were Super Bowl champions. They won again in his fifth year—matching Landry's total—then Johnson left months later following a spat with owner Jerry Jones.

While Landry distanced himself from football in general and the Cowboys specifically, he never held a grudge against Johnson.

"I visited with him a time or two, asked him for advice a time or two, and like always, he was first class and very cordial," said Johnson, the first coach to win a college national championship and a Super Bowl. "It was not a close relationship, because we weren't close before. But it wasn't hostile or anything. He understood."

Johnson took a year off, got back into coaching with the Miami Dolphins, then retired after another four seasons. He said he never again spoke with Landry after moving out of Dallas.

"After I left the Cowboys, I don't know if I talked to anybody," he said, laughing.

In February 2001, Johnson was inducted into the Texas Sports Hall of Fame in Waco. Standing in the Tom Landry Theater, in front of a display case featuring one of the coach's trademark fedoras, Johnson remained in awe of the man who created the Cowboys' winning tradition that he restored and continued.

"Tom Landry was one of the greatest people that's ever been. There's no need to compare. He'll always be looked upon as one of the greatest to ever coach the game."

Barry Switzer

Barry Switzer didn't directly follow Tom Landry in the head coach's office in Dallas, just like he didn't directly replace Bud Wilkinson as head coach at the University of Oklahoma.

Yet, in both jobs, Switzer felt like he was working in their shadows.

"The success they enjoyed made your job tougher," Switzer said. "They created the tradition. They made it a good job to have, but a tough job to try maintaining the excellence they established.

"Bud created the monster, I had to feed it. People expected you to be successful and to win. Dallas fans were no different. They expected you to be successful because they'd enjoyed tremendous success."

Switzer led his personal life far differently than Landry and Wilkinson. On the field, though, he lived up to their standards by leading the Sooners to multiple national championships and winning a Super Bowl with the Cowboys.

Switzer's best days at Oklahoma came in the 1970s, when Landry's career in Dallas was also at its peak.

"They won a couple of Super Bowls in the '70s and we were winning national championships," Switzer said. "I remember Tom once saw us play in the mid-70s and he had a quote about us. He said something about Oklahoma being better than the team he was playing that week."

Switzer and Landry first met in 1960 when Switzer was an assistant coach at Arkansas, his alma mater, and one of his former college teammates, Jim Mooty, played for the Cowboys. The coaches remained casual acquaintances over the years.

"I knew Coach Landry from a distance," Switzer said. "When I became coach at Oklahoma, I would go by the Cowboys' offices every once in a while and I'd go to Coach Landry's office. I'd visit with him a few minutes then go about my business."

Chan Gailey

Chan Gailey's football mentor was Dan Reeves, whose mentor was Tom Landry.

But when Gailey took over Landry's old job as coach of the Dallas Cowboys, he wasn't able to produce Landry-like success.

Gailey was fired after going 18-16 and failing to win a playoff game in his two seasons. He left with the dubious distinction of being the first coach in team history not to win a Super Bowl.

Gailey said he was never intimidated by the mystique of carrying on the Cowboys' tradition that Landry began.

"But I don't think I ever forgot it either," Gailey said. "It was probably some of both.

"I think there was a tremendous amount of respect for that position, but I didn't let that overwhelm me—because I didn't think Coach Landry would let that overwhelm him.

"I can't imagine him ever being overwhelmed or intimidated by anything."

Not even the bomber missions he flew over hostile territory in World War II?

"You have to think that in the very first one of those he flew, he knew exactly what he was going to do. He had a plan to do and he carried it out," Gailey said. "In my mind, that's how I see him doing it."

When Gailey was hired, much was made of his similarities with Landry. He'd been an innovative coordinator on a successful team and he was a kind, modest guy devout to his Christian upbringing and active in the community.

Landry smiling into microphone . . .

"I promise you, my name and his name didn't deserve to be in the same sentence," said Gailey, now the offensive coordinator for the Miami Dolphins. "It would've taken a lot of years of a lot of successful football and being a positive role model for me to deserve to be in the same sentence with him."

Gailey first met Landry through the FCA.

"I was with him at two or three functions and was able to sit down with him," Gailey said. "We talked more family and FCA than football. He didn't want to talk football much. I don't think he wanted to put his nose where he thought it might not belong. He respected other people and their positions.

"I would've liked to have known him better. I certainly had a great deal of respect for him."

Reeves was Gailey's Little League baseball coach in their hometown of Americus, Georgia. Reeves later gave Gailey his first NFL job as an assistant coach with the Denver Broncos. They spent six seasons together.

"Dan wouldn't use his name publicly or in front of the team," Gailey said. "But in individual discussions about the way things were done, he certainly used Coach Landry and the way things were done in Dallas as examples all the time."

. . . and steely-eyed on the sidelines. (Photos courtesy of Denne H. Freeman)

Gailey always wanted to emulate Landry's calm, composed demeanor.

"When you're a young coach, you are looking for people who you feel you want to be like. He was one of those guys," Gailey said. "It wasn't just the wins and losses. The respect people had for him and the way he impacted lives—that's what is amazing. That's what people will remember."

Dave Campo

Since the Dallas Cowboys began in 1960, either Tom Landry or Dave Campo has been on the coaching staff every year.

But the first and the current coach of the Cowboys never worked together. Campo joined the team in 1989 as the last hire on Jimmy Johnson's initial staff. He worked his way up from defensive assistant to secondary coach to defensive coordinator, then became the fifth head coach in team history in January 2000.

Over the 11 years Campo worked as an assistant in Dallas, he met Landry at several banquets. Much to Campo's regret, they never had more than a casual conversation.

"It was mostly in social settings," Campo said. "He mentioned that he'd heard some good things about what we were doing, that kind of thing."

Campo's admiration for Landry dates to his childhood. He was a New York Giants fan growing up in Connecticut after Landry had left the team. Still, he learned plenty about Landry's days as a Giants player and coach.

"When I was a young boy, my family would get together every Thanksgiving and we'd watch the Dallas Cowboys and Coach Landry find a way to win," Campo said. "And he always did."

Campo's career path was much more winding than Landry's. He started at his high school alma mater, then worked at 11 colleges, his last one being Miami with Johnson before reaching the NFL.

Along the way, Campo got a couple of up-close glimpses of Landry at work.

One of the college staffs he was on spent several days watching the Cowboys train at Thousand Oaks, California; another time, he visited team headquarters in Irving.

"The thing that sticks out to me is that he was such a classy person," Campo said. "You'd like to win, but you'd like to win with class, too. I'd like to think there will be more people like Tom Landry, but things have changed. There probably will not be another Tom Landry."

Could Campo be another Tom Landry?

"My demeanor is a little less stoic," Campo said. "I think you have to be yourself. But there's a way of being yourself and doing it the right way, too.

"I'm really not looking to fill anybody's shoes. At the same time, I'm a history person, and I don't think there's any question that when you look at the Dallas Cowboys, the history is so strong that you can't help but be somewhat excited because of the people who've gone before you.

"Tom Landry was the Dallas Cowboys. He built the team, along with Tex Schramm, Gil Brandt and the former owners. There's no question that makes this an exciting position to be in."

Chapter Seven

PRESS BOX PERSPECTIVE

Tom Landry might not have been the most colorful coach in the NFL, but he was always accessible and courteous, and those are the two things reporters appreciate most.

Landry faced his share of media critics, especially in his later, losing years. But he understood his relationship with the press better than most and knew it was the coach being criticized, not the man.

He didn't play favorites among reporters and he never lied. Sure, he withheld information about injuries or personal problems, but that was his duty as a coach.

Landry wasn't big on hitting "softball" questions, ones that are designed to draw a humorous response. But he did take the bait once when asked about a bomb threat in the press box at Yankee Stadium.

What would've happened, Coach, if there had been an explosion and all the scribes were obliterated?

"I suppose we would have observed 30 seconds of silent prayer," he said. "Then we would have continued play—with enthusiasm."

Frank Luksa

Of all the sportswriters to ever cover the Dallas Cowboys, none spent as much time around Tom Landry as Frank Luksa.

Yet Luksa's fondest memory came from watching Tom and Alicia eating dinner at a restaurant.

"I think it was Philadelphia, although the city could have been some other place, like Washington or New York," said Luksa, who joined the beat in 1962. "I do remember it was a long-ago Saturday night before a Cowboys game on the road.

"Our group retired to a restaurant for the usual pre-kickoff ritual. On this evening, we were seated, glanced about and saw a couple situated in a quiet corner. They had eyes only for each other. Never gave us a look. Their gaze locked over the light of a single candle. Even from a distance, I could feel the emotional exchange taking place across their table."

Luksa recalled that Alicia was "all things to Tom . . . wife, mother, devoted companion and, everyone suspected, the eye who saw that her husband dressed to impeccable standards."

Times spent with and around Landry fill Luksa's memory. He joked that stories "jostle for their place in recall."

One that won the battle comes from the last time he interviewed Landry.

They met in the office Landry shared with his son. His illness had set in, yet Landry appeared in good condition considering the state of his health.

Among the things they discussed was whether Landry could coach today's NFL players.

"I'm sure I could adjust to it," Landry said. "But I don't think it's something I'd like. There's too much money and do-your-own-thing now. Those things we didn't have in our era."

They talked about games won and lost. Luksa expected one of the three Super Bowls lost by a combined 11 points to be the biggest disappointment. Instead, it was the 1981 NFC championship lost when Dwight Clark made an amazing touchdown grab in the back of the end zone, putting the upstart San Francisco 49ers into the Super Bowl.

"The 'Big Catch' to me was really devastating," Landry said. "Win that one, and we might have won a couple more Super Bowls."

Landry said losing his job didn't hurt as badly as losing that game.

"I never got that low being fired," he said. "I just picked up my books and left."

Luksa saw Landry's famous facade come tumbling down several times. One of the most illustrative was on a cutdown day in 1975, when Landry had to release three likable veterans to clear roster spots for the rookie crop known as "The Dirty Dozen," which included players such as Randy White, Thomas Henderson and Bob Breunig. Among those released was linebacker Ken Hutcherson, a Landry favorite who carried a Bible with his playbook to meetings.

"Upset over what he'd done, Landry strode down the hall and met White, Henderson and Breunig," Luksa said. "Walking past without breaking stride, tears in his eyes, he impaled the rookies with a brief glance and said, 'I hope you're worth it.'"

Another seemingly out-of-character moment came when Luksa saw Landry at the Super Bowl in January 1999.

"What are *you* doing here?" Luksa said, jokingly implying that Landry had no connection to the NFL.

"Oh, no, not you!" Landry replied in mock horror.

A few mementos of Luksa's sportswriting career adorn the walls of his home office. There are pictures of Nolan Ryan, Magic Johnson, Muhammad Ali, Mel Renfro, Darrell Royal and Charlie Waters. There's also one of Landry taken when he filmed a Western-themed commercial for American Express that included a punch line about being "surrounded by Redskins."

"The picture shows Landry astride a horse in full cowboy gear," Luksa said. "He could be mistaken for a rugged Marlboro Man.

"Landry's inscription means the most to me because it reflects his highest compliment: 'Thanks for being a professional.'"

Blackie Sherrod

Blackie Sherrod, another newspaperman whose career covered the entire Landry era, coined the phrase "Mount Landry" in his columns about the stoic Cowboys coach.

"It seemed to fit the stolid, unflappable and dependable, durable object he had become," said Sherrod, whose work appeared in the *Fort Worth Press*, *Dallas Times Herald* and *The Dallas Morning News*. "He was there in his unflinching granite form, yesterday, today and tomorrow.

"Strange, it was the same veneer that made Ben Hogan intriguing and respected by millions, but it seemed to work the opposite with Landry. Some critics were perplexed—'We cut him, why doesn't he bleed?'

"In the face of mistakes, the coach seemed unperturbed."

Sherrod remembered that Landry had "constant courtesy and utter lack of individual resentment toward his media critics."

"After a defeat on the road, there were none of these curt answers and angry stompoffs as Mike Ditka had been known to do, and Bill Parcells and Chuck Noll and John McKay and even Vince Lombardi was capable of doing," Sherrod said.

"Landry always met with familiar and strange reporters alike and gave thoughtful attention to questions, no matter the downgrading implications. Regular Cowboy media took this for granted; foreign press continually was impressed and appreciative."

It wasn't just a show Landry put on to impress the outsiders.

"On the local front, Landry made no distinction between critics who might call him senile and faltering and downright dumb and those less impetuous," he said. "Landry was a strong, decent and good human."

Verne Lundquist

Tom Landry knew Verne Lundquist first as a sports anchor for a local television station, then as the radio voice of the Cowboys and, in later years, as an announcer for a national television network.

"It was just a great association I had with Tom," Lundquist said. "He was always wonderful to work with. He treated you with respect and had a great sense of humor."

When Lundquist began announcing NFL games for CBS, it required him to visit with Landry a day or two before to collect background.

"It was funny," Lundquist said. "I would come walking in the door with Terry Bradshaw or somebody and he would get that little crinkle in his eye. He'd greet us, then he would say, 'I don't know what you need me for. You've got Lundquist here who has been covering this team since the 1960s. He knows everything about us and what we're going to do. You don't need to talk to me because Lundquist knows it all.'

"We'd all get a big laugh out of it because Tom would do it every time. Then, Tom would give us what we needed. It showed you his great sense of humor."

Lundquist recalled that back in the days with WFAA-TV in Dallas, he had a reporter named Gerry Oher who convinced Landry to play along on all kinds of offbeat stunts.

"He could get Tom to do these silly little features, like wearing a crazy hat or interviewing Oher," Lundquist said. "Oher would call from Thousand Oaks and say he had got Tom to do so-and-so and I'd say, 'You got Tom to do what?'"

Lundquist, who was the voice of the Cowboys from 1972 through 1983, said Landry's patience with reporters was what impressed him.

"My favorite early memory of Tom was at those press luncheons on Tuesday at that place just off Central Expressway," Lundquist said. "He would do the writers press conference, then do television interviews. It didn't matter if you were a golden throat from Dallas or Waco, he would always give a straight answer and never belittle anybody. He always gave them the dignity of a response."

At first, Lundquist and his cameraman were the lone representatives of the TV world.

"For a while, it was only me and Jack Murray shooting the luncheons on 16-millimeter film," Lundquist said. "Then other stations followed suit and stations started coming in from all around Texas. I told (public relations director) Doug Todd that he was killing Tom. Sometimes he would do as many as eight or nine one-on-one interviews.

"Tom just kept on doing them."

Lundquist remembers Landry going out of the way to help him with a golf tournament in Colorado in the early 1980s.

"It was a real honor for him to play in our charity golf tournament for three days," Lundquist said. "It was great sitting around talking to him after the rounds. He was such a pleasant guy."

Lundquist had the honor of being with Landry to witness two of the momentous events of the 20th century: the resignation of Richard Nixon and Neil Armstrong's walk on the moon.

"I remember we were at Thousand Oaks in what we called the 5:30 Club when the Nixon speech was televised," Lundquist said. "It was August 9, 1974, and is doubly etched in my mind.

"I was sitting on the arm of a sofa right next to Tom, who was a staunch Republican. He was a solid Nixon supporter and had voted for him. Tom was typically stolid throughout the speech, very serious. There was no banter. Once the speech was over, Tom got up and walked out without saying a word. He went back to watching film."

Five years earlier, Lundquist and Landry were glued to the television as Armstrong planted his footprints onto the moon.

"We were all overwhelmed," Lundquist said. "It was wonderful to share those two events with Tom."

Lundquist added: "I loved Tom. He was an impressive guy. We in the media were all lucky to have covered a coach like him."

Brad Sham

Brad Sham has been in the radio booth for 23 seasons calling the highs and lows in Dallas Cowboys' history. His favorite Landry memories, though, all came away from the games.

Start with the good piece of advice the coach once gave him.

"After Frank Glieber passed away in 1985, it fell on me to do Tom's television show," Sham said. "There was a column in the *Dallas Times Herald* saying the set was clearly designed to have Tom's chair higher than mine, all the better to make him look superior.

"Well, that hit my hot button because it wasn't true. I was in Tom's office one day going on and on about how the newspaper could be that demeaning. I wouldn't let it go and Tom got a bemused look on his face as my rant continued. Finally, he just threw his head back and laughed out loud."

Then Landry gave Sham a piece of advice it had taken decades for him to learn: Let the media shots bounce off him like rain off a tarpaulin.

"Haven't you learned by now not to let what someone writes bother you?" Landry said.

"You could tell he was kind of tickled that it bothered me," Sham said. "It was a great insight to Tom, how he had learned to live with media criticism and was passing along some of his experience to me."

Sham recalled a great example of Landry's sense of humor.

Every Tuesday, at interviews with the television and broadcast reporters, Tom Hedrick would fire off the first question: "Tom have you ever seen Calvin Hill run like that?"

"Hedrick would do it every week without fail," Sham said.

One Tuesday, Hedrick was a no-show. So Verne Lundquist jumped in and asked the traditional opening question.

After the gales of laughter died down, Landry deadpanned: "No, *Tom*, I don't think I ever had."

Then there was the strong human side of Landry that Sham witnessed.

"My most enduring memory of him, and the most defining of him for me, came on the day of Glieber's funeral," Sham said.

Glieber, the longtime voice of the Cowboys, had passed away while jogging. After the funeral, Sham and his wife Peggy went to the Glieber home to console his sons, Craig and Mitchell, as well as his widow Cathy.

"Peggy and I turned around in the kitchen to see Tom standing there with an arm around both those big, strapping kids," Sham said. "The boys were emotional wrecks and Tom was cooing to them like a mother hen, reassuring them.

"It said more to me about Tom than anything. Here was the so-called 'plastic man' who wasn't supposed to have a human side comforting these two young men who had lost their father. It was a most enduring and revealing memory."

Dale Hansen

Dale Hansen discovered that Tom Landry could give as good a needle as he had to take.

"Landry had a great wit," said Hansen, a popular sports anchor for WFAA-TV who was a color analyst on the Cowboys radio network. "The thing about it is that you had to wait for it and pay attention. You had to wait to find that pearl."

Once, Hansen was emcee at a charity banquet and decided to do a little roasting of Landry to go along with the roast beef.

"You know, every time I go to a charity banquet, Tom is there," Hansen told the audience. "Every time I go to a charity golf tournament, Tom is there.

"One of these days, Tom is going to forget about charity and start coaching again and get the Cowboys back to the Super Bowl."

The crowd oooohed and aaaahed at Hansen's dig.

"Half the crowd was saying, 'You can't say that about Landry,' and half the crowd was agreeing with me," Hansen said.

A smiling Landry quickly defended himself. He put Hansen, who shortly before then had been fired from a Dallas television station, squarely in the bull's-eye.

"With impeccable timing," Hansen said, "Tom shot back: 'Dale, you're pretty mouthy for a guy who only has one television station left in town where he can work.'"

The crowd fell out of their chairs laughing.

"It was great," Hansen said. "He really nailed me."

Another memory comes from a year when the Cowboys were preparing to play the Minnesota Vikings on the road.

"[Reporter] Chris Arnold says to him, 'Coach, you're getting ready for a big game on the road against the Vikings up in Minnesota. Are you concerned weather might be a problem?'"

Landry's straight-faced response: "Since we play inside a dome, I don't think it will be a factor."

Then there was the time Hansen had the bright idea of doing a story on Landry as the man of steel, someone who could leap tall buildings in a single bound.

"I decided to do this story that Landry was actually Superman," Hansen said. "I thought it would be a lot of fun. I had in there that Landry was Clark Kent, Tex Schramm was Perry White and Gil Brandt was Jimmy Olson.

"I had all kind of props set up and everything. I even got a big rock and painted it green for the kryptonite—you know, that stuff that was supposed to make Superman weak.

"I stood near Landry with the rock while he was riding an exercise bike at the Thousand Oaks training camp. We filmed him, then we slowed it down in the studio to make it look like the stuff was causing him to lose strength."

The plot thickened . . .

"We wanted to get Tom to look like Clark Kent before he changed into Superman," Hansen said. "Tom was being interviewed by a guy from *The New York Times*, but he knew we had a plane to catch so he excused himself to help us.

"We got him to run down a hallway, look around nervously, then loosen his tie and duck into another room. Then, on the film, we dubbed Superman flying out of a window. Then Tom did the reverse coming out of a room, putting his tie and coat and hat back on, while Jack Murray filmed it."

Landry was cooperative, but curious. He wanted to know the point of his "acting."

"Tom, you really don't want to know," Hansen told him. "It's a little something we're doing."

The Landry "Superman" film was one of the funniest ever done on the coach. It aired locally and got a big response.

A week later, at the weekly press conference, Hansen was standing by the door when Landry walked in.

Without a smile, Landry said: "Superman, huh?"

"These are just a few reasons of why Landry was the classiest guy around. He would help the media the best he could," Hansen said.

There's also the story about the day that Landry had to loan money to Hansen.

Former Cowboys assistant Dan Reeves was hired as the head coach of the Denver Broncos and Hansen wanted to get Landry's reaction.

It was late, so Hansen went to Landry's house. The coach came to the door wearing a robe.

"After the interview, I got to fishing around in my pocket for toll change," Hansen said. "I could only find one quarter. It took two. My cameraman didn't have any money either."

Landry shook his head and found another quarter for Hansen.

"They don't pay you very much do they?" Landry quipped as handed the money over. "Ask 'em for a raise."

Randy Galloway

Randy Galloway's initial impressions of Tom Landry were wrong, which is difficult for the advocate of "wimp free," straight shooting writing and talking to admit.

"I started observing Tom from afar," Galloway said. "I was a baseball beat writer and I would switch over and do Cowboys sidebars once the hardball season was over.

"I always had immense respect for him, but the impression I got from afar was that I didn't think I wanted to deal with this man because, basically, all he was going to give you was name, rank and serial number. At least, that's what I thought."

Galloway learned otherwise when he became a columnist for *The Dallas Morning News* in 1981 and was around Landry and the Cowboys on almost a daily basis.

"I flipped 180 degrees on Tom then," said Galloway, who now writes for the *Fort Worth Star-Telegram* and hosts a popular radio show on WBAP-AM. "It all goes back to the oldest notion of all and that's don't prejudge people. I found him to be a delightful human being."

Galloway said Landry knew sportswriters had jobs and tried to help them as much as possible—within certain limitations.

"Tom was fine to deal with, and he liked to have fun, despite his image," he said. "Oh, you were always at arm's length with Tom, kind of like the players, who will tell you the same thing. But he would always give you what you needed to get the job done.

"He was one of the best I've ever been around at having some kind of working relationship with you. He had dealt with all kinds of media and you weren't going to trick him—and, please, don't try."

Galloway said Landry would usually give you a golden nugget to go on.

"You were only going to get what Tom told you, but if you would listen, he would tell you a lot more than you originally thought he did," Galloway recalled. "He talked in a kind of a code. Once you broke the code, you knew he was giving you something.

"I found Tom to be a very refreshing guy. One of the things I liked is there was class and honesty in dealing with Landry. Maybe he wouldn't always tell you everything on some football-related item, but I give Landry that right. I just don't want 'em (coaches) to lie.

"I put class and honesty above everything, and that includes how good a coach can coach.

"Tom started off with class and, later on, added the coaching part like a big piece of icing on a cake."

Mickey Spagnola

Mickey Spagnola will be forever grateful to Tom Landry for letting him off easy.

Spagnola came to work for the *Dallas Times Herald* during the 1984 season. His first assignment was to call Landry at home—at night.

"I had to watch one of those weird Saturday night national television games which had a bearing on the Cowboys season—win or lose," Spagnola said. "Then I was supposed to call Tom at home.

"I was really dreading it. I didn't know him and he didn't know me."

Spagnola decided the prudent route would be to warn Landry that he was going to need some quotes.

"Sure," Landry said.

"It was a huge relief to me because Landry could be pretty intimidating for someone coming from Jackson, Mississippi," Spagnola said.

Still, Spagnola was nervous.

"I remember I had a lot of high anxiety, and when I called the phone was busy," Spagnola said. "I felt like a young kid calling a girl on a date.

"I finally got through and he answered the phone himself. He was as nice as he could be. He knew the drill, and it was surprising to me because all I had ever heard was all this stoic stuff. He was most gracious."

Despite it being their initial interview, Spagnola knew when it was time to stop.

"I talked to him for about five minutes," he said. "There was no small talk with Tom. Finally, he said, 'OK?' It was his way of telling me the interview was over. It was the first time I ever got OK'd by him. As I was later to learn, that was Tom's way of saying he was ready to go."

Spagnola said he would rate Landry as the best he's met in dealing with the media.

"The popular concept was that it was a cold organization, but Tom and Tex did their best to help you," he said. "It was a breath of fresh air."

Then, there was the day at training camp in Thousand Oaks when Spagnola first became a target of Landry's famed bullhorn, which he carried up to the tower.

"It was real hot and we all had our shirts off," Spagnola said.

Suddenly, Landry screeched through his bullhorn: "You guys on the sidelines, get your shirts back on. This *isn't* the beach."

Among those scrambling to dress was Schramm.

Spagnola also remembers an incident in the 1985 season in which Landry had to wear a flak jacket because of a death threat in Los Angeles.

"Tom coached the whole game with a flak jacket on," Spagnola said. "He tried to play it down, but it took a lot of nerve for him to go out there with some nut running loose.

"But that was Tom. Nothing bothered him."

Carlton Stowers

Tom Landry didn't get hung up much on trophies. You could go into his office and not find any trappings of the man's many sporting accomplishments.

Except for one: The Door.

That's what Carlton Stowers recalls from his daily dealings with Landry while working for *The Dallas Morning News* as the Dallas Cowboys beat writer.

"I remember the door to his office had a Super Bowl trophy on one panel and a Cowboy helmet on another. It was a beautiful thing," said Stowers, who traded in his newspaper job to become an award-winning mystery author. "Some big fans came to him after the Cowboys won Super Bowl XII and wanted to do something. They said they would like to build him this heavily paneled door with some expensive wood, like mahogany.

"They made the door and Tom loved it. From then on, if he had a picture taken with somebody, he would have it taken in front of that door. When the team moved to Valley Ranch, Tom ordered that the door be taken along."

Fast forward to February 1989 when Jerry Jones fired Landry.

"The next day, Tom was packing up all his belongings and as he was ready to leave, a security man came up and asked if there was anything he could do," Stowers remembered. "Tom said there was—he'd like that door sent to him. The security man had it done and to this day that door is at the Landry Investments office, which proves that even Tom had a trophy he loved."

Having discovered Landry's sentimental side, Stowers also encountered the humorous side.

Stowers cited an example from Cowboys training camp one summer when most of the writers, and even publicity man Doug Todd, decided to grow beards.

After a blue-white scrimmage, this motley group approached Landry to get his analysis of the event.

Landry waited, hands on hips, staring at the approaching journalistic mob.

Then Landry shook his head and said, "Every time I see you guys coming, I think I ought to call security."

Stowers said he was amazed at how accessible Landry was.

"You could call him at 10 p.m. and he would answer questions because he knew we needed it for our jobs," Stowers said. "He knew what our responsibility was.

"Win, lose or draw, he would stand in there in the locker room until the last question was asked. He claimed he didn't read the newspapers, but he knew exactly what all of us were doing. I think Alicia would read the paper and then point out something that he needed to know about.

"It was great covering the team with Tom as the coach. You could criticize him and he would never call you or mention it one way or another."

Bob Taylor

A cartoon poking fun at Tom Landry's stone-face features was one of the most memorable of award-winning cartoonist Bob Taylor's long career at the *Dallas Times Herald*.

It ran October 24, 1971, and was 11 panels of Landry trying to get his legendary "game face" on.

"Ain't had th' right emotional 'feel' lately," the cartoon coach says.

"Gotta get th' team 'up' . . . in a mean mood."

Yet, for seven panels, Landry maintains the same stoic expression he had in the first three panels.

Finally, in the last panel, Landry says, "Wanna see me do it again?"

The cartoon became a coast-to-coast sensation because Taylor was nationally syndicated.

"It was the most requested cartoon I can remember doing at the paper," Taylor said. "It was a common notion everybody carried that the expression on his face just never changed, even when he got excited. People called and wrote from all over wanting copies of it for their refrigerators and scrapbooks.

"I must have done 100 cartoons about the great stone face. I even had things breaking off his face like little chips falling off Mount Rushmore."

Taylor remembered the cartoon infuriated club president and general manager Tex Schramm.

"I was at a driving range when Tex and [team publicist] Al Ward showed up," Taylor said. "I walked over to be friendly, but Al said Tex didn't want to talk to me."

What did Landry think of it?

"He never called me or anything, but I don't think he liked it," Taylor said. "I can remember running into Tom after that at a Salesmanship Club outing in East Texas. We were on the same footpath. Tom just stared at me with a little smile, but didn't say anything."

Taylor was the target of that stare one other time.

He and a colleague, Steve Perkins, were caught raiding the ice cream stash in Landry's refrigerator late one night at the Cowboys training camp.

Landry stayed in good shape, but ice cream was one of his passions. The media always knew where he kept the goodies.

"Tom just gave me that frozen stare again and left," Taylor said. "I think it melted my ice cream."

Bob Taylor hit the mark—and some nerves —with his lampoon of Landry.
(Cartoon courtesy of Bob Taylor)

George Dunham

George Dunham's first interview with Tom Landry was very revealing.

"I went down the hallway to the coaches entrance and knocked on the door," Dunham said. "I didn't hear anything, so I knocked again. I still didn't hear anything, so I opened the door and there was Tom standing stark naked.

"He was changing clothes to go to workout. I mumbled my apologies as I backed toward the door."

Landry's response: "Are we going to do that interview right now or can I get dressed and do it?"

"By all means, coach," Dunham said. "Go ahead and get dressed.'"

"I guess I'm the only media guy who ever saw him naked," Dunham said. "It was a very uncomfortable moment, believe me."

Dunham said another memorable moment came during his first training camp covering the Cowboys.

"I was 21 and just out of North Texas," said Dunham, now the host of a popular morning sports show on KTCK-AM, as well as the public address announcer for Cowboys home games. "I thought I had died and gone to heaven to get to cover the team, even though I thought they had no idea who I was.

"I was in the coaches dorm and fed some tape back to the studio in Dallas. I decided I would step out on the balcony and see what was going on back on the field. All of a sudden, there was Landry standing by me.

"He tapped me on the shoulder then said, 'It looks pretty much the same every day out here, doesn't it, George?'

"You could have knocked me over with a straw. I had been in camp only two days and Tom Landry knew my name. You can imagine how that made me feel. It gave me goosebumps. I was a nobody, but he took the time to find out who I was. He knew who I was. I couldn't believe it."

Dunham said he always used to get a kick out of some of Landry's pet phrases.

"Craig Way and I used to die laughing because Tom would use the transitional phrase *'in there'* all the time," he said. "We would count how many times he would use it. Tom would say, 'We've got a tough schedule in there,' or, 'The Redskins have good linebacking in there,' or 'The offense is going to have to move the ball in there.'

"We would always look forward to those Tuesday press conferences."

A few months after Landry's death, Dunham honored the coach's memory by naming his son Scott Landry Dunham.

"I always had a lot of respect for him, particularly the way he treated people," Dunham said. "He never put anybody down and that would have been easy to do with some of the questions I heard asked of him on Tuesdays.

"What a great man."

Jim Dent

Jim Dent remembers the last day Tom Landry spent at the Dallas Cowboys' training camp in Thousand Oaks, California.

"Little did any of us realize this was going to be Tom's final camp because of the owner change at the end of the season," Dent said. "But it was a day branded forever in my mind."

As usual, Dent would join Landry in a fenced-off area to ride exercise bicycles.

"Everybody was gone but me and Tom," recalled Dent, then a beat reporter for the *Dallas Times Herald*. "We were grinding along when I noticed two shaggy guys with long hair, no shirts and no shoes hanging onto the fence while I talked to Tom.

"The bell rang on the bike, which meant he was done. He said he would see me later."

Landry opened a big gate and walked out.

"These two dirty beach bums were dying to see him," Dent said. "I guess they figured he would be cold and stuck up, but they asked for autographs anyway.

"Much to their surprise, he obliged them. I can still see it now. The sun was setting over the Pacific and you could see the silhouette of Tom Landry walking between two hippies laughing and talking and having an animated conversation. I thought, 'If the public could see this, they would have an insight into the real Tom Landry.'"

Dent recalls another real Landry moment he witnessed.

"Tom was a hands-on guy and he decided to show Roger Staubach how to run a bootleg," Dent said. "So, he took the snap and ran the play around end, limping all the way because of an old knee injury."

Then it was Staubach's turn.

"Roger took the snap, ran around end and started limping downfield. Nobody could keep from laughing. Even Tom got a big kick out of it."

Another time there was a long news conference in which Dent made the embarrassing mistake of asking the same question twice.

"Tom got up from behind his desk, came over and knocked on my head like he was at a door and said, 'Anybody there?' Everybody laughed. I never saw him get mad at a reporter, only a little perturbed."

Another time, Landry ran into Dent on his way to a news conference before an NFC championship game. Dent was carrying a can of beer and didn't want Landry to see it.

"Tom walked right toward me and I nervously stuck the beer down in my jeans pocket," Dent said. "It leaked all over my pants. He just smiled. He knew what had happened."

Dent recalls a news conference Landry once held on a September 11, his birthday.

Landry noticed the absence of reporter Gary Myers, who sometimes could get under Landry's skin with pointed questions.

"Where's Myers?" Landry asked.

"That's your birthday present," Dent answered. "He's not here."

"Tom got a big kick out of it," Dent said.

Dave Campbell

Although Dave Campbell was from Waco, a medium-sized city in Central Texas, Tom Landry was as courteous to him as any visiting journalist.

"He treated me like I was from the *New York Times* or the *Chicago Tribune*," Campbell recalled. "He was very cooperative and helpful over a period of several days when I was doing a four-part series on him.

"I liked Tom very much. He had a good sense of humor and wasn't the grim man you saw on the sidelines."

Campbell, the longtime sports editor in Waco and the founder of *Texas Football* magazine, was struck by Landry's composure after games, win or lose.

"He was very obliging with the sportswriters," Campbell said. "I don't ever remember him storming at a questioner or storming out of the door. He was a very self-contained man. Very controlled."

Landry once told Campbell about his World War II days, including the story of his plane running out of gas and making a crash-landing.

"Tom said he was flying against a Germany which had lost most of its air force and wasn't as strong as it had been," Campbell said. "He left the impression things would have been tougher if he had had to go against what he called 'the first team.'"

Campbell and wife Reba were once driving Tom and Alicia Landry to Ridgewood Country Club in Waco for a charity golf tournament.

Somehow the topic turned to cancer, which had stricken the Landrys' youngest daughter Lisa.

"Why can't they do something about cancer?" Campbell recalls Alicia wistfully asking.

Nobody answered.

"Isn't it ironic that many years later, cancer is also what got Tom," Campbell said.

Jim Reeves

Early in his career as a *Fort Worth Star-Telegram* columnist, former baseball beat man Jim Reeves found out fast what his readers thought of Tom Landry.

"As a young columnist, I was still trying to learn the ins and outs and all the rules," Reeves said. "I wrote a column that was semi-critical when he wore those pink-tinted sunglasses, saying basically that it was not a good look.

"It was only a mild critique. But, my gosh, the fan mail I got was as if I'd vilified a saint. I learned that you just don't say anything bad about Tom Landry."

Reeves became a columnist in 1987 after covering the Texas Rangers for 12 years. The following summer, he went to training camp with the Cowboys for the first time.

Reeves had been to his share of spring trainings with the Rangers in Pompano Beach, Florida, but he soon learned not to expect the same laid-back environment with the Cowboys in Thousand Oaks, California.

"I got out there and heard all the stories about Landry getting on the megaphone and yelling, 'This is not the beach. Put your shirts on,'" Reeves said. "By the time I started going, nobody was taking their shirt off. They knew better."

Chuck Cooperstein

Radio host Chuck Cooperstein isn't awed by much. His first meeting with Tom Landry fits in that small percentage.

"I was incredibly intimidated," Cooperstein said. "I was working for KRLD, which was the Cowboys flagship station at the time. He did so much stuff with us. He was very nice and proper—but, wow, for me, it was like, 'This is Dallas. I am in Dallas and this is Tom Landry.'"

Cooperstein regrets that he didn't get to spend more time around Landry.

"I never did a one-on-one, long, sit-down interview with him. But I did once get to host his 15-minute Monday radio show when Brad [Sham] lost his voice," Cooperstein said, laughing. "I wish I still had that tape."

Cooperstein's first day at KRLD was in 1984, the day Randy White ended a long holdout. A few days later, the Texas Rangers fired general manager Joe Klein and hired Tom Grieve.

"What a week," Cooperstein said. "I remember asking someone, 'Is it always like this around here?'"

Ken Sins

One of Tom Landry's foibles was an inability to handle certain names. In his dozen years covering Landry, Ken Sins remembers hearing plenty of botches.

For example, sportswriter Frank Luksa was always "Luska" even though Landry had known him for decades.

Some of the others:

Don Smerek became "Smirkie."

Gary Hogeboom was "Hogan-bloom."

Phil Pozderac was "Pozdrak."

Raul Allegre became "Rawl Allegro."

Dick Vermeil became "Vermillion."

Landry also had his own Texan way of pronouncing cities like "Wershington" and "Sant Louis."

"Sometimes," Sins said, "when Landry would butcher a name, a wise guy reporter would raise his hand and say 'Now Tom, about those new players . . .' Landry would just laugh and shake his head."

Landry never made pals with the media, but he didn't treat reporters as enemies, either.

"He knew we had a job to do and he let us do it," said Sins, who covered Landry for the *Fort Worth Star-Telegram* and the *Dallas Cowboys Weekly,* and is now associate editor of the fan magazine. "Landry always treated us with respect. There was never a question so dumb that it was deemed unworthy of comment."

Sins occasionally called Landry at his home. Some of those calls were made rather late at night.

"Never was he grumpy," Sins said. "Landry figured you were doing your job and he was doing his."

Mike Rabun

Tom Landry's final preseason news conference in 1984 was fascinating.

Throughout training camp that year a debate raged as to whether Danny White or Gary Hogeboom should start at quarterback. Landry was supposed to settle the issue at that gathering of reporters.

"The exact wording of his edict is no longer contained in the memory bank, but the look will always be there," recalls Mike Rabun, who covered the Cowboys for United Press International for much of the Landry era. "A few beads of sweat appeared to add to the uncomfortable nature of the occasion as Landry announced his decision."

Finally, Landry announced his choice: Phil Pozderac, who had been fighting for a job on the offensive line.

"It might have been argued that Landry mentioned Pozderac's name on purpose as an attempt at comic relief," Rabun said. "But his face said otherwise."

Ron Spain

Tom Landry shed his game face once he got on the golf course.

Ron Spain, now the editor of the fan magazine *Dallas Cowboys Weekly*, had the good fortune to draw Landry in his foursome once at a Byron Nelson media day event.

"It was such an honor to get to play with Tom," Spain said. "And what a great personality he had. He felt at home on the golf course, and you could tell it relaxed him. "

Spain said Landry was the star of their foursome.

"He could really give the ball a good belt. He was a really good player."

Spain said Landry was relaxed as could be on the golf course.

"Tom wasn't anything close to being the stoic figure you saw on the sidelines," Spain said. "He was joking and having a great time. There was a big change in his personality when he was comfortable being around people."

One thing about Landry didn't change: winning.

"Tom took us to a victory that day in the tournament," Spain said. "He played great."

Landry shares a laugh with reporters during a Super Bowl gathering. (Photo courtesy of the Gen Long collection)

Chapter Eight

NEW YORK YEARS

Tom Landry was a professional football player by the time he walked off the field following his final college game.

It was January 1, 1949, and Landry's Texas Longhorns had just beaten the Georgia Bulldogs 41-28 in the Orange Bowl. Landry had the best game of his career and as he headed for the locker room, he was met by Jack White, an assistant coach for the New York Yankees of the All-American Football Conference. White pulled a contract from his pocket and Landry signed it.

The Yankees and their in-town rivals, the New York Giants of the National Football League, both drafted Landry in 1946, which is when his class would've graduated had it not been for the war. Both teams still had his rights and whichever signed Landry first would get him.

Landry's first season with the Yankees was the last for the team and the league. The NFL absorbed the AAFC in 1950 and the Giants were allowed to pick five Yankees; once again, they selected Landry.

Landry played six seasons as a defensive back and punter, making All-Pro in 1954. The Giants made the playoffs his first season, but lost to Cleveland, which had moved to the NFL from the AAFC.

The Browns of that era were dominant. Led by Otto Graham and Marion Motley, and coached by Paul Brown, Cleveland forced NFL teams to find a new way to play defense. New York coach Steve Owen came up with the idea of a formation featuring six lineman, one linebacker and four defensive backs, instead of the predominant 5-3-3. However, he wasn't sure how to make it work.

Landry figured it out and taught his teammates. The basis of Owen's 6-1 "Umbrella" was to trick the offense into thinking the middle of the field would be open, but two of the front men would drop back. Years later, that led to the 4-3 front that was Landry's first major coaching innovation.

In 1954, Jim Lee Howell replaced Owen as head coach. Howell hired an assistant from Army named Vince Lombardi to run his offense. Nobody knew the Giants' defense better than Landry, so Howell made him a player-coach. At 29, Landry was the youngest assistant in the NFL.

Landry did double duty for two years, then became strictly a coach in '56. The Giants won the championship that season and the defense led the way.

With rookie Sam Huff playing the newfangled position of middle line-backer, fans became as excited when their team did not have the ball as when they did, prompting the birth of the now-common cheer, "De-fense! De-fense!"

Two years later, New York was back in the championship, this time against Baltimore. After four quarters, both teams were still tied at 17. The Colts scored on Landry's defense in overtime of what's remembered as "The Greatest Game Ever Played."

Howell knew how great he had it with Landry and Lombardi as his assistants, even joking that his job was to keep balls pumped and to enforce curfew. Howell acknowledged Landry as "the best defensive coach in the business," so he wasn't surprised Landry had his choice of coaching jobs for the 1960 season, a year after Lombardi became the head coach at Green Bay.

Howell already had decided that 1960 would be his final one with the Giants. His third-to-last game before retiring was a 31-31 tie against Landry's Cowboys in New York, where fans cheered the rival coach prior to kickoff. The final score was significant to Dallas because it was the first game that wasn't a loss. Afterward, Howell upgraded his previous compliment, saying: "Tom Landry is the best coach in all of football."

In 1989, Landry's first year out of football, the only game he attended was between the Cowboys and Giants—in New York. He watched a 15-0 New York victory from the private box of Giants owner Wellington Mara, who remained a close friend.

The Giants also were part of Landry's first game back at Texas Stadium. In 1993, New York—then coached by Landry protégé Dan Reeves—was the opponent the day Landry was inducted into the Ring of Honor.

Here are the statistics from Landry's seven-year playing career with the Giants and Yankees:

RUSHING—26 carries, 131 yards, one TD, long of eight yards.

PASSING—11 completions, 47 attempts, seven interceptions, 172 yards, one TD, long of 70 yards all with '52 Giants.

RECEIVING—six catches, 109 yards (all with '49 Yankees).

INTERCEPTIONS—32, 404 return yards, three TDs, long of 55 (career-best eight INTs in '51, '52 and '54).

PUNTING—41.4-yard average, 384 attempts, five blocked, long of 69 (2,249 yards in '49 led the AAFC).

Frank Gifford

Frank Gifford spent enough time around Tom Landry as a teammate, player and broadcaster to have a good idea about what made him tick.

"He had that engineer's analytical mind and, being a pilot, he had great discipline," Gifford said. "He also had the intelligence to realize he wasn't fast, he wasn't necessarily big and he wasn't very quick. So if he was going to cover somebody, he had to know where that guy was going to go. Necessity is the mother of invention and from his own necessity grew his whole defensive concepts of reading and anticipating.

"I think the same understanding of the game and burning intensity that drove him to be a pro football player is also what made him, in my estimation, maybe the greatest coach of all-time. He's certainly right up there with Lombardi.

"He was very mild-mannered. Never swore. I saw him only a couple times raise his voice, and he never exploded out of pure frustration like most coaches. But, inside, this guy was an intense competitor. He wanted to win, he wanted to play right and he wanted to be the best he could be.

"Most people never recognized Tom as being that kind of competitor because he had such great personal control. He didn't rant and jump around like Mike Ditka. But that doesn't mean he wasn't burning inside to win just as much as they were—and, in many cases, I

Everything Frank Gifford knew about playing defense he learned from Landry. (Photo courtesy of the New York Giants)

think more. My wife and I played a lot of bridge with Tom and Alicia, and it was fun. You could see the same intensity in the bridge games."

Gifford constantly came to Landry's defense during Monday Night Football broadcasts, especially when he shared the booth with Don Meredith.

"Don is one of my best friends—he's my little boy's godfather—but we got to where we couldn't even talk about Tom," Gifford said. "Don and Tom had this oil-and-water relationship. But that didn't keep me from saying what I wanted on the air.

"Our views were totally opposite, but I knew Tom in a different way. Don certainly had every right to feel what he felt, although I don't know what it was because we've never discussed it."

Gifford became Landry's teammate in 1952 when the New York Giants made him a first-round pick out of Southern California.

Gifford had been an All-American running back, but the Giants already had a star ballcarrier in Kyle Rote. So, Gifford wound up being Rote's backup at offensive halfback and the top backup at defensive halfback.

Gifford had little experience on defense, so Landry—who was two years from becoming a player-coach—taught him the basics.

"His system was mainly about discipline. That's the best way I can put it," Gifford said. "You read offensive sets then took your key from what would happen. As a defensive player, you would key on different players.

"Before him, I had never heard of it and I don't think anyone else had. The things they do now are more complex, but every team that has some sort of 4-3 goes back to Tom and his keys."

Landry was so devoted to his keys that he'd rather a player miss a tackle within the system than make a play while going outside it. There are many stories supporting that, but Gifford has the best one.

"I intercepted a pass one time, lateraled to him and he scored a touchdown—and he still chewed me out the following Monday for being in the wrong position," Gifford said. "It seemed like I was always doing the wrong thing—yet, somehow or other, I did pretty well with it."

Because the Giants knew how tightly Landry held to his keys, they were able to use their knowledge against him in a game during his early days in Dallas.

"All we did was reverse the keys in the huddle," Gifford said. "It was really fun."

The inspiration for Landry's defensive diagnoses was epic battles with the Cleveland Browns. Gifford believes that Landry watched so many Cleveland films that he eventually became in tune with the thinking of the brilliant offensive mind of Paul Brown.

"When you're playing in a Tom Landry defense, you really have to understand the offense," Gifford said. "That's how he realized the strengths and weaknesses of various offensive sets."

Gifford said pro football still seemed like a pickup game until Landry turned it into a chess match. Soon after, fellow assistant and future rival Vince Lombardi adopted many of the same ideas.

"Lombardi learned from Landry the intelligence of doing the right thing, following the keys, the discipline of doing that instead of giving in to the pure emotion of the game," Gifford said. " Once you can accomplish that, you can bring the emotion back into the game."

During Gifford's two-way days in New York, he had the incredible experience of being coached by both Lombardi and Landry.

"I was very fortunate," said Gifford, who was the NFL Player of the Year in 1956 and later became a Hall of Famer. "Even though they weren't all that close, they weren't enemies or anything. They were both competitive and both were off-the-charts intelligent. I think each complemented the other."

Despite Landry's success in New York, Gifford said some Giants were skeptical whether he would succeed in Dallas.

"I didn't know either," he said, "particularly when he took over the offense. He had them doing all that jumping up and down and the multiple shifts—it looked like a fire drill out there.

"At first, instead of being a hitting type of team, they were a finesse type of team. But when they were at their height, they had good people who could hit and could survive Tom's mental gymnastics. They knew what they had to do and Tom didn't really tolerate anything less."

By the time the Cowboys became America's Team, Gifford had a great view from the press box as a broadcaster for ABC. He was no longer the only one in Landry's corner.

"I said many times how totally misunderstood he was, and I really felt that," Gifford said. "Some head coaches call offensive plays, but I don't know any who call defensive plays. Well, Tom did both. At the height of his career, he was running it all.

"Consequently, you looked at him and he looked like a machine because he wasn't responding. But if the ballcarrier fumbled or if one of his players got hurt, Tom's thinking about the next defensive play or getting the right replacement on the field. Football doesn't allow a whole lot of time for retrospect. I knew that. And I knew Tom and how much he loved Alicia and his kids and what a great father he was and what a wonderful person he was."

Pat Summerall

Pat Summerall said Tom Landry helped him with his placekicking, broadcasting and baptism.

Placekicking came first.

"Tom was my kicking coach with the New York Giants," Summerall said. "He summoned me to his apartment in 1959—we lived in the same hotel—and told me he was leaving to take the head coaching job with the Cowboys.

"Then he got down to business like he usually did. He said, 'You'll probably beat me someday, but don't ever kick without supervision. Have somebody make sure they watch so you don't fall into the bad habits we talked about in practice Now, if you miss to the right, this is what you're doing wrong, and if you miss to the left, this is what you're doing wrong.'

"It was pretty incredible. He wanted to make sure I didn't forget my kicking keys."

Landry was right about his buddy beating him. Two years later, Summerall and the Giants beat the Cowboys.

"We had always had a great association, but he had his famous game face on that day," Summerall said. "His kicking tips came in handy."

Next came the broadcasting help at the start of Summerall's storied second career.

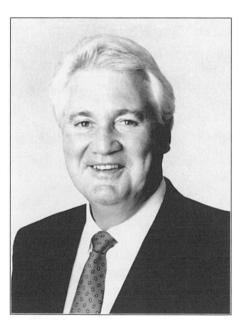

Pat Summerall will never forget . . . um, uh . . . Landry. (Photo courtesy of the New York Giants)

"I was an analyst and we were doing a game in the Cotton Bowl with the Cowboys and the Cardinals," Summerall said. "In those days, the analyst would be on the field introducing the players. They would run up to the camera, smile and I'd announce their names.

"I was a little scared at first, but I got through the Cardinals lineup OK, finishing off with coach Charlie Winter.

"I got through the whole Cowboys lineup and Tom stepped up. I drew a total blank. I couldn't remember his name. Here was somebody I had been on the same team with and I froze on his name."

Summerall said Landry "finally realized what was happening."

"He said, 'I'm coach of the Dallas Cowboys.' And then, it all came back to me and I announced Tom's name. He always kidded me about it."

Landry later inadvertently added an inside joke to Summerall's on-air chatter with longtime broadcast partner John Madden.

"One time, we asked him about Doug Cosbie. We told Tom we heard Cosbie was hurt," Summerall said. "Tom came back and said, 'I don't know what's exactly wrong with him. You know I think he has some kind of a combilation up there.'"

Madden and Summerall never found out what a "combilation" was. But they still use the term.

"To this day, we use that if somebody is nursing some sort of a mysterious injury," Summerall said. "We just say, 'I guess ol' so-and-so has some kind of a *combilation* up there he can't get over.'"

Finally, there was the religious conversion that made Landry more proud of Summerall than any game-winning field goals.

"The last time I saw him was at his golf tournament in Dallas," Summerall said. "I had just been baptized into the church. I wanted to tell Tom because I knew it would make him feel good.

"Tom had his picture taken with each group and when our group was waiting to be photographed, I said, 'I've got some news for you. I was just baptized last Sunday.'

"That was the biggest smile I ever saw on his face. My wife said later that Landry told her, 'I couldn't be more proud of Pat.'"

Wellington Mara

When Tom Landry was considering leaving New York for Dallas, Giants owner Wellington Mara gave a strong recommendation to Cowboys owner Clint Murchison and team president Tex Schramm.

Later, Mara questioned his generosity.

"There was many a day he made me regret my recommendation," said Mara, who was the team's personnel director in Landry's early years then became the club's president.

Mara said that many of the qualities that made Landry a great coach in Dallas were evident during his days as with the Giants.

"The thing that always stood out about Tom is that even though he held his

Wellington Mara and Landry never let football interfere with their friendship. (Photo courtesy of the New York Giants)

emotions in check, I know how intensely competitive he was. I knew that from his days as a player with us," Mara said. "The other thing I remember about Tom is how completely confident he was without being cocky.

"Regardless of what happened on the football field, we always felt he could handle it. . . . And, to my knowledge, he always did."

Although Landry compiled a 35-16-2 record against the Giants, becoming their No. 1 division tormentor, Tom and Alicia Landry remained great friends with Wellington and Ann Mara. The couples often dined together when the Cowboys visited New York.

"He was always a close friend of ours," Mara said.

Kyle Rote

For anyone who wonders what it was like to have Tom Landry and Vince Lombardi on the same coaching staff, Kyle Rote tells a story that illustrates what it meant for head coach Jim Lee Howell.

During training camp, Rote walked down a hallway and saw Lombardi showing films and talking offense. In another room, Landry was going over defenses with his players. Then Rote came across Howell, who had his feet up while reading the newspaper.

"That's a classic story," Rote said, laughing. "He had Tom and Vince running things for him, so he really didn't have to pay that much attention. No one would really say anything about it in a serious way, but everyone knew he had a great staff."

The staff helped each other for the benefit of the team. For example, it was Landry who suggested that Lombardi move Rote from halfback to flanker.

"He looked at what would be the most difficult position to cover me from," Rote said. "That added eight years to my career."

Rote respected Landry as a player, coach and friend.

"Tom was one of the best defensive players I ever saw. He gave a lot of comfort to those around him," Rote said. "He also was one of the best coaches.

"He had a good sense of humor and was a very decent, decent man. I really admired his football knowledge and his personal values. I was fortunate to be there when he was."

Andy Robustelli

Andy Robustelli and Tom Landry were part of one of the most unique carpools in automotive history. This group that drove to Yankee Stadium from the Connecticut suburb Stamford also included a revolving cast of Giants players and a lawyer breaking into sportscasting, a guy named Howard Cosell.

"Ballplayers would come in from out of town and probably didn't have cars. The fortunate ones who had would pick up the players," Robustelli said. "Tom was one of them, although he was probably one of the only coaches.

"He was always silent. He was never one to take over in a crowd. He was a very quiet person, regardless."

Landry wasn't big on pep talks, even in his days with the Giants. Robustelli, a Hall of Fame defensive lineman, remembers Landry emphasizing old-fashioned principles like hard work and self-confidence.

"You don't have to be a rah-rah guy if you're looking at the team you're playing and you know you're better," said Robustelli, who later coached New York's defense and was the team's director of operations for 12 years. "I think that's probably why the thing he pointed to the most was good execution.

"The coaching philosophies that he had were conducive to believing in him. So, if he believed, you had to believe."

One of the best examples of Landry's methods paying off came in the 1958 playoffs. The Giants beat the dreaded Browns 13-10 in the final game of the regular season, then met them again in the next game to determine the Eastern Conference championship.

Landry's precise game planning and the players' perfect execution led to a 10-0 victory. New York held Jim Brown to just eight yards and shut out Cleveland for the first time in eight years.

In the locker room after the game, Robustelli was holding the game ball. He gave it to Landry.

A week later, the Giants lost to the Baltimore Colts in what's remembered as "The Greatest Game Ever Played." Landry remained in New York one more year before moving south to start the Cowboys.

"He was a success with the Giants. He just took what he was good at and brought it to Dallas," Robustelli said. "I think Tom's theory was you play the game with what you do best and you design your defense for the best."

Allie Sherman

Tom Landry's first dose of football innovation came in 1950, his first season with the New York Giants. Coach Steve Owen decided to try shaking up the Cleveland Browns with a defense that featured six men up front, one in the middle and four deep backs.

Teaching the 6-1 scheme known as the "Umbrella" wasn't easy, recalls then-assistant coach Allie Sherman.

"It was our off week and I told the backs, 'We're going to do something so totally different from anything you've ever learned.'"

"As a result, during this week, you may look like you should never be near a ballclub, let alone be playing for one. But let's have faith because it's so different that it'll arrive and we'll be ready next week," Sherman said.

"Of all our defensive backs—and all of them were very good and experienced—Tom showed that he had more understanding, vision and feel for what we were trying to do. He was the one who showed the strongest instinct. As a result, we nominated Tom to call the coverages for us out there."

The key to the 6-1 was that when Otto Graham went back to pass, two of the six defensive ends would drop back eight yards and 45 degrees—essentially giving the defense three linebackers. Thus, the seeds were planted for the 4-3 defense that Landry made famous, and the movement later led to the Flex.

The original Umbrella had a lot of intricacies, such as varying the number of players that would drop off and how far back they'd go.

"The purpose was to disturb the rhythm of the passers and the receivers," Sherman said. "Tom was the one who had to make those percentage calls."

The defense was as new to Sherman and the coaches as it was to Landry and his teammates. What amazed Sherman was that Landry not only understood it, but he was able to improve on the ideas and was able to teach everyone how to do it. In a nutshell, that's what coaching is all about.

"You can draw up a lot of things and understand why you want to use them against ballclubs or make it a basic part of your team, but you've got to be able to teach it so that other people can understand it and use it," Sherman said. "Not every coach who understands the concepts and techniques can

Allie Sherman won five of his first six meetings against Landry, then lost seven of the last eight. (Photo courtesy of the New York Giants)

teach it. In my mind, teaching is where there's a big difference in the degree of coaches."

Sherman went to the Canadian Football League after the '53 season. Landry was a player-coach the next two years, then was in his second year as the defensive coach when Sherman returned as a scout in 1957. He was amazed by the way Landry taught football as if it was industrial engineering.

"He was so precise," Sherman said. "If you were a defensive tackle, he'd say, 'The first step you take with your right foot is six inches. The next step with your left foot is six parallel inches. As you take those two steps, you deliver the blow right under the numbers.'"

Landry and Sherman were assistants together for one year, then Landry went to Dallas. The following season, Sherman replaced Jim Lee Howell and was named Coach of the Year his first two seasons. Had Landry remained, he probably would've gotten the job over Sherman and had a much easier start than he had in Dallas.

Landry ended up going 8-6-1 against Sherman, winning seven of the final eight meetings after losing five of the first six.

Sherman said he wasn't surprised that Landry succeeded with the Cowboys. What did surprise him was how quickly it happened.

"There are a lot of good people in football coaching and some who are just fair. I figured he'd be one of the real good ones," Sherman said. "He had the ability, the vision, to understand offense and defense. He was a complete football man."

Chapter Nine

THE EARLY YEARS

Mission Eagles, Texas Longhorns, 8th Air Force

GROWING UP IN MISSION

Thomas Wade Landry was born September 11, 1924, in the far South Texas town of Mission. He was the third child of Ray and Ruth Landry, about four years younger than brother Robert and a year and a half younger than sister Ruthie. Another brother, Jack, joined the family in 1931.

Ray Landry's family had moved from Illinois to the Rio Grande Valley around the turn of the century because of the warmer climate. Ruth's father was a farmer, and he trekked the family through several states before settling in Mission in 1915.

Ray Landry was a mechanic by trade, but he also was the chief of the local volunteer fire department and the superintendent of the Sunday school at First United Methodist Church. Many folks in town called him "Uncle Ray."

He was such a stalwart in the community that locals still say they consider Tom a celebrity because he was Ray's son, not because of his other accomplishments. When they created a Man of the Year award, Ray was the first recipient. A park was named in Ray's honor 12 years before a downtown street and the high school stadium were named for Tom.

Ray and Ruth were married 55 years, until her death in 1975. Ray died in October 1978, nine months after attending Tom's second Super Bowl victory.

When Tom was growing up, the United States was in the clutches of the Great Depression. He was a senior in high school when Pearl Harbor was bombed. His brother Robert enlisted in the military soon after and died while ferrying bomber planes to England.

In junior high, Tom met one of the biggest influences of his life: Bob Martin.

Just 22 when he moved to Mission, Martin had been a star center on the 1933 Breckenridge High Eagles and a letterman at San Marcos State Teachers College, now known as Southwest Texas State. His first job was coaching the junior high at Mission, and he lived in a garage apartment two doors down from the Landrys.

The high school football stadium in Mission bears the name of its most famous alumnus. (Photo courtesy of Jaime Aron)

Martin was the ultimate hands-on coach. He wore a uniform but no pads and dared the team to try tackling him. That was how they practiced defense. On offense, he borrowed formations and strategies from the successful college teams of the day.

The first day Martin spoke to the team, he said he needed someone tough and smart to handle the ball at the start of every play. Landry volunteered, so Martin made him the center. He later proved more valuable as the quarterback.

That switch came when Martin was promoted to head varsity coach before Landry's junior year. The Mission Eagles promptly won the district championship, but lost in the bi-district round of the playoffs.

The following year, Mission allowed only one touchdown—and it came on a controversial play involving Landry. The Eagles went 12-0 to claim the regional championship, which was as far as teams could go back then. In his final high school game, Landry ran for three touchdowns—including a 63-yarder—and threw for another in a 33-0 victory over Hondo.

Landry never forgot his old coach. When he was inducted into the Hall of Fame in 1990, Landry thanked his family for their support, then talked about Martin.

"He taught me a lot about football," Landry said. "He taught me the fundamentals, he taught me values, he taught me to pay a price to win. He contributed greatly to my success."

Ruthie (Landry) Lowrie

The ideal life Tom Landry led can be traced back to a wonderful childhood.

"I think so," said his sister Ruthie Lowrie. "We had a terrific mother and father, good surroundings and a lot of encouragement from the people all around us. We were all together as a family in a small town and we just loved it. We didn't have the peer pressure that children have today."

Ruthie has many fond memories of days spent playing with her older brother Robert and younger brother Tommy.

"The three of us had such a great time playing together," she said. "We played football in the front yard, climbed trees, dug tunnels and did all sorts of things.

"We'd walk to the swimming pool and swim all afternoon. My mother lost her brother when he was young, so she was determined that all of us would learn to swim. And we did, we learned to swim quite young. We had enough money to go and swim all day long.

"We didn't have a lot, but we thought we were rich.

"We only lived a block off the main street. My dad's garage was right behind the house, so we'd run over there and do whatever we needed to do over there, then come back home. He always came home for lunch, ate and went back to working in the garage again.

"We spent an awful lot of time on Saturdays going to the movies. We'd pay a nickel and stay there all day practically. On a Saturday night, Daddy would park the car on the main street and we'd go up there and watch the people go by.

"Of course, Daddy was a fireman, the fire chief. I can remember many Christmases when the fire alarm would go off and Daddy would disappear. We'd wait for him to come back again."

Ruthie admits, "He was my brother, and brothers and sisters fight." But, in general, she and Tommy got along well during their younger days.

"Tommy was always so reserved and so quiet, even as a child," she said. "He was popular with the boys and girls, although he was very shy, especially with the girls."

Ruthie left Mission for nurses training in Dallas while Tom was still in high school. Because they never again lived in the same city, it was difficult to maintain a tight bond.

Tommy Landry

THOMAS WADE LANDRY

Thomas Wade Landry was born in Mission, Texas September 11, 1924 and has lived in Mission exclusively. Tommy, as he is known to everyone, is an attentive and diligent student. He has not only brains, but he also has brawn. Handsome Tommy is six feet tall, weighs 165 pounds, and has brown hair and gray-green eyes.

With the exception of the fifth grade, Tommy has been a student of the Mission Schools exclusively and is now an outstanding junior in Mission High School.

Tommy's activities in Mission High School have been mostly athletic, but he also makes above average grades. Tommy, a center and later a quarterback, was a member of the Junior High Football Team from 1938 to 1940. This year Tommy started what appears to be a brilliant Senior High Football career by being an important member of this year's championship team and by winning a place on the All-Valley First String Team. For two years Tommy has been a first string member of the Senior Basketball Team which this year won the Rio League. Tommy has also been active in Track and Softball. He is an active Hi-Y member.

In 1940 Tommy received the Sophomore Boy Service Award, which is the highest honor that can be given a sophomore boy. He was president of the Sophomore Class in 1939-1940, which shows his leadership ability. In 1939 and again in 1940 he was voted the Cutest Boy in Mission High School.

After he is graduated from Mission High School, he plans to enter college.

Mission High produced its own Who's Who book in the 1940-41 school year. (Photo courtesy of Gen Long Collection)

"As Tommy got older and went to the University of Texas and to war and on with the Cowboys, he was so busy that we didn't have much chance to be together," she said. "And, if we were, there were just too many people around for us to have the closeness."

Being related to Tom Landry brought along a celebrity status that Ruthie and the family didn't always enjoy.

"It was very exciting, but awfully hard," she said. "I remember one time, somebody called my mother and chewed her out about something. I felt so bad about that, to think someone would do something like that just because the Cowboys lost a game."

Ruthie and her family were with Tom and his family for his Hall of Fame induction in 1990. Another special time together was a party for Tom and Alicia's 50th wedding anniversary. She spent a few days with her brother at the end of his life, but his condition had already overtaken him.

She was in Dallas in the days following his death. She heard and read many things about her brother that she didn't know, things that made her appreciate him even more.

"We're so proud of him and the legacy he's left," she said. "People still look up to him.

"I was out playing golf the other day, and one of the girls told me that a friend of hers was going to have a grandson the next day and they were going to name him Landry Matthew because they were such great football fans and Tom Landry fans."

Jack Landry

While Tom Landry was coaching the Dallas Cowboys, anyone who met Jack Landry couldn't help but ask whether he was related to Tom.

"When I said yes, there was disbelief," he said. "Most people usually let it go at that because I don't look anything like Tom—different size and everything. But I never found it to be offensive. I was very proud of Tom."

Jack Landry wasn't all that close with his brother. A nearly seven-year gap in age was part of it. Jack also was admittedly "kind of a loner" who didn't marry until his late 40s.

"Whenever I asked Tom for advice, he was always there to give it to me. He tried to help as best he could and he was right most of the time," Jack said. "But he was barking up the wrong tree lots of times. That wasn't his fault—that was mine.

"He understood people, I think, in a big way. He had a very good perspective on life. He tried to give me good advice as far as how to get along in this ol' world, but I just wouldn't take it."

Jack was in grade school when Tom starred for the high school varsity squad. The youngster went to all the games, home and away, as did most people in town.

"We all went to the regional finals on a train. Everybody from Mission went to see that ballgame," Jack said. "It was the first big trip of my life. I was impressionable enough to enjoy it. I don't remember the specifics of the game, but I know they won big."

The summer of 1948 was the last time Jack and Tom lived in their parents' home together.

"He played baseball for a team they had there in Mission," Jack said. "He hit home runs and he pitched. I guess he could've been a pretty good baseball player if he'd put his mind to it."

Jack wasn't much of a football player. Although he was a starter his junior and senior years, he wasn't fast enough to make an impact. His contribution instead came as president of his class.

Jack said he never felt any pressure to live up to his brother's standards.

"I was always Tommy's younger brother, but my father also was well known and highly respected. He also carried a big load as far as the town was concerned," Jack said.

The headlines in Mission on December 7, 1941, were about an upcoming playoff game. (Photo courtesy of A.B. Ward)

Jack said Tom had a lot in common with their father.

"Tom and Robert both took a lot of dad's traits," Jack said. "Tom definitely seemed to have the patience. Daddy would love to talk to people. Tom had that same ability. You know, people say he was standoffish and all that stuff, but I don't think that was true if you were with him one-on-one. He had the patience of Job to listen to your troubles or talk to you. Daddy did too."

Wade Spilman

Tom Landry was the best friend Wade Spilman ever had. He proved it for the umpteenth time during the late stages of illness that claimed his life.

At the time, Spilman wasn't feeling so great himself. He'd ruptured both Achilles' tendons and was suffering through a lung problem.

"I think it was about the third time he was back in the hospital for treatment when he called me one day," Spilman said. "He said, 'Hey, I got to thinking about you, and I wanted to call and see how you're doing.'

"Here's this guy in his kind of condition and he wants to know how *I'm* doing. I said, 'That's not the question, Tom. How are *you* doing?' He said, 'I'm hanging in there.'

"You know, that was Tom Landry—a very unselfish person his entire life. This was not just a phenomenon in recent years or after he dedicated himself to Christ. He was always this way, even as a boy growing up."

Spilman would know. He and Landry were born a month apart and became inseparable friends soon after.

"Our families went to the same church, so we were thrown together immediately," he said. "All through our lives, we remained very, very dear friends. I guess we both regarded the other as our closest friend and maintained that kind of relationship right up to Tom's death.

"We never had any argument, any dispute, any controversies between us. If we'd go months and not see each other, when we got back together, it was just like we'd never got apart. That's a rare treat and an extraordinary experience to have."

As kids, they played a lot of sports together. Spilman was too slight to play football, but he became a star tennis player. They both loved golf.

During one memorable stretch, they played golf together nearly every day. Both had just gotten out of the military and they had some time off before returning to the University of Texas.

One day, Landry suggested they spend the evening across the Mexico border in Reynosa.

"Tom and I hadn't exactly been the party boys growing up. The only way we

Wade Spilman and Landry were lifelong friends, from childhood in Mission to retirement in Austin. (Photo courtesy of Wade Spilman)

ever went out with a girl is if she asked us to a prom or a junior or senior dance," Spilman said. "But, here we were, men of the world coming back from the service. We thought, well, we probably ought to go over to Reynosa and see the big shows and the dancing girls and the really big parties. So we said, 'Let's do it. We owe it to ourselves.'

"Well, we go over there and we don't get through the first little old drink when Tom said, 'What are we doing over here? This is ridiculous.' So we went back home, got up early the next day and played 45 holes of golf."

At Texas, Landry became a star football player. Yet he was so humble that he didn't even brag to his parents.

"I was home one time and his mom asked how he was doing. I said everybody thought he hung the moon," Spilman said. "She asked if there'd been any articles in the paper because Tom never told them anything. So, after that, I was the guy who furnished any kind of report about Tom from the newspapers."

Spilman and his wife occasionally flew to Dallas for Cowboys games. They stayed at Tom and Alicia's house, and Landry always gave them personal attention.

"Here he is, football week in Dallas, maybe going into a game that was just critical, and lo and behold he'd meet us on a Saturday afternoon at the airport and just not think anything of it," Spilman said.

"One time, he met us at the airport and had to go back to a team meeting that night at the hotel where the team was staying. He invited us to go down there and wait in a suite the hotel made available to the team, then we'd go downstairs and have a nice dinner.

"We get to that hotel and I've never seen so many people who came up wanting his autograph, wanting to talk to him. It was just amazing to see. We could've eaten in the suite, but, no, he was willing to go right back into the public.

"Having been through this on other occasions, I said, 'Tom, are you sure you want to go?' He said, 'Oh yeah, it's no problem. It doesn't worry me.'

"My wife and I were with him so many times and saw how graciously he responded to requests for autographs or would acknowledge people who came up to us in restaurants, hotels or wherever we were. He was just delighted to do it and tried making them feel good. He wasn't gushing all over the place. He just recognized that was his responsibility because of his celebrity status."

Landry recognized his status, but he didn't relish it. He mostly preferred avoiding the spotlight.

A good example came in the hours after the January 1978 Super Bowl in which the Cowboys beat the Denver Broncos 27-10. Spilman and his two sons had watched the game from 50-yard-line seats, along with Ray Landry.

"I saw him right after the game and he said to come by the team hotel," Spilman said. "So my boys and I drove out there. He'd been there 45 minutes, and he'd already taken a nap.

"Tom, his dad, my boys and I visited for a while. He'd just won the dadgum Super Bowl, but he took the time to enjoy it with us! Then he said he'd like to stay and visit, but there was a team party and he had to go make an appearance."

As close as Spilman and Landry were, Tom never tried convincing his pal to follow the same religious path he'd chosen.

"Not once did he make any effort to admonish me in any way, shape or form," Spilman said. "Never did he say this is something I want to encourage you to do. I think that was typical of his relationships. He led by example.

"He witnessed in a different way. He didn't go out and read scripture to you or quote the Bible. He personified it by the way he lived, which a lot of us try to do, but don't have the same religious zeal, conviction and motivation he had."

Spilman became a lawyer and served four terms in the state legislature. Both worlds are filled with people who say one thing and do something else. Spilman, though, knew someone who was above that.

"Tom never wavered," Spilman said. "There was never any letdown where he just went along to get along. He believed what he believed.

"I guess that's why he was loved and admired by everybody at every stage of his life and always greatly respected."

Don Bentsen

Don Bentsen spent much of his teen years hanging out with pals Wade Spilman and Tom Landry. Sports were their main form of recreation. Troublemaking never was.

"We horsed around, had fun, but there were never any scrapes or problems," said Bentsen, the younger brother of former U.S. Senator Lloyd Bentsen. "I know it would be more interesting if we had, but I never saw Tom in any kind of out-of-line situations.

"It just didn't seem to occur to him to do those things. He just wouldn't think of doing anything that would embarrass his family. The thing that's really special is that he didn't plan it that way. It's just the way he was.

"He was a natural so far as being considerate, thoughtful, concerned about other people. Everything always looked like it was easy for him. He didn't need a lot of advice. He backed his own judgment and he had good judgment."

That good judgment extended onto the football field, where Landry displayed his trademark calmness, even in high school.

"I saw him play football and saw him play hard," said Bentsen, a high school teammate. "But I never ever saw him upset. I know other players got excited, upset, worked up to do well, but that was never Tom."

Bentsen was with Landry on the teams coached by Bob Martin. He, too, remembers the impact Martin had on his players.

"Everybody played their heart out for Bob," Bentsen said. "I think Tom had excellent training under Martin; we all did. I have a doctor friend who says, 'I'd have never made it without Bob Martin.'

"Martin taught fundamentals, and he worked the daylights out of you. He wanted his players in good condition because he didn't want them to get hurt. No one minded the hard work because he was a nice guy and the motives were right.

"He put himself pretty much on your level. He listened to everyone, but he knew more than anybody else did. He enjoyed the fellowship and liked to work to gain people's respect. He was honest, straight forward, no baloney. It all seems so simple when it's like that."

Bentsen remembers how Martin enjoyed challenging players to tackle him. He also remembers Martin donning gloves and boxing with any player willing to take him on.

"He could use you for a punching bag, but he didn't," said Bentsen, who, like Landry, later won an intramural boxing title at the University of Texas.

Bentsen and Spilman were roommates at the University of Texas and have remained close. Time and distance kept Bentsen and Landry apart after college, but they remained fond of each other.

One of Bentsen's favorite memories of Landry came just a few years ago, when Landry was in South Texas to speak at an FCA banquet.

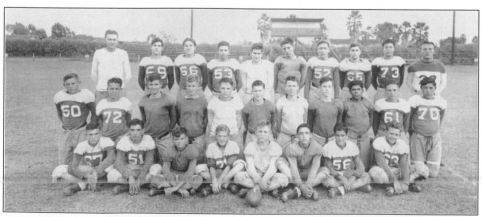

Landry's ninth grade team photo from 1938, the first under Coach Bob Martin. Landry is in a grey sweatshirt in the middle of the second row. Martin is on the far right end of the top row. Don Bentsen is on the far left end of the second row, and A.B. Ward is on the far right of the bottom row. (Photo courtesy of the Gen Long Collection)

"I took my grandson to this banquet and he brought a little friend with him," Bentsen said. "Before the banquet, I had a chance to say hello to Tom. As we started walking toward Tom, my grandson's friend was shy and dropped back. I turned to Tom and said hello and introduced my grandson. Tom said, 'Nathan, I'd like to meet your friend.' Of course, Nathan calls his friend over, and he got excited and ran over.

"It wasn't special for him to be considerate of someone. That's just the way he was. You just can't exaggerate what a great guy he was. There will never be enough people like him."

Marvel Deen (Dooley) Rhodes

Marvel Deen Rhodes remembers the one thing that would set off Tommy Landry.

"He loved his funny books and he didn't like to share," she said with a big laugh. "Oh, he really loved those funny books, Captain Marvel and all the ones that were popular in the late '30s and early '40s. He'd always say, 'What do you want to read my funny books for?'"

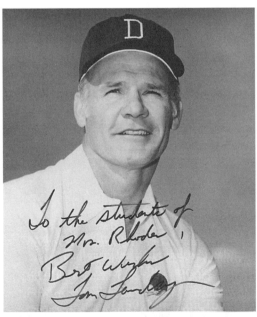

Childhood friend Rhodes used Landry's gift as a teaching tool for her third grade class. (Photo courtesy of Marvel Deen Rhodes)

The Dooley family and the Landrys lived around the corner from each other and were so close that people thought they were related. Ray and Ruth Landry were the best man and maid of honor in Marvel Deen's parents' wedding, and she later made them the godparents of her children.

"They were wonderful people," she said. "His mother and daddy had a lot of influence on him, his daddy especially. His mother was super at making chocolate pie. And Tommy loved that chocolate pie with big, thick meringue. His daddy was a good cook, too. He made all these big, thick biscuits and fried fish."

The kids spent most of their summers at Crystal Waters, a city-run watering hole. The Dooleys and the Landrys also took vacations together at the cottage they shared at Walker Lake.

"We all went out there even after Tom and Alicia were married; they'd bring their kids out there, too," Rhodes said. "We'd have picnics and fishing and swimming. It was fun. They were real happy days."

Tom, who was a year older than Marvel Deen, often played golf with her husband whenever the family visited Mission. She became a third-grade teacher, and she used her childhood friend to help discipline her students.

"We had a little game going," Rhodes said. "I had a playing field and made little Dallas Cowboys helmets for it. Each student had a helmet. When they got extra achievements, they went forward. If they misbehaved, they had to go back a yard. When they got too many backwards jobs, that's when I sent them to 'talk to the coach.' That meant they had to talk to a picture of Tommy that he had autographed. He wrote on it, 'To the students of Mrs. Rhodes, Best Wishes, Tom Landry.'

"Tom also sent me a lot of little things they had there at the Dallas Cowboys, like pencils and little emblems that I gave out to the children for achievement."

When Landry was inducted into the Hall of Fame, Rhodes sat in the front row with his family.

"It was the highlight of my life," she said. "I loved it. He just had a twinkle in his eye. During the ceremony, he looked down and saw me sitting there next to Lisa. I never will forget that."

A.B. Ward

A.B. Ward was the beneficiary of one of Tommy Landry's first football brainstorms.

Landry was the holder and Ward the kicker on the 1940 and '41 Mission teams. Tees weren't legal at that time, but Landry came up with another way to help improve Ward's accuracy.

"He kept a dime stuck in his belt loop," Ward said. "He would draw an X down on the ground with his finger, then put the dime down in the middle of the X. He could see the dime shine. And then he'd set the ball on there and I'd kick it. It wasn't illegal, because it wasn't a tee. It was just to mark the spot.

"That was just between him and me. We made a lot of scores that way."

Ward, however, missed a PAT early in the 1940 bi-district championship game. Mission ended up losing to Alice 7-6.

"After that, Don Albrecht stood up and said, 'Next season, we won't let anybody score on us!' Turned out he was right."

The only points the Eagles allowed in 1941 came in a 13-7 victory over Donna. That touchdown, though, came courtesy of the officials.

"They were on about the two- or three-yard line and we set them back and set them back," Ward said. "Then it was fourth down and they were on about the 14-yard line. They passed into the end zone and Tom went up and hit the ball with both hands and knocked it clear into the stands. After he had hit the ball, he knocked the receiver down, but that was perfectly legal as long as you hit the ball first.

"But the official called it pass interference, which was a 15-yard penalty. So he just walked across the goal line and held up his hands for a touchdown. They kicked the extra point and that was the only points scored against us. But they never should've been able to kick that."

Landry was innovative all the way back to his days as a holder for Ward. (Photo courtesy of A.B. Ward)

Landry never forgot that play. But what also probably stuck with him was the way Martin reacted—or, rather, didn't react.

"The only emotion he ever showed was that time," Ward said. "But he knew if we lost, he could protest the game."

Landry absorbed much of Martin's coaching style.

In addition to the stoic sideline demeanor, other Martin traits visible in Landry were emphasizing fitness for himself and his players, insisting that players be fundamentally sound, using lots of shifting on offense and a four-man line on defense, and treating the team like a family.

"He made Tom a lot of what he was," Ward said. "He taught him all about defense. For two years when we were in high school, Tom would take his study hall period and he and Coach Martin would study defensive theory."

One of Martin's pet phrases was "play your position," which meant he didn't want defenders roaming from their assigned area. That later became the staple of Landry's Flex defense.

On offense, Ward shared the backfield with Landry, but Landry was the signal-caller. Before every play, Landry would say, "Everybody block."

"That was Coach Martin's idea for him to do that. Coach Martin was very into repetition," Ward said. "He'd tell you, 'Get to where you can do this automatically.'"

Although Martin was stern, he also showed patience and a controlled temper.

"He never belittled you," Ward said. "He called everybody 'Honey.' He'd tell you what you did wrong, then show you how to do it right. The only thing would be if you said, 'I thought so and so.' He'd say, 'There you go thinking again.'"

After the 1940 season ended in disappointment, Martin united the team with the motto "Eleven brothers are hard to beat." He painted it on the back of baking flour posterboard and hung it above his desk. Soon after, he sent every player a Christmas card with the following inspirational poem entitled "You," which Ward still has in his scrapbook. It reads:

You are the fellow who has to decide,
Whether you'll do it or toss it aside;
You are the fellow who makes up your mind,
Whether you'll lead or linger behind;

Whether you'll strive for the goal that's afar,
Or just be content to stay where you are.
Take it or leave it! There's something to do!
Just think it over, (player's name)
It's all up to YOU!

Landry upheld the poem's message when he tried to continue playing despite having broken his jaw early in a game against Harlingen.

"He got kicked while he was on the ground," Ward said. "He still punted the ball right after his jaw was broken. He told the center, 'Be sure you put it right here in my hands, because I can't see real good.' And then he punts the ball about 50 yards in the air."

Ward and Landry also ran track together and played softball in junior high. Landry also was on the basketball team, which played in unusual conditions.

"We didn't have a gym, so we played outside," Ward said. "They cut holes in dishpans and used them as reflectors for the lights."

Landry and Ward first met in the early days of grade school. Although they were in different grades, the school was so small that they often shared the same classroom. The two also went to the same church.

Ward's family lived on a farm about a mile from downtown. They grew two crops of tomatoes each year, and when it was time for canning them, the Landrys were among the folks from Mission who sometimes came to help.

"People from the church would come out to our house and we would can 1,000 to 1,500 cans of tomatoes a day," Ward said. "Tom and I would stoke the fire and put the big pots on the stove. This was during the Depression, in '34 , '35, '36, '37."

In the summer of '44, Ward and Landry happened to be at home from the military at the same time. The pair decided to go visit Martin at his new school in Brownsville, where he eventually became such an institution that a high school was named for him.

"We didn't have a car available, so we hitchhiked," Ward said. "It wasn't anything. We just shot onto that highway that runs up and down the Valley and got rides in the back of pickup trucks and in the trunks of people's cars. We'd get out of a car and be out for just a couple of minutes because both of us were in uniform.

"We spent the day with Coach Martin, then hitchhiked back."

Ward followed Landry's career from afar. There were a couple reunions, but they often came during football season and Landry couldn't make it. Still, he let his old pals know he was thinking about them.

"He waved at us," Ward said. "As he was leaving the field for halftime, he waved at the crowd, but we really knew he was waving at us. Nobody watching the television but us knew what he was waving at."

Gen Long

Gen Long had a simple reason for commissioning a larger-than-life tribute to Mission's favorite son.

"It was just the right thing to do," said Long, a city council member and businesswoman.

"We had a blank wall that was 140 feet long and the wall was located on Tom Landry Blvd. My husband and I have traveled quite a bit and we were really impressed with the murals that we saw in Vancouver, Canada. So we decided we would like to have a mural of Tom Landry showing his early life in Mission and following through his life."

Gen and Bill Long began their project in 1993. They had only briefly met

Creating the Landry mural in Mission. (Photo courtesy of the Gen Long collection)

Landry, yet admired him from afar. They contacted him first to make sure he approved.

"He seemed very humbled, very honored that we wanted to do this," she said. "A close friendship grew as we worked together."

Artists were asked to submit proposals. The Longs narrowed it to two, then let Landry make the final decision.

He chose one by Manuel Hinojosa that was like a timeline of his life, beginning with a drawing of the family home and ending with his induction into the Hall of Fame. In between, there are images of Landry as a player at Mission High, the University of Texas and the New York Giants, as well as various scenes from his days with the Cowboys.

The mural, which took more than a year to paint, was unveiled in September 1995. Landry was on hand, as were several of his former players. They all left imprints of their hands and feet in the cement beneath the massive drawing.

The mural has been a popular attraction ever since. When Landry died, it also became a natural place for local residents to mourn.

"That evening, people were already gathering at the mural. They were leaving flowers and candles," Long said. "At one time, I counted 32 people at the mural or across the street looking at it.

"I think we probably had over 3,000 people over 10 days. I visited with quite a few of them who were from as far away as Europe, Canada, Mexico, New York . . . just all over."

The mural facing Tom Landry Blvd. is a pictoral history of the coach's life. **(Photo courtesy of the Gen Long collection)**

LIFE AS A LONGHORN

Tom Landry went to college in the fall of 1942 and lasted only one semester before serving his country in World War II. After returning in the spring of 1946, he had some very busy years.

Landry earned a degree in business and two letters in football. He was a member of the Delta Kappa Epsilon fraternity and a service group known as the Cowboys. He participated in many intramural sports, once winning the light heavyweight boxing title and excelling in swimming, wrestling and basketball.

But the most important thing that happened to him in Austin was meeting Alicia Wiggs.

A football teammate who also was a fraternity pledge brother arranged for the blind date between Landry with the pretty blonde freshman in October 1947. On January 28, 1949, the two were married in Houston.

Growing up in Mission, Landry hadn't thought much about picking a college until his senior year of high school.

A prominent businessman in Mission suggested the University of Texas. A former teammate of Landry's older brother Robert pushed Mississippi State. Landry visited Rice and also considered Southern Methodist.

Landry (No. 24) and Bobby Layne (No. 22) surrounded by the rest of the starters for the Longhorns as they prepared to face Alabama in the Sugar Bowl on January 1, 1948. (Photo courtesy of Denne H. Freeman)

He went to Texas partly because it was closest to Mission and partly because he had friends going there. His freshman year was devastated by Robert's death. Robert had enlisted in the war effort early that year and was ferrying planes to Europe in the Army Air Corps when his plane disappeared near Iceland.

Tom enlisted in the reserves in November 1942 and four months later was training to become a pilot, just like Robert had been. Landry would go on to fly more than 30 bomber missions in a B-17 and escape several brushes with death.

He returned to college as a 21-year-old sophomore. Injuries limited him that season, but he became a prominent player the following fall.

Landry began the 1947 season as the backup to star quarterback Bobby Layne, then became the starting fullback after injuring his throwing hand. He also started in the defensive backfield and was the punter.

The Longhorns' only loss was by one point to SMU. Texas was driving for the win when Landry slipped in a puddle before taking a handoff on a critical play late in the game. The Longhorns capped the season in the Sugar Bowl, trouncing Alabama 27-7.

In 1948, Landry was voted one of two team captains, but it ended up being a disappointing fall. Texas went 6-3-1, yet somehow earned an invitation to play in the Orange Bowl.

In his collegiate finale, Landry had his best game, rushing 17 times for 117 yards as Texas silenced its critics by upsetting No. 8 Georgia 41-28 on January 1, 1949.

Landry wanted to be a quarterback at Texas, but settled for fullback. (Photo courtesy of the Dallas Cowboys)

Landry's affiliation with the school continued through the years.

In 1971, Landry and Dick Harris, his co-captain on the 1948 squad, were inducted into the Longhorn Hall of Honor together. Coincidentally, Texas' quarterback that season, Eddie Phillips, later became Landry's son-in-law, marrying Tom's oldest daughter Kitty. In 1973, Landry earned the Ex-Students' Association's Distinguished Alumnus Award.

Landry maintained a home in Austin and remained friends with several of his former teammates and other college pals. He rooted for his alma mater from afar, even when one of his former Cowboys assistants, John Mackovic, became the Longhorns' coach.

Lew Holder

Lew Holder was behind the nicest thing anyone ever did for Tom Landry. He's the one who arranged for the blind date between Tom and a freshman named Alicia Wiggs.

Holder's girlfriend at the time, Gloria Neuhaus, lived at Wooten Hall and was friends with Alicia. Lew knew her, too, and figured she'd get along great with his teammate.

"I told Gloria I wanted to get Tom a date with Alicia, so she got them a blind date," Holder said. "We all went out together to Hamilton Pool and had a little picnic. After that, I don't think either one of them ever went out with anyone else."

Holder had the honor of being Tom's best man when he married Alicia in January 1949.

Holder and Landry met their first semester in college, then both left for the military. They returned the same time and together were pledges in the Delta Kappa Epsilon fraternity, known as the "Dekes."

During the war, Holder was a fighter pilot instructor in Phoenix, Arizona. He sent home his paychecks, and by the time he got back he had a nice stash waiting.

"The first thing I did was get me a new Lincoln," he said. "Living at Hill Hall, the athletes' dorm, people thought they were paying me to play."

Holder became such good friends with Landry that he gave Tom a set of keys to the car, which made it easier for he and Alicia to go out on dates.

But because Holder's car was so recognizable, people often thought they were seeing Holder taking out Alicia. Sometimes the mistake was made the other way, where folks thought Landry was with Gloria.

"Alicia was blonde and Gloria was a brunette, so people could tell them apart. But I guess Tom and I looked enough alike that people were always teasing us that they saw one of us with the other's girlfriend," Holder said.

Holder and Landry remained good friends through the years. Landry occasionally would fly to Horseshoe Bay, a resort community outside Austin where Holder lived, and they'd take in a round of golf.

"He would come over here and get his plane worked on," Holder said. "He had this mechanic he liked at our airport, so he'd bring it in about every year and we were able to keep in touch."

George McCall

George McCall spent the spring of 1947 catching passes from two future members of the Pro Football Hall of Fame: Bobby Layne and Tom Landry.

Layne was the incumbent starter, while Landry was trying to win the job after returning from World War II. McCall also was just back from the war and trying to win a job as an end.

"Tommy could really hold his place real well competing with Bobby," McCall said. "But then he hurt his thumb and couldn't grip the football real well. So he concentrated on playing fullback and halfback. Of course, Tommy was real good at just about everything they wanted him to do in football—quarterback, kicker, defensive back."

The relationship between McCall and Landry went far beyond football. Along with Lew Holder and Bobby Koy Lee, the foursome hung out together and all dated girls who were friends.

Landry enjoyed playing golf with his pals George McCall (second from left) and Spilman (second from right). (Photo courtesy of Wade Spilman)

As close as the group was, McCall had no idea about Landry's war heroics.

"He never talked about it," McCall said. "He wasn't boisterous whatsoever about anything. He was a very solid person. You just couldn't find a more trustworthy person than Tom Landry. And he was such a nice person.

That's why he got elected captain of the '48 team."

McCall was invited to Landry's wedding, but couldn't get off work. He occasionally visited the couple when they were living in Houston, then followed his friend from afar when Landry played and coached in New York, then Dallas.

Landry later bought a second home in the Austin area, and the two renewed their friendship.

"We picked up right where we left off," McCall said.

Dick Harris

When Tom Landry returned from war and rejoined the Texas Longhorns, many of his teammates were fellow veterans.

But some, like Dick Harris, were straight out of high school.

"I was 18 or 19 and he was in his 20s," Harris said. "He was like a babysitter for some of us."

Landry was an older, wiser person who always tried keeping the youngsters out of trouble. Yet, he did it in a way that commanded their attention and respect.

"If Tommy told you to do something, you did it," Harris said. "If you were doing something he told you not to do, you didn't do it again. He was that kind of a person.

"Discipline is something that some people can give and some can't. He certainly could. He had the vocabulary to tell people exactly what he wanted or didn't want and they listened. He didn't do it because he could, he did it because it had to be done."

Harris said Landry was such a strong leader that no one ever questioned his motives or his tactics.

"He was pretty tough and could hold his own at whatever he wanted to do," said Harris, who played offensive tackle and linebacker. "No one ever tried him on for size with a fist or a hard word, at least, not that I ever saw."

In 1948, Harris and Landry were the team captains. They became close enough friends that each was in the other's wedding.

Until Landry was married, he lived in the athletic dormitory. Harris recalled that the coaches basically left Landry in charge of the place.

"They looked to Tommy for guidance when somebody was raising hell or fighting or drinking," Harris said. "He was just that kind of person. I respected him for it tremendously."

Rooster Andrews

As manager of the Texas Longhorns, Rooster Andrews' main responsibility often was taking care of his best friend, quarterback Bobby Layne.

Layne was a carousing quarterback whose off-field exploits became as legendary as his on-field success—and he made All-America in football and baseball. Most stories involve late-night drinking followed by heroics in a game the next day.

Layne's lifestyle was the exact opposite of Landry's, which could've been a problem when Landry was Layne's backup. But Landry never made an issue of it.

"I don't think Tom objected so much as he didn't want to do it himself," said Andrews, who in addition to his manager duties also occasionally kicked extra points. "Bobby would be drunk and Tom would just go on. He was never critical. The worst he'd say was, 'Gosh, I wish he hadn't done that.'

"I think Bobby was real fortunate that his coaches accepted him for what he was and what he was going to do. They realized he had more strong points than weak ones, so they let him go."

Andrews recalls being with Landry at a Doak Walker Award ceremony soon after Layne died.

"And Tom took the ball in the discussion about Bobby," Andrews said. "Tom Landry just knew how to see the good in everyone he met."

Andrews was a sophomore and Landry a freshman when they lived next door to each other at Hill Hall, then UT's athletic dormitory. Landry made a lasting first impression.

"You knew from the firm way he shook your hand and looked you in the eye that he had to be a great guy," Andrews said. "And I honestly believe that the day Tom Landry passed away, he was the same quiet gentleman and good guy he was when he came in here as a freshman in 1942."

Andrews has remained in Austin and owns four sporting goods

Landry and Rooster Andrews shared happy memories as well as sad ones. (Photo courtesy of Rooster Andrews)

stores that bear his name. His second-story office overlooking his main location is a shrine to the stars he's befriended through the years. There are so many autographed pictures, plaques and other mementos that wallpaper isn't needed. An autographed picture from Landry hangs in a location above Andrews' desk, directly over his head as he faces visitors. Landry's photo is located above a drawing of Layne and beneath a picture of former Texas coach Darrell Royal.

Andrews and Landry saw each other several times a year, mainly at banquets such as the Doak Walker Award. One of their most memorable conversations came at one such get-together following the death of Landry's daughter.

"He knew I had a daughter die too," said Andrews, who lost 28-year-old Susan following a long battle with anorexia a few years before Tom's daughter Lisa passed away. "He said, 'It's tough. It's the toughest thing I've ever faced.'

"I saw a side of him I hadn't ever seen—but I knew it was there."

SERVING HIS COUNTRY

Tom Landry's final high school football game was played six days after Pearl Harbor was bombed. Two years and two months later, Landry was in Wichita Falls, Texas, going through basic training at Shepherd's Field.

After earning his wings and getting other training in the United States, it was time to cross the Atlantic. Landry spent his 20th birthday as a member of the 493rd bomb group, the 93rd bomb wing of the 8th Air Force, based near Ipswich, England.

Landry sat behind the controls of a B-17 bomber, a plane so big and strong that it was known as the "Flying Fortress." He flew in 30 missions. In addition to avoiding enemy fire, he survived a crash landing and a near-ejection that was avoided when Landry revived a jammed instrument at the last second.

Lieutenant Landry returned home late in 1945.

Fifty years later, Landry again faced a dire moment in the air, this time while he was controlling his own single-engine Cessna.

As he often did, Landry was flying wife Alicia and granddaughter Christina between Dallas and Austin. Except this time, the engine went out. With no airport in sight, Landry smoothly landed the plane in the football field at Ennis High School.

While that was Landry's most frightening post-war experience on a plane, he did have another stomach-churning ride—this one courtesy of the Blue Angels, the Navy's precision flight squad.

After holding on through some loops and rolls, Landry ran the controls for a bit. It reminded him of the power of the Flying Fortress, but with much smoother controls. The power, by the way, ended up being a bit intense—Landry blacked out for a short stint.

Mark Oristano

Tom Landry downplayed his World War II experiences.

It just wasn't Tom's style to play the war hero. He figured risking his life while flying bombers over Germany and Czechoslovakia was his duty.

Landry wasn't completely private, though. He often used certain tales in public speeches.

In 1981, Mark Oristano coaxed Landry into discussing his dangerous wartime missions during a weekend radio show on the Texas State Network.

"I called up and Tom said, 'OK,'" Oristano said. "I was kind of surprised and excited he consented to do the show."

What followed was a 90-minute interview about days as a pilot of the B-17 bomber.

"It was fascinating stuff about six-hour flights to the target, 30-second bombing runs and six-hour flights back to home base outside of London," Oristano recalled. "Tom was a co-pilot, but sometimes a higher-ranking officer would step in if the plane was leading a large flight.

"Several times, Tom would have to sit in the turret gun bubble, where he had a bird's-eye view of the flak flying past. Tom said it was a 12-hour flight where you were freezing to death in the high altitudes and scared to death."

Landry told about the day the fuel ran out and the plane had to belly land in France.

"Tom said the plane had both wings sheared off by trees," Oristano said. "He said one tree ended up a foot in front of his face. Everyone walked away. There were no fires or explosions because there was no gas. Nobody got hurt.

"I knew then why third-and-long didn't scare him."

Oristano remembers Landry telling him that takeoffs and landings were the most dangerous parts of a mission.

"On takeoffs, if they were the lead plane, they had to keep circling until all 300 to 500 planes got off the ground. Occasionally, they would have collisions," he said.

Landry said just coming home was a dice roll, too.

"You can imagine 2,000 airplanes all coming back to England, which is socked in with fog, and they're all trying to find their airfields. That was about as scared as you can be, I think, coming back and trying to find your own field," Oristano said.

Landry told Oristano the anti-aircraft fire was fierce.

"Flak would bounce your airplane around," Landry said. "It was much worse than air turbulence. You could see it, those puffy black clouds. You knew for sure they were shooting at you. The flak was the main threat to our safety because the Luftwaffe had been pretty much neutralized, although, on occasion, a fighter plane would make an appearance.

"The first mission we went on was into the Mersburg oil fields outside Berlin. I never saw anything like that. It was like flying inside a thunder-cloud, only it was flak. We got out of there as quickly as we could."

Landry knew he was lucky to survive 30 missions.

"Your odds of making all your missions was 5-to-1," Landry told Oristano.

Oristano said Landry's bomber group was called on to help during the Battle of the Bulge, but was grounded 20 straight days because of snow and fog.

"They kept scrubbing missions because we couldn't see our hands in front of our face," Landry remembered.

They would warm up their planes and sit in them until they got the stand

HOW

"My Military Training Enabled Me To Do My Duty Because The Lives Of My Crew And The Destiny Of My Country Depended On It."
-Tom Landry

Landry's military career prepared him for the rest of his life. (Photo courtesy of Lew Holder)

down. Finally, they got to bomb the Germans to help General George S. Patton beat back Adolf Hitler's final surprise attack of the war.

Oristano recalled that Landry told him that the ruggedness of the B-17 helped pull the fliers through.

"It was a great airplane," Landry said. "You could get a couple of engines shot out and still get home on just two engines. It really was a 'Flying Fortress.'"

Landry told Oristano that he would have returned if needed.

"I could see myself doing it all again if our country was threatened the way it was at that time," he said. "Goodness gracious, everybody just went to war. Whether you came back or not was not the important thing."

Oristano said he thought back to the interview after Landry died.

"Tom was a great football coach," Oristano said. "But he was a great man long before he coached the Cowboys."

Chapter Ten

"WINNING SOULS FOR CHRIST"

Tom Landry didn't miss football one bit after he left the Dallas Cowboys. He found something better to do.

"I have a new passion and that is winning souls for Christ," he told Howard Hendricks, the Cowboys' chaplain during most of the Landry era and a leader of the Dallas Theological Seminary.

Spending Sundays at church was part of Landry's life from his earliest days. His family attended the First United Methodist Church in Mission, Texas, and his father Ray was the superintendent of the church's Sunday school.

Yet it wasn't until early 1959 that Tom Landry truly found God.

Landry was an assistant coach with the New York Giants, but he spent his off-seasons in Dallas. One day, a friend named Frank Phillips invited him to a Wednesday morning men's prayer breakfast that he regularly attended.

Landry was hooked after his first visit. He suddenly realized that a relationship with Jesus Christ was missing in his life. He then became enthralled by the Bible and made his faith the most important thing in his life.

Landry spent the rest of his years spreading the word in a way that typified his class, dignity and grace. He never pushed his beliefs on others, instead choosing to tout the importance of God in his life and hope others made the same choice.

Landry became highly involved in the FCA and the Billy Graham Evangelistic Association, using those organizations as platforms to spread his message.

He lent his immeasurable influence and counsel to many other faith-based groups, including the Highland Park United Methodist Church, where he'd been a member since 1956, and the Dallas Theological Society.

The majority of Landry's efforts were for the FCA. Outside the group's founders, he's considered the most influential person in the organization's history and the person most responsible for its phenomenal growth.

Landry's drawing power, captivating personal testimony and behind-the-scenes work also added another dimension to Graham's already popular crusades. His specialty was going into cities days before the event to help build momentum.

Tom Landry changed the way football is played through his many innovations. Through his dedication to his faith, he changed many more lives.

Billy Graham

For many years, Tom Landry and Billy Graham consistently ranked among the most respected men in America. If they had a vote, each would've listed the other.

Landry respected Graham so much that he kept a picture of the evangelist on his office wall. Graham respected Landry so much that he had the coach speak at 54 crusades.

Landry spoke at 54 of Billy Graham's crusades, including the 1971 event at Texas Stadium, where this photo was taken. (Photo courtesy of the Billy Graham Evangelistic Assocation)

It should be no surprise that the two became friends. They have a lot in common.

Both grew up in small towns during the Depression, then became leaders in their field by their early 30s. Although they were famous worldwide, they remained humble. Each dramatically impacted those they came into contact with, yet also touched the lives of many more they never met.

Landry first became involved with Graham's crusades in San Antonio in 1966. His last appearance was 1999 in Indianapolis. In between, he became a key figure as both a speaker and coordinator. Landry's biggest responsibility was overseeing the Greater Billy Graham

Southwest Crusade at Texas Stadium, which ran for 10 days in September 1971.

The night Landry died, Graham released the following statement:

"The death of Tom Landry has come as a shock to me and to Christians everywhere.

"Tom was one of the greatest Christian gentlemen I ever knew.

"He was associated with me in many of my crusades and often went weeks ahead of us to address the leaders in each city and urged them to put their trust in God and support our ministry when we arrived.

"His wife Alicia is the granddaughter of one of the greatest evangelists in American history, Dr. R.A. Torrey, and she helped inspire Tom toward Christian service.

"He will probably go down in sports history as one of the greatest football coaches we have ever had.

"I join with thousands of others not only in mourning his passing, but in the joy and anticipation of seeing him again in heaven."

John Corts

The last conversation between Billy Graham and Tom Landry was rather dramatic.

"They talked not long before Tom's death," said John Corts, president and chief operating officer of the Billy Graham Evangelistic Association. "Billy told me they had a wonderful talk. He told me that he said to Tom, 'I'll see you in heaven.' They smiled about that."

Corts had the privilege of being part of several conversations between Graham and Landry. A memorable one came following the death of Landry's daughter Lisa.

"They were talking about many of the difficulties she went through," Corts said. "Billy was so compassionately interested and Tom sounded as though he was looking for someone he could pour it out to.

"It was almost like a pastor-parishioner type conversation, but there wasn't anything official about it. It was just like a group of friends."

Corts joked that "Billy doesn't understand football as well as Tom understood the scriptures." But, he added, they shared many positive qualities.

"One of the nice things about Billy Graham is that he's what you think he is, there aren't any surprises," Corts said. "I found that to be true of Tom Landry. It's obvious why they got along so well."

Graham's crusades became national sensations in 1949. Adding Landry to the roster two decades later was still a nice boost because he consistently drew crowds of 10,000 to pre-crusade rallies.

"There was an enormous amount of respect for Mr. Landry through-out the Dallas region, and we found it translated throughout the nation," Corts said. "I think it was more than just what he had to say; it was the consistency of character he demonstrated across the book. Even that quiet demeanor on the sideline that everybody remembers—the guy with the hat who sort of bites his lip when everything goes wrong—it was consistent.

"Even though he was quiet, he was a very persuasive guy. People would go away saying, 'You know, Tom Landry's right. I need to be involved here. I need to put some legs to my prayers and be involved with my commitment.' He had enormous influence, far more than he realized."

Landry was especially effective with his target audience: men.

"Men seem to have a lot more difficulty articulating things of the Christian faith, particularly men who aren't real deep in their faith. So to hear Tom Landry stand up and talk about his faith in God was a big experience for them," Corts said. "They might have been drawn to hear him speak by the football, but they went away impressed by his sincerity."

Corts met Tom Landry at the '71 event at Texas Stadium. Landry was the chairman and Corts was the association's local representative.

Planning for the event overlapped with football season, but Landry handled both duties deftly. The crusade was a smashing success and the Cowboys—who moved into Texas Stadium a month after the crusade—won their first Super Bowl that season.

"He was very sincere and very, very committed to being a chairman," Corts said. "He was excellent at it—one of the best we ever had."

Landry often held crusade planning meetings at team headquarters because he didn't have time to get away. Usually, he invited Corts and others to join him for lunch.

The group had their heads bowed in prayer before one meal when a player interrupted and asked Landry a question.

"Tom looked up from a bowed head and said, 'Shut up, we're praying.' That big ol' football player stood there and kind of folded his hands and bowed his head. He waited for the prayer to be over and said, 'I'm sorry Coach.' He was just like a whipped puppy.

"That was early on in my experience with Tom, and it made me say to myself, 'Wow, these guys really know where he stands.'"

Landry's popularity within the community also came in handy.

"We look to a chairman to make key appointments, and Tom had a marvelous network of people," Corts said. "He was very astute in understanding whether someone's commitment to a project was real or not. He had a great way of sorting that out. He'd get someone committed to a task, then call me and say, 'I've got them signed up. Now you tell them what to do.'"

It wasn't always that easy. Here's what Corts went through in trying to work with an oil executive.

"Who are you?" the man's secretary said.

"I'm John Corts with the Billy Graham Evangelistic Association," he said.

"I don't know how to spell your name."

"C-o-r-t-s."

She put him on hold.

"I have a list of people that I can put through, and I can't put you through because you're not on the list," she said.

"Ma'am, how do I get on the list?" he said.

After putting him on hold several more times, the secretary became exasperated.

"Sir, I don't know how to help you. I really don't think I can," she said.

Corts, who was equally exasperated, said: "I was just trying to talk to the man because Tom Landry had asked me to call him and tell him about the crusade."

"Who?" she said.

"Tom Landry."

Corts picks up the story from there.

"The next thing I heard was this happy voice saying, 'Boy, John, it's good of you to call. Tom told me you'd be calling. It's wonderful to hear from you.' All I had to do was say the magic of Tom Landry's name."

Corts once told that story at an FCA dinner that Landry attended.

"Tom sat there and laughed and said, 'Oh, no, it's not really like that,'" Corts said. "That was part of the genius of the man."

Corts and Landry saw each other often at crusades around the country. Whenever they gave speeches together, they always told people, "We both have an Alicia in our home who means a lot to us," referring to Corts' daughter and Landry's wife.

Although Landry was a speaker in high demand, he remained most faithful to Graham's crusades and the FCA. Whether it was intentional or not, it made his message even stronger.

"He had a focus about life. He knew what he wanted and went after it. He was a goal-oriented guy, for sure," Corts said. "He assured us time and again, 'I'm very committed. Anytime you guys need me, I want to give that high priority any time I can.'"

"The last time I saw him, he said: 'The Billy Graham Evangelistic Association has given me a marvelous platform that I have been delighted to use.' And I said, 'If that's the case, then we rejoice because you've been a wonderful influence for us, as well.'"

Charlie Riggs

Tom Landry was in charge of the first event at Texas Stadium, but it wasn't a Dallas Cowboys game. It was a Billy Graham crusade.

And if it wasn't for Landry, the crusade might have had to find a different home.

Here's the explanation from longtime crusade director Charlie Riggs:

"The stadium was about two-thirds finished when the plumbers union went on strike. Before they would settle it, they needed a lot of agreements," Riggs said. "Tom asked the union to meet with the Billy Graham team members, some committee members and the board.

"He got the union to come around, but they said we could only use so many toilets, so many faucets, etc. So the agreement was made and we moved in there."

Riggs was at 53 of the 54 crusades Landry was involved in, missing only the final one. Riggs remembers there were often interesting circumstances behind getting Landry to the events.

Such as the time they met in Graham's hometown of Asheville, North Carolina.

"We went to the airport to pick him up Friday afternoon and Tom got off the plane and could barely talk—but he came anyway. We took him to a hospital, got him on a respirator and put him to bed at eight o'clock. The next morning, he got up before the crowd and said (in a raspy voice) 'I don't know how long my voice will last,' but little by little it came back."

And then there was the time they met in Spokane, Washington.

"We went to meet his plane and he wasn't on it! Around 10 o'clock, we found him in his hotel room. We said, 'Tom, what happened?' He said, 'It was raining cats and dogs in Dallas. When my plane got out on the runway, we were No. 21 in line to takeoff. So I said to the captain, I can't wait. I've got to get to Spokane.' So that guy pulled his plane out of line, contacted another plane that was ready to go and put Tom on that plane going nonstop to Seattle."

Riggs always enjoyed hearing Landry give speeches.

"He had an amazing knowledge of the scriptures. He'd quote one after another," Riggs said. "He also was a very humorous man. He'd have those guys laughing one minute, then he'd get real serious and say, 'The apostle Paul said . . .' He quoted the apostle Paul a great deal. Paul was a great leader."

Riggs met many great people in his years with the Graham association, yet he puts Landry way up on his list.

"He had a tremendous walk with God," Riggs said. "I never met anyone with more integrity than Tom."

Bill Krisher

Whenever the FCA needed Tom Landry, he always came through.

Landry was actively involved in the organization on a local, state, regional and national level. He traveled the country spreading the group's message, helped put together major events and was instrumental in expanding the FCA to middle-school campuses and the inner-city and in getting females involved.

Landry helped start the Dallas chapter and made it the strongest in the country. He jump-started chapters from Fargo, North Dakota, to the state of Illinois, and many points in between. He was chairman of the national board from 1974-76 and was a lifetime national trustee.

While former baseball executive Branch Rickey was involved in launching the FCA in 1954, Landry's involvement turned it into the powerhouse it is today: teaching a commitment to Christ and spiritual growth to more than 300,000 students on the campuses of nearly one-fourth of all schools in the country.

"Coach Landry more or less carried on Branch Rickey's dream and desire to see athletics used as a platform to witness a person's faith," said Bill Krisher, director of the FCA's Western region, who worked closely with Landry for four decades, including starting the Dallas chapter together. "Coach realized that he could use the Fellowship of Christian Athletes as his pulpit to express his faith before a lot of young people."

Krisher said Landry was attracted by the FCA's purpose: "Present to athletes and coaches, and all whom they influence, the challenge and adventure of receiving Jesus Christ as Savior and Lord, serving Him in their relationships and in the fellowship of the church."

Landry made the FCA a major part of his life after speaking at a National Camp in Estes Park, Colorado, in 1962. As he stood before more than 1,000 youngsters, Landry recognized the impact he could have on future generations by simply telling them about his own experiences and values.

Krisher came to the FCA with a football background. He'd been a two-time All-American at Oklahoma, played for the Pittsburgh Steelers in 1958 and '59, then spent two years with the Dallas Texans. While in Dallas, Krisher often attended the same Wednesday morning prayer breakfast that had spurred Landry's dedication to Christ in 1959.

Krisher gave up football and joined the national FCA office in Kansas City, Missouri, in 1963. He moved back to Dallas and became director of the Southwest region in 1968.

Krisher and Landry made a great tandem from the start.

In 1969, they organized the "Weekend of Champions," which drew 365,000 people over three days. It included 70 schools and 105 churches and helped lead to the creation of a Dallas chapter in 1972.

For many years, the leaders of the Dallas group met in Landry's office at Cowboys headquarters at 7 a.m. on the first Friday of every month.

"Tom really brought a beacon to Dallas and the Southwest about what the FCA was all about," Krisher said. "His effort was remarkable. He was always willing to make a priority of doing whatever we needed him to do, whether it was to get on the phone and call people or go visit with people.

"If there's anything I can give Coach Landry total credit for, it was focusing on the junior high program and getting it started nationally. He believed in working with kids while they're young and getting them involved. That's really where his heart was."

Krisher said it was easy to see what made Landry so dynamic.

"His reputation as a Christian probably was greater than his reputation as a coach, although his reputation as a coach carried a lot of weight," he said. "I think his consistent walk with the Lord and his consistent talk to the Lord are what drew people to him more than anything else.

"His sincerity and humility were so outstanding. What you saw was what you got."

Krisher said Landry felt he gained from being able to help others.

"In the early years, we'd be flying somewhere and I'd say, 'Coach, why are we on this airplane? Where are we going? Why aren't we home with our families?' And he'd say, 'Bill, I guess the Lord just wants us to be where we're going.'"

Dal Shealy

Tom Landry's impact on the FCA is immeasurable. However, there is one eye-popping figure that helps put it into perspective: $108 million.

That's how much the FCA raised from the mid-1970s through 1999 strictly from a fund-raising effort known as "Tom Landry Associates."

"That's a miracle in itself," said FCA president Dal Shealy, who has been with the corporate office since 1988 and knew Landry through coaching since the '70s. "The Lord really used him and put him in that special spot to make the FCA grow."

To be a Tom Landry Associate, someone must give the FCA at least $10,000 in one year. Anyone giving $100,000 over the course of the years becomes a Lifetime Landry.

The program began when Ron Morris, then the director of development, was looking for a way to boost donations. The top honor was $1,000 and that just wasn't enough.

"Ron had this vision that if we were going to keep growing, we needed some bigger dollars. He came up with the idea of having the Tom Landry Associates and approached Coach Landry about it," Shealy said. "He said,

'Coach, what we'd like to do is start a major-donor level of giving and call it the Tom Landry Associates.' Coach, being kind of modest, said, 'Shoot, nobody is going to give money to the FCA under my name. Suppose I mess up somehow.'

"Ron said, 'Coach, you're kind of Mr. FCA and you have the marquee name.' Tom was still kind of reluctant. He said, 'Nobody is going to write out a check just to be a Tom Landry Associate.'

"Then Ron reaches into his pocket, pulls out a check and shows him one for $10,000 made out to Tom Landry FCA Associate. Then he pulled out about four or five more. And Tom said, 'Well, if they're already doing it, I can't very well say no.'"

Every year, the Tom Landry Associates gather for a special weekend in their honor. Because the event is usually in the fall, it was difficult for Landry to be there when he was coaching.

But he always was.

Sometimes the gatherings were planned in Dallas for a weekend the team had off. Many times, they took it on the road with the Cowboys, gathering in places like Denver, Washington and Chicago.

Landry tirelessly traveled the country for the FCA, spreading the organization's message and planting seeds for further growth. Although fundraising was always part of the agenda, he was focused on something more important than the bottom line.

"He'd tell a couple jokes, tell about the Cowboys, but then he'd get into the Fellowship of Christian Athletes and his personal testimony and he'd offer his plan of salvation," Shealy said. "He always closed his talks with a prayer and he'd encourage people to make a dedication, to get with our staff to follow through with the FCA or to get plugged in with a church.

"When we'd get ready to leave, he wouldn't ask how much money did he raise. He'd say, 'Let me know how many people made a faith commitment.' Because he really wanted to know that, through sharing his faith, people were coming to the Lord. That's what kind of special man he was."

The FCA could use Landry's magnetism to help fund its latest major project: The Tom Landry Worship Center, part of a proposed $8.3 million expansion of the organization's headquarters in Kansas City, Missouri.

The idea came up in a board meeting a week after Landry died.

"It was a very emotional meeting," Shealy said. "We spent a lot of time talking about Coach Landry."

They also talked about doing something special to honor his memory. At first, there was talk of sprucing up the chapel and naming it after Landry. The more they talked, the more ideas they had. That was when they decided that considering all he'd done for the FCA, they might as well go all out.

"It will include a prayer garden, a foyer where we'll have memorabilia and a chapel," Shealy said. "Outside, next to the prayer garden, there will be a reflecting pool and fountain."

The center, which will hopefully open in fall 2001, will be near the front of headquarters. At the entrance will be the bust of Landry created for the Excellence of Character award the Dallas FCA chapter started in 1999.

"We in the FCA miss him greatly, not because he was a great teammate but because of his friendship," Shealy said. "It was really, really kind of surprising how my spirit was reacting. I told Alicia I have the same kind of emptiness as when my mom and dad went to be with the Lord."

"But even though he's gone, the impact he had and the model he set will live on through the FCA."

Dan Goddard

It's no coincidence that the strongest FCA chapter in the country is in Dallas, the city where Tom Landry lived.

Landry was the chairman of the Dallas chapter's board of directors from its inception until his death. Through his leadership, the FCA has a presence in nearly 400 schools in the Dallas area, a penetration level of nearly 80 percent, triple the national average. The FCA's first junior high chapter started in the area as did the first girls chapter.

Landry helped get the first full-time staffer hired in 1968 by asking 15 businessmen to invest $1,000 in the organization. There are now 14 full-time staffers and an annual budget of more than $1 million; both figures are the most of any FCA local chapter.

The chapter's biggest fund-raiser every year is a golf tournament that began in 1978 as the Dallas FCA Open and three years later was renamed the Tom Landry FCA Open.

The first one raised less than $10,000. The first one with Landry's name brought in about $50,000. The 2000 event raised in excess of $640,000.

In 1999, the Dallas chapter began the "Tom Landry Excellence of Character Award."

"It's a national award to honor someone who has shown the same types of qualities and character that Coach Landry showed throughout his life," said Dan Goddard, the FCA's area director for Greater Dallas and northeast Texas, who was involved in creating the award when he was president of the Dallas chapter.

The first recipient was Jim Myers, Landry's longtime colleague with the Cowboys, who has long been the backbone of the Landry Open. The 2000 honoree is another person near and dear to Landry's heart: Billy Graham.

The award winner receives a bust of Landry that the coach helped design. The sculpture is made out of bronze and has a rugged finish. The coach is wearing a hat, of course, and has little expression on his face. He's wearing a tie to look professional and an overcoat to signify he's not a fair-weather person. A copy of the bust resides proudly at the Landry household.

Unfortunately, Landry wasn't able to make it to the first presentation in November 1999, which was billed as "A Golden Evening with Tom & Alicia." Part of the celebration was for his 75th birthday, which came two months before, and the couple's 50th wedding anniversary, which had been in January.

The 2000 golf tournament was held April 17, exactly two months after Landry was remembered at two memorial services.

Landry's absence loomed large. It especially hit home to longtime tournament participants who missed taking their annual picture with Landry on a picturesque hill between two holes.

"He would stand out there all day long, from early morning to late afternoon," Goddard said. "Roger Staubach talked at our banquet about how it took awhile to go up that hill. He had to gather himself. That happened to a lot of people. It was the realization that coach was no longer here."

Goddard came to the chapter office after working in the school system in nearby Plano, which is widely known for its powerful football program under Coach John Clark. Clark also started the FCA's involvement at the school.

"When he signed up, he figured they'd send him brochures and other things to get started," Goddard said. "About two weeks later, a man named Tiny Goss called him and said he'd like to come out and bring a speaker. Coach Clark was really surprised that they'd come all the way out and help like that, so he got all the kids together. To more than his surprise, the speaker was Coach Landry."

Goddard learned through the years not to be surprised by such gestures. Landry always made the FCA a priority and was a true gentleman wherever he went.

"There was always something about him," Goddard said. "Just his very presence in entering a room changed the atmosphere in the room. I think it was that great excellence-of-character quality he had, and people recognized it."

The first Tom Landry FCA Open after his death raised more than $640,000. (Photo courtesy of the Fellowship of Christian Athletes)

John Erickson

John Erickson thought the FCA's search committee wanted to talk to him about a candidate he'd recommended to run the organization.

Actually, the group headed by Tom Landry wanted Erickson to have the job.

"I remember asking him what kind of person they wanted," said Erickson, who at the time was general manager of the NBA's Milwaukee Bucks. "Tom said, 'We're looking for a head coach and you know what that means.' He looked at me across the table with those steely eyes and I knew right away what he was talking about."

Erickson became president in 1972 and remained in charge until 1988. He worked closely with Landry the entire time, especially early in his tenure when Landry was chairman of the national board of trustees.

One of his favorite stories shows Landry's impact on the organization as well as his sense of humor.

"There was a man in Fargo, North Dakota, who said if we could have Tom Landry come speak, he'd give me $50,000 to support the funding of a staff person in the state," Erickson said. "Well, Tom didn't know about that part of the arrangement, but he did know that he had to speak.

"We landed in Fargo around noon. They let all the kids out of school so they could hear Tom, so there was a real big crowd. When he finished speaking, I saw the man who had called me come forward and he handed me an envelope. Inside was a check for $50,000 made out to the Fellowship of Christian Athletes.

"I handed it to Tom and said it was from Mr. So-and-so for your coming here today. And Tom looked at me and said, 'Wow! I must be getting to be a pretty good speaker.'"

Landry never lost that touch.

In the late 1990s, Landry visited Erickson's hometown, Rockford, Illinois, and helped do what the former FCA president couldn't do: spur the start of a regional office.

"I was born and raised in Rockford and was known well. I'd speak there when I was FCA president, but we could never get a staff person there," said Erickson, who joined the organization in 1959. "Tom went in and that was really it. His presence brought them from out of the woodpile."

Landry was a major drawing card, even when paired with other celebrities.

"I think of all the coaches who've been in the movement—and we've had Alonzo Stagg, John Wooden, Tom Osborne, Bobby Bowden, George Halas and so many others—Tom was the key coach," Erickson said. "Many coaches have done many things, but Tom attracted and influenced so many people."

Erickson said the time that Landry reserved for the FCA was unbelievable considering the demands on him.

"Some coaches would make an appearance, then because of their busy schedule they'd have to leave," Erickson said. "But when Tom would come to a conference or something, he would take in every speech and every activity. He really gave of himself. He'd sit around and answer questions late at night."

Erickson's time with Landry did uncover a weakness.

"He could not sing," Erickson said, laughing. "But he loved Christmas carols."

Erickson discovered this one Christmas at Landry's church, Highland Park United Methodist.

"We sang together with the big crowd. I remember he just boomed them out," Erickson said. "The people didn't even look around to see who was off-key because they knew it was Landry."

Erickson's presidency began at a crucial point in the organization's history. The FCA was growing fast, but so was its debt. A poor corporate structure was part of the problem, so Landry and Erickson worked together to reorganize it.

They merged two separate boards into one board of trustees, which Landry headed. He remained a board member most of Erickson's 16-year presidency. When Landry was the board chairman, Erickson held meetings in Dallas so the coach could attend without disrupting his football schedule.

"We were in a growing stage. There were a lot of big decisions to make, and we just didn't have funds to do everything," Erickson said. "Tom never lost control or lost emotions while making difficult decisions."

Erickson said he never knew of Landry accepting payment for his appearances and often wasn't even reimbursed for his travel expenses.

Landry was able to devote even more time to the FCA after leaving the Cowboys. Erickson noticed that in Landry's later years, his speeches became even more focused on religion.

"In the last two or three years before his passing, the intensity of his faith life was growing every day," Erickson said. "Looking back, it seemed like he kind of knew what God had in mind. He didn't want to just talk and tell funny stories. He wanted to witness for Christ."

Many of Erickson's memories of Landry came back to him while attending the funeral.

"As I listened to others and remembered things we did together, I really felt fortunate to have known and been in the presence of and worked with a truly, truly wonderful human being," Erickson said. "At the time, I knew he was a terrific fellow and a Christian man, but as I listened to players, teammates and members of community, I realized he was much more than that."

Grant Teaff

Grant Teaff brought Baylor University out of the football wilderness to Southwest Conference titles and Cotton Bowls.

But he said his collegiate football miracles on the Brazos River were minor compared to what Tom Landry did in the NFL.

"There are few people I would class in the genius category, but in football, he was," said Teaff, who along with his wife, Donnell, has been a close friend of the Landry family for decades. "He was far ahead of the curve in the game."

On a personal level, Teaff and Landry shared a passion for the FCA, and they attended many functions together. Teaff was once the emcee for an FCA banquet honoring Landry.

"We had a lot of similar interests in life," Teaff said. "We got to be close. The coach and I spent a lot of time together. He gave a good portion of his time for FCA money raising."

Teaff introduced Landry at his 70th birthday and the occasion provided a chance to tell a favorite story.

"We had won the SWC title for the first time in decades, played Alabama in the Cotton Bowl and had an outstanding season in every way. We were feeling pretty good and went to services at the First Baptist Church in Waco.

"As Donnell and I were walking out of church, a member, Bill Nesbitt, came up the aisle and said he wanted to introduce his three boys. Bill said 'Boys, I want you to meet the greatest coach in America!'

"With that, his six-year-old boy looked me in the eye and asked: 'Are you Tom Landry?'"

Teaff said: "Tom loved that story. It really made him laugh."

Six months later, there was a humorous sequel when Donnell was in Abilene, Texas, speaking to a Baptist convention.

"She told the story about the little boy in church and everybody loved it," Teaff said.

In the audience was Sandra Covington, the wife of the team doctor. Sitting beside her was an elderly lady from Mississippi. She leaned over to Mrs. Covington and said: 'I certainly know who Grant Teaff is, but who is that Tom Landry fellow?"

"Tom got a big kick out that story when I told it to him," Teaff said.

Teaff, the president of the American Football Coaches Association, recalls the painful lesson that Landry learned by not following up on his recommendation to draft Mike Singletary, who went on to a Hall of Fame career with the Chicago Bears.

"When Mike was a senior, I called Tom and Gil Brandt," Teaff said. "I told them usually I don't try to get into anybody's business, but I would give anything if you guys would draft Singletary. I told them he would lead them to a title and be the best leader they ever had.

"Tom was polite, but noncommittal. The Cowboys, with the help of computers, already had criteria worked out. Singletary was 5-foot-11 3/4 inches. He got kicked out of the computer.

"The rest is history."

The intense Singletary became one of the greatest linebackers in NFL history and took the Bears to a Super Bowl championship.

Landry later told Teaff that the Cowboys had been blind in not seeing Singletary's talent and desire.

"Tom told me: 'If you ever call me again on a player, we're going to throw the computer out in the backyard.'"

Years later, Teaff called Landry on a receiver, Ray Berry.

"However, Ray went to a team picking ahead of the Cowboys," Teaff said. "Tom had Gil call me from the draft room explaining they had done everything they could to get him."

Then there was the funny incident when Landry and Teaff were playing golf in Tom's FCA tournament.

"We both hit balls near a lake on a downslope," Teaff said. "I thought I parked the cart correctly, but in the middle of my backswing, it started rolling toward the water."

Teaff, who played small college football, said he threw down his club and met the cart head-on halfway down the hill.

"I broke down like a middle linebacker and stuck the thing good and it quit rolling," Teaff said.

"Tom couldn't keep from laughing the rest of the day," Teaff recalled. "He said, 'I knew you were tough, but not linebacker tough.'

"I just knew I couldn't let that cart go in the drink with his golf clubs in there. I'd never hear the end of it."

Teaff added, "He was a special man. It's too bad everybody in this country didn't get to know him on a personal level."

Donald Carter

Tom Landry warned Donald Carter.

"When I started the Dallas Mavericks, got the original franchise and put my money down in '78, he asked me if I knew what I was doing," Carter said. "I kinda told him no. He said, 'Well, you're going to have lots of trials and tribulations. There's going to be times you wonder why in the world you ever did this.'"

One of those times came in 1987 when Dick Motta quit as the team's coach after their best regular season was followed by a first-round playoff elimination.

"I was stunned," Carter said. "I was raised up around the original Dallas Cowboys and around Tom Landry, so I thought Dick Motta would be my coach until I died.

"I saw Tom a couple days after, and he said, 'I told you it was going to happen.'"

So Carter asked Landry for advice.

"Bear with it, bear with it," Landry told him. "Don't forget where you came from and what the Lord has planned for you."

When the Cowboys were for sale in the 1980s, Carter did his best to buy the team. Told that he couldn't own franchises in the NBA and NFL, he offered to put the Mavericks in his wife's name. Things in Dallas might've been radically different had he been able to pull off that deal.

The relationship between Landry and Carter goes back long before Carter's days in pro sports.

"I first got to know Tom when the Billy Graham crusade was at Texas Stadium," Carter said.

Over the years, they worked together on FCA boards and were involved in starting a youth home outside of Dallas on land that Carter owned. Carter later became the first $1 million donor to the FCA.

"The real joy I had with him was through the FCA, working together on boards," Carter said. "We just had great prayer time, sharing the Lord and his gifts and blessings."

Carter said even Landry's death had a positive impact on others.

"He's really made us look back and think about some good memories and about the things this guy tried to teach us while he was alive," Carter said. "He's teaching us even more now that he's in heaven.

"The lesson is that if you will stay with your commitment and truthfully not deviate and not think that you have to change steps because of the way the rest of the world is marching, then the Lord will continue to give you the beat to walk to."

Kyle Rote Jr.

Kyle Rote Jr. had reason to be grateful to Tom Landry at an early age.

"He changed many of my diapers," Rote said.

Rote's dad was Landry's teammate on the New York Giants and the two families lived in the same suburban neighborhood. In later years, both lived in Dallas. As Kyle became older, he gained an even greater appreciation for Landry.

"I love Coach Landry," Rote said. "In the middle of his great Super Bowl runs, my mother was very sick. She had a stroke in her late 30s and was in a wheelchair. Alicia and Tom, in the middle of the insanity of a head coach's life, they always kept in touch with my mom. They were never too busy to stay in contact with people of that era."

Landry's biggest impact, though, was serving as a role model for Rote in his days as a soccer star, and even still now in his days as a high-profile sports agent.

"The story of his own conversion is so classic for those of us in competition in sports or business," he said. "Essentially, he thought the significance of life came in victories, but when he got to the level of success, he found he wasn't satisfied.

"He was a great high school player, but he wasn't satisfied, so he figured it would be better in college. He was successful there, made All-American, but it still didn't satisfy him, so he thought maybe it would be different in the pros. Then he went to that prayer meeting and discovered what was really missing was that he didn't have a strong relationship with God."

Rote's story was similar.

"As a young Christian in my teens or early 20s, his example was to show me that success in life was not in success itself but in love of God," he said. "That saved me a number of years, if not decades, so I could quickly learn that peace and significance in life is not going to be a best-selling book or winning the Superstars competition or scoring more soccer goals.

"Sports success is a wonderful goal, but a horrible God. He modeled that a generation ahead when very few people did."

Rote attended a Bible study that primarily included Cowboys players but also had athletes from other pro sports. Landry never went.

"I asked him why and he said it was because he didn't want players showing up just to get into his good graces. They should be there to seek and learn," Rote said. "As much as he and Alicia would have enjoyed it, he had the wisdom to understand the learning environment would've changed.

"Think about the purity of that. He deprived himself what would've been a very rich, fun environment for him. It just took me years to appreciate that kind of servant leadership."

Another bit of Landry wisdom that Rote admires was the coach's intense devotion to a few causes.

"I'm involved in some way with something like 185 organizations and I can't do it all," Rote said. "He figured out that he was more effective devoting himself to a few organizations rather than being cut up into pieces and not having a significant impact anywhere."

Dennis Conner

Tom Landry was so humble that he seemed to go out of his way to avoid giving himself even the slightest pat on the back.

"In working with him since 1978, we'd often sit down and discuss his availability for certain things," said Dennis Conner, the Dallas FCA director from '78 to '84, then the state director for 16 years. "Whenever he could not be someplace, all he would say is, 'I can't do that one.' He'd never elaborate.

"Later, I would find out by reading in the newspaper or seeing on the news that Coach Landry was in New York to receive a Man of the Year award from some organization, or he was in Los Angeles to be on television.

"It would've been very easy for him to say, 'Aw, Dennis, I'm going to New York to receive this award,' but he never did. He never dropped names or told anyone how important he was. He was terrifically humble, the most humble individual I've ever been around of that stature. That was the personification of the Lord in him—to serve, not be served."

With all the accolades and attention in his life, Landry's humility got quite a workout.

"One time I went to El Paso with him," Conner said. "We had a twin-engine private plane that was going to take us, but when we got to the airstrip at Love Field we found it was a real small one.

"We had a three-hour flight in that plane to get to El Paso, then a press conference, reception, banquet and the flight back, and he never complained. You couldn't help but be influenced to be as gracious as he was."

Landry signed every autograph, posed for every picture and shook every hand. It seemed he could go on forever making others happy.

Yet, there was a limit to his patience.

"In dealing with Coach Landry, you always knew when a meeting was over," Conner said. "He didn't come out and say it, but everything became monosyllable answers: 'Yes.' 'No.' 'OK.' That was a funny thing about him."

Gary Lower

Imagine spending a day enjoying the fresh air and majestic scenery of the Rocky Mountain National Park with Tom Landry. Gary Lower and his wife Elaine had that privilege.

It was the early 1990s and Lower, the FCA's vice president of ministry projects, was at the FCA camp in Estes Park, Colorado. Landry was there, but his wife Alicia wasn't. So the Lowers invited Landry to join them for the afternoon.

"He said, 'I'd love that,'" said Lower (rhymes with "flower") "So we picked him up and off we went. We had the best time, just talking, shooting the breeze and totally relaxing. This was not the coach of the Dallas Cowboys or a Hall of Famer. It was just a friend, talking about family and fun and all his years with the FCA.

"We stopped by the side of the road and there were a bunch of mountain goats over there. They were pretty tame, so he got out and stood among them and we took his picture. Then we went up to the top of the mountain. We walked into this place they have up there and I don't think a soul even recognized him. And he was having the time of his life by not being recognized.

"Then, all of a sudden, a little boy probably nine or 10 years old walked up to him and said, 'Aren't you Coach Landry?' And he said, 'Yes, I am.' The boy asked for his autograph and he said, 'You bet.' So they walked over to a chair where he could sit down and he signed something for the little guy. I thought, 'This is Tom Landry. He'll take time for anybody, even though he was enjoying not being recognized, knowing full well that was going to open the floodgates for everyone else around who hadn't recognized him.'"

Another time, the Lowers and Landrys were at an airport. The four of them were talking when again a youngster approached looking for an autograph.

"The little guy said, 'Would you sign your name on my T-shirt?'" Lower said. "Coach always carried around one of these pens that would write on just about anything. So he pulled it out, but Alicia said, 'Just a minute, Tom.' She said, 'Young man, does your mother know you're getting ready to have your T-shirt signed? Why don't you go ask her first.'

"So he went over to ask his mom. She smiled and nodded her head, then he came back. I thought, there's a wife and mother wanting to make sure that the boy didn't ruin his brand-new T-shirt."

Bunny Martin

Tom Landry couldn't be phased, not even by a disrespectful 19-year-old juvenile delinquent.

"I hate the Dallas Cowboys," the teen told Landry during a prison visit.

"I hate the Washington Redskins," Landry answered.

"And then we all giggled," said Bunny Martin, who had taken Landry to the youth correction center as part of the prison ministry work they shared. "That's the kind of guy he was. You just didn't rattle Coach Landry any time about anything."

Martin and Landry met at an FCA camp in 1964 and struck up a long, meaningful friendship.

Martin, a yo-yo champion and magician who also does motivational speaking, became involved in the Cowboys' team chapel services for 21 years, often working Thanksgiving Day.

"Coach always sat in the front row, arms crossed, glasses on and never said a word," Martin said.

Their bond became closest under the worst of circumstances. In the early 1990s, Martin's daughter-in-law fought cancer about the same time as Landry's daughter Lisa. Their battles were very similar, except that Brenda Martin's diagnosis came following childbirth, while Lisa was still pregnant when her tumor was discovered.

Although Brenda and Lisa never met, Bunny and his wife remained in contact with Tom and Alicia, each sharing their pain with someone who could truly understand what they were feeling.

"During Brenda's final days, Tom and Alicia called us and we spoke for an hour," Martin said.

After Lisa died in 1995, Bunny saw Tom during a viewing at the funeral home.

"I walked up to Coach and he looked at me and said, 'You've been through this. It's tough.' I reached over and hugged him and he hugged me back," Martin said. "Now Coach wasn't a huggy-touchy person. I only hugged him twice in my life. The other time was after one of the Super Bowls."

Martin was active in youth prison ministry for many years, then in the mid-1990s started his own group, "Reaching America's Youth."

"When I thought of people I wanted on the advisory board and the executive board, Coach Landry was one I wanted," Martin said. "So I wrote a letter, then called him, and he said he'd be happy to do it. You could always depend on him."

Landry served on the advisory board and also joined Martin for occasional ministry appearances.

"He'd talk to the inmates from a platform and he'd go around and speak to them one-on-one," Martin said. "He just did good everywhere he went. He could fit in anywhere.

"The man was just one of a kind. I told Alicia after the church service, 'The greatest thing about Coach Landry was that he was great and he never knew it.' That's a very valid statement. He never knew how great he was—humble and great.

"The press always wondered about what was going on in the head of the man under the hat. But what was so complicated about Coach Landry was the fact he was so simple. There was nothing to figure out. I've met very few men with the moral caliber of Tom Landry. He was in a league of his own."

Martin and Landry traveled together often, and Martin said Landry heard him speak so often, the coach probably knew all his punch lines.

But Landry never asked for any yo-yo or magic lessons.

"He would ask me on occasion how to do a card trick," Martin said. "I'd show him and he'd just smile and giggle and say, 'Isn't that something.'"

FINAL WORDS FROM THE COACH

Now that everyone else has had their say about Tom Landry, it's time to hear from the Coach himself.

Here's what he had to say during his induction to the Pro Football Hall of Fame, his induction into the Ring of Honor and to a prayer breakfast before a Billy Graham crusade in 1985.

PRO FOOTBALL HALL OF FAME

The Pro Football Hall of Fame makes players wait five years after they retire to be eligible for enshrinement. Coaches, however, are eligible as soon as they retire. So it was no surprise that in January 1990, the first election after Landry was forced into retirement, the voters for pro football's highest honor chose him to

Landry was inducted into the Pro Football Hall of Fame as soon as he became eligible. (Photo courtesy of the Gen Long collection)

be part of a class of inductees that included Buck Buchanan, Bob Griese, Franco Harris, Ted Hendricks, Jack Lambert and Bob St. Clair.

Landry received his bust and yellow jacket that are the Hall's trademarks on August 4, 1990. He was introduced by Roger Staubach, whom Landry had introduced at his induction five years earlier.

"A little over 20 years ago, a dream came true when I first stepped on the field at Cowboys training camp as a rookie, finding I was being coached by the very best," Staubach said. "It is my pleasure to introduce coach Tom Landry."

"Thank you very much," Landry said to loud applause. "Without my hat on, some of you might not recognize me. But, you know, they're taking bets on whether or not I will show any emotion today and the odds are very heavy that I won't.

"They told me this was going to be a great experience for me, and having been here to introduce several players into the Hall of Fame, I thought I would handle it very well. But when you're on this side, it's a little bit different.

"It's really a thrill for me to be here. If I don't show emotion, it's all on the inside.

"It makes it a little special today to have Roger Staubach present me for introduction into the Hall of Fame. I could talk for hours about Roger Staubach and all the great guys who played for the Dallas Cowboys.

"I would like to recognize the enshrinees for the tremendous jobs they did. They're all the players; I'm the coach.

"It makes it a little different going in from a coaching standpoint. I wish I'd have been a good enough player to go in as a player; that would've been super. I wasn't, unfortunately, but I'm glad to be here, though, as a coach.

"I had the pleasure of coaching against all these guys or playing against them. I coached four Super Bowls against them. I understand now why Pittsburgh beat us twice: Their whole team is going to be in the Hall of Fame before too long. They were a great team and they deserve it.

"Can you believe I played against Bob St. Clair? That ages us both. They told me he ate raw meat for his pregame meal. I didn't want to get too close to him because I didn't know what would happen. But, boy, he was a great player, and I'm just delighted to go in with these guys.

"Of course, the selection committee, if they hadn't selected me, I wouldn't be here. I would certainly like to thank the Hall of

Fame and its selection committee for inviting me to be a part of this great, great Hall of Fame.

"You know, it's hard to name all the people who've helped you be successful. But the most important to me is my family. The coaching business is very tough and your family is so important to you. And I'm going to introduce my family very quickly: my wife Alicia, this beautiful gal right here; my son, Tom Jr.; my oldest daughter, Kitty; Lisa, my other daughter; and my sister's here, too, Ruthie.

"There's two people who are not here today who would've loved to be here, and that's my parents. They both passed away in the '70s. My dad had the chance to see us win our last Super Bowl, against Denver. He was a great sports fan and he enjoyed it so very much. It's amazing how as we get older we understand how important family is. I'm just glad that God gave me such a great mother

"I'm talking about all the junior high and senior high coaches in America—what an impact they have, really, on all the youth in America, where we need the impact today."

and dad. It made a lot of difference in my life.

"Others who made great impact in my life, I think probably the one man who made the greatest difference was my coach in junior high and high school. I only had one coach when I was in junior high and high school. He graduated from San Marcos and came to Mission, Texas, to coach when I was in junior high school. Then, as I moved up to senior high school, he moved up as head coach. But he taught me a lot about football—he taught me the fundamentals, he taught me values, he taught me to pay a price to win. He contributed greatly to my success. I'm talking about all the coaches—all the junior high and senior high coaches in America— what an impact they have, really, on all the youth in America, where we need the impact today.

"It was a pleasure for me to really play for only two teams. I went up with the New York Yankees of the All-America Conference. I was there for only one year before they folded into the NFL, then I went to the New York Giants and the Mara family. The Mara family really meant a lot to me personally. The Mara family, the Halas family, the Rooney family—they're part of the NFL. And to be a part of that team and to see the type of family atmosphere that they had—you know, we didn't always agree, but like most families we would always make up. I had the chance to play, I had the chance to be a player-coach for them and then be a defensive coach.

"Those were the days. When I first came up, we didn't even have television. Can you believe it? Television was not there in 1949, '50 and the early '50s. I coached all the way through the '50s with the New York Giants. Vince Lombardi and myself, we coached. Vince handled the offense and I handled the defense until he went to Green Bay. We had some great teams with the Mara family. Wellington and Ann Mara, probably here today, they're some of my best friends.

"But as I moved to the Dallas Cowboys, I had the real pleasure to have an owner by the name of the late Clint Murchison.

"Clint Murchison took over the Cowboys in 1960 and was with us until he passed away recently. He never once criticized me or second-guessed me in the whole time I was with the Dallas Cowboys. I remember after the 1963 season, we had only won five games after four years in any one season. They called a press conference and I remember we went and everybody said, 'Well, Landry's gone.' Then Clint walked in and said I'm going to give him a 10-year contract with one year left. Now that's loyalty, that's support.

"I believe that Clint Murchison was probably the one person who enabled us to go 20 years with winning seasons because he took the pressure off of me, he took the pressure off of Tex Schramm, he took the pressure off the organization. That's what makes great teams or great dynasties. It was really a pleasure for me to have that.

"Others in the Dallas Cowboys, Tex Schramm was a tremendous or-

> *"They called a press conference, and everybody said, 'Well, Landry's gone.' Then Clint walked in and said I'm going to give him a 10-year contract with one year left. Now that's loyalty, that's support."*

ganizer. He's contributed greatly to the NFL in so many ways, and he was always responsible for our organization. Gil Brandt was another one who came in at the same time. His scouting helped us tremendously in the early years as we developed as a football team, and that was very important to me personally.

"Of course, the last year has been a very, very interesting year for me. I got fired and I'm in the Hall of Fame, all in one year. So you coaches remember there's always good things at the end of the rainbow if you stick at it.

"I think our coaching staff was another reason that we were very successful. I had coaches who coached with me for 29 years—Jerry

Tubbs did. I had Jim Myers and Ermal Allen who coached with me for almost 25 years. I had Gene Stallings for 14 years. Danny Reeves came up as a player and went all the way through as a coach before he went on to Denver. Of course, Mike Ditka did the same thing. He came to us as a player and now he's coaching the Bears.

"All these guys were with me more than 15 years as coaches, and that's what made the Cowboys what they were."

THE RING OF HONOR

Tom Landry became the eighth inductee into the Cowboys' Ring of Honor at Texas Stadium on November 7, 1993. Fittingly, the Cowboys were coming off one Super Bowl title and were on their way to another, and they were playing the New York Giants, Landry's first team. Adding to the perfect

Landry and his fellow Ring of Honor inductees: (from left) Staubach, White, Renfro, Howley, Perkins and Lilly at the 1999 Tom Landry FCA Open golf tournament. (Photo courtesy of the Fellowship of Christian Athletes)

scenario was the fact that Landry protégé Dan Reeves was coaching the Giants and Pat Summerall, one of Landry's pupils when he coached in New York, was broadcasting the game for CBS. Summerall handled the public-address duties for the occasion, which included introducing the other seven honorees, all of which were in attendance.

Jerry Jones had asked Landry to go into the Ring of Honor in 1989, but he declined. Then, in early 1993, Landry bumped into Jones at a golf tournament and the offer was extended again. After much thought—and after reading hundreds of letters from fans divided over whether he should or shouldn't accept—Landry decided the time was right.

"I think it would be foolish for me to say I'm not going to go in the Ring of Honor because I'm mad at Jerry or somebody else—because I'm not at all," Landry said at a July news conference announcing the honor. "I would've gone in way back when Jerry first asked us, after the first year, if I'd felt that was the right time. But it wasn't the right time.

"I was so busy doing what I was trying to do in building our business up that I really didn't have time to think about it one way or another. You, the press, were the only ones who reminded me of it most of the time. They seemed to remind me of it all over the country. Really, that didn't both me at all because I knew I'd be directed that way whenever the time was right. The time is right, right now, as far as I'm concerned."

The news conference was the first time Landry had been back at Texas Stadium since he was fired. He'd yet to attend a game there, but that was mainly because he knew he'd be mobbed by fans if he tried.

"I'm still surprised that, after four years, people still like me," he said.

Being back at the stadium triggered some fond memories.

"When you come in here, you start thinking about the great games that we played here," Landry said. "When you think about those great games—Roger Staubach against Washington, bringing us back in the last minute—it thrills you a lot to be able to say, 'Well, I'm back at Texas Stadium.'"

The honor turned into a weekend of activities. There was a party on Saturday night at Texas Stadium that was basically a big reunion.

When the ceremony began, the fans booed *"I'm still surprised that after four years, people still like me."* Jones. The jeers turned to cheers when he began reading a list of Landry's accomplishments.

"That great record is only transcended by the fact that you represent for sports what we all in sports would like to be represented, and that is a higher cause and a bigger meaning. You've done it all on a competitive basis," Jones said.

"Our Ring of Honor stands for the men who built this franchise and had it called America's Team. This would not be the Ring of Honor without you, and without you in it."

Then, a curtain rose to display the permanent marker: Tom Landry, 1960-88. A tiny fedora hangs to the left of his name, in place of the jersey number listed for the others.

After several minutes of applause, it was finally time to hear from the guest of honor.

"Well, I want to say this is really an outstanding day for me personally," Landry said. "I don't know how you can thank all the people that are responsible for putting this thing on here. I do think that this is one of the great times. I'm honored to be in the Ring of Honor.

"You know, I look at those names up there and at these guys here that I'm so proud of. It was amazing what they contributed to the winning seasons that we had.

"When you take Don Meredith, Don Perkins and you start out with that team that started 0-11-1. Boy, we were really moving in those days. They took a lot of beating through the years.

"Bob Lilly was our first pick in the draft. He went through a lot of tough seasons against the Green Bay Packers. I remember when we got to our first Super Bowl, with Baltimore, and we thought we had the game won. We thought we would finally win and they kicked the field goal that beat us. Bob picked up his helmet and threw it about 70 yards. He threw it farther than our passer could throw it in that particular game.

"These guys were all great. Mel Renfro, a tremendous person. Chuck Howley was the Most Valuable Player in our first Super Bowl win on defense and that's one of the few times that's ever happened. I'll tell you, when you take Roger Staubach and you watched him play, everybody was on the edge of their seats every time Roger was there. You know, Lee Roy was the smallest middle linebacker in the league, but he was one of the best in there.

"I think it's a tremendous thing . . . I know they wouldn't be here, and I wouldn't be here, if it wasn't for all the other players. We had the alumni in this weekend. All those guys—the coaches and all who did so much for the Dallas Cowboys—I'm just sorry that the late Clint Murchison is not here. He would've enjoyed this day tremendously.

"And, of course, with his leadership and Tex Schramm's leadership, we set our sails for what we did through all those years and made it possible that we could achieve all those things. We had a great organization and we had a lot of good people working for us in those days.

"I would like to really take this opportunity, since the New York Giants, my old team, are here, I'd like to thank Wellington Mara and Ann Mara, who've been great friends of mine through the years. They prepared me with the New York Giants to become the coach of the Dallas Cowboys.

"So I'm just delighted to be here today. I want to thank Jerry for all he's done to make this a special day. Thank you very much."

MEN'S PRAYER BREAKFAST

(part of a pre-crusade rally for Billy Graham's visit to Southern California in the spring of 1985)

Tom Landry was involved in 54 Billy Graham crusades, mostly as a pre-crusade speaker. It was his job to help drum up support for the event.

A typical speech was given in Anaheim, California, in the spring of 1985. A barbershop quartet warmed up the crowd with several songs, including a tribute to Landry.

His performance was typical: a bit of humor and a few football anecdotes, followed by his own story of how he found religion—including tales of near-death experiences in war—and what it means to him. He frames it all around ways others can be champions for God.

Some of the stories might sound familiar from the previous chapters, but those who heard Landry speak often enough will read this text and hear him saying the words, which makes it rather powerful.

There are many Bible quotes, yet Landry sprinkles in humor throughout—especially two great stories involving George Halas and Dick Butkus.

"I'm delighted a few of the girls showed up, because it improves this audience tremendously.

"I tell you, after hearing the quartet, I forgot what I was going to say. Y'all got me so shook up here. I think I could improve my image if I could get one of those bow ties from them. That would really look good on the sideline, I'll tell you that. . . .

"I realize I'm in Ram country down here, but you better not go north. We've got a little stronghold up in Thousand Oaks, California. That's Dallas Cowboys country. But I notice this year the Raiders are moving in to the north of us, so we're getting surrounded again.

"The Rams and Dallas have had some great, great games through the years. You've watched them and we've had some exciting times together. I think one of the greatest teams I ever saw were the Rams in the '50s. Some of y'all are not old enough to remember those great teams. They had [Bob] Waterfield, [Norm] Van Brocklin, [Tom] Fears, [Elroy] 'Crazy Legs' Hirsch, Deacon Dan Towler, all of them. I was just breaking into New York that time for the New York Giants. We had a really bad team in the early '50s. They would come into New York for a game we had for charity, and, boy, it just worried the heck out of us every time they came in because we knew we were in for it.

"I was playing left corner and Dick Nolan, who coached the 49ers and New Orleans and is now on my staff, was playing the right corner. They had a little strategy they used when they came into the goal line. They put in what they called the 'elephant backfield.' This was three of their biggest guys, who would line up in a straight-T. My good friend Dan Towler, who's been on our board with the FCA for many years and is a great, great friend of mine, he weighed about 235 or 240 and he played one of the fullbacks, and Tank Younger played the other halfback—that gives you an indication of how big they were. He was about 245. They just lined up in a tight T and ran off left tackle or right tackle every time. Well, I knew they were going to be coming at Dick Nolan or myself, and I knew they would go toward Dick because I was so tough on the other side.

"Dick and I talked all week about how we were going to try to stop them, but we couldn't find any solutions. So we kicked off to them and here they come down to the five, and here came that elephant backfield. In those days, we had those wooden posts on the goal line. I was leaning on one and Dick was leaning on the other. I said, 'Man, here they come.' I hollered at Dick, 'Watch out!'

"They snapped the ball and sure enough, they handed it to Towler, and those other big guys led him off toward Nolan, off tackle. The hole opened real great. You know how you do when you're trying to make that last yard: You lower your head and just cover that ball up. Dan just came roaring in there—and hit the goal post solid.

"I looked over there and the goal post started (shaking), but it held. It threw back and Dan went back, lost the ball and one of our guys took off downfield and all the Rams were chasing him. Here was Towler, laying on the ground, shaking his head. He got up and said, 'Golly, what happened?'

"And Nolan told him, 'If you come my way again, next time, I'll really hit you.'

"Every time Dan gets with me and I tell that story, it just kills him because it's true!

"But you know, in 1984, we didn't have a very good team in Dallas. We were out of the playoffs for the first time in 10 years. We had a 9-7 record, which is not very good in Dallas. We had a terrible offense. I had to go back to 1964 to find the time when we had scored less points than we scored last year.

"I felt a little bit like the coach who was a failure one season and wanted to get some help, so he went to a psychiatrist. The psychiatrist said, 'Sure, come on in and lay down on the couch and start talking about whatever is on your mind.' After listening for a couple of hours, he says, 'I know what you're problem is: You're a poor motivator.' Well this upset the coach terribly. No coach likes to hear that he's a poor motivator. So he says, 'I want a second opinion.' The psychiatrist says, 'I'll give you a second opinion—you're offense stinks, too!' I really feel like that, too.

"Football coaches, I know we have some in here today, and baseball managers, we have the most unsecure jobs in America. We don't last very long if we're not successful. I was talking to Billy Martin the other day after he came back with the Yankees. He said, 'You know, I don't mind Steinbrenner writing my name on my office door in chalk. The thing that worries me the most and really kind of irritates me is that wet sponge he hangs up there behind it.' So, I tell you, we're in a tough business.

"I'm going to share with you a little bit this morning what I've entitled, 'A Champion For God,' and I'm going to give a personal testimony so you really will understand where I'm coming from.

"I was raised down in Mission, Texas, which is a small town in the tip of Texas, down by Brownsville in what we call the Rio Grande Valley. It's much like California as far as citrus fruit and winter vegetables; a wonderful place. I was raised down there and I really hadn't ever gone farther than San Antonio.

"My dad was a mechanic, had his own garage, his one-man auto repair shop. My parents were wonderful people. I remember in the Depression years, we had six in

> *"I thought the way to be successful in life was to be the best at whatever you could do. I thought if I reached the top of my profession, I'd have everything that life had to offer."*

the family and we ate every day with $1.50. It's hard for anybody to believe that, but we ate well—mainly because he traded the farmers automobile work for their vegetables.

"I went to church every Sunday, really. We were just a half-block from the Methodist church and my dad was the superintendent of the Sunday schools. But we really never studied the Bible in our home. We didn't pray too much. We did when we had guests over for dinner or something, but it didn't really mean much.

"I thought the way to be successful in life was to be the best at whatever you could do. I was a football player in high school and I wanted to be the best football player I could be. I thought if I reached the top of my profession, I'd have everything that life had to offer. I had a chance to go to the University of Texas, which was a big step for me coming from a little, small school. I went to the University of Texas in '42 and made the team and was very excited about that. That was during the war, as you know, and we all joined the reserves. I joined the Air Force reserves at that time. A few months more, we went into the service. They called up our reserve.

"Looking back, I believe God protects us and prepares us for something, even though we may not want to hear it yet. I know he got me through the war because I was flying out of England over Europe in a B-17 as a copilot, and one time we had to go to Czechoslovakia, which was about 10 and half hours away, which was about the range of the B-17. We went over there and we usually cleaned out our mixture coming back to be sure we'd get across the [English] Channel before we ran out of gas. On that particular day, we'd been flying three or four hours coming back and were almost over Holland at the time and all four of our engines stopped at one time. We were losing altitude quickly, and we rapidly checked all the instruments and everything, and the gas and gas gauge were pretty much on empty. The pilot said, 'Well, we've got to bail out.' As I start to get out of my seat, for some reason, I reached up and pushed the four mixtures forward. They'd been lean; we'd overlooked them. I didn't know why I did it, but I just pushed it forward—and all four of those engines caught on. By then, we were very low, and we went over Amsterdam with the Achtung shooting at us.

"That's amazing, you know, that that happened.

"Another time, we came back the same way and we were running out of gas. It was after Normandy and we had an alternate airport and we were supposed to go into it. So we tried to get into that airport. But when we got there, it was completely stocked in. We tried to find it, but we couldn't. We were skimming over the trees and finally ran out of gas and hit into the field. We went through those trees and cut off both engines, got out of the airplane and all nine of us walked out without a scratch.

"So I just believed that God had a purpose for me at that time."

"When I came back from war and went to the University of Texas, we again had great teams, went to the Sugar Bowl and Orange Bowl and won them all. Every time, it was exciting. But the thing that was creeping into my life at that time was an emptiness and a restlessness after the excitement of achieving these things.

"My only rationalization was that I hadn't reached the top of my profession. I thought I could reach that. So I went into pro football and I had a lot of success. I had the privilege of being in Pro Bowl games and being All-Pro; we won the world championship in New York against the Bears and I was at the top of my profession, very excited about it. But there was still an emptiness and a restlessness in my life.

"So I was thinking about getting out of football. I came back to Dallas and a friend of mine met me one day on the street and he said, 'Tom, how about attending a Bible study that meets at the Melrose Hotel on Wednesday mornings.' I thought the guy must be crazy. I knew the Easter story and the Christmas story and I'd been to church every time I could get into the church, but I'd never read the Bible

> *"We . . . went to the Sugar Bowl and Orange Bowl and won them all. . . . But the thing that was creeping into my life at that time, there was an emptiness and a restlessness after the excitement . . ."*

before. He was persistent, so I went to study the Bible and started to study the Bible for the first time.

"We happened to be in Matthew, on the Sermon on the Mount. Jesus was saying, 'Do not be anxious about your life, what you shall eat or drink, or about your body, what you should put on. Isn't life more than food and body more than clothing? Seek first the kingdom of God and his righteousness, and all these things will be given to you.'

"Well, I got excited because this was the first time I'd ever read anything like this. I went on to read the parable about the builders, where Jesus explains the importance of a strong foundation. He says, 'Anyone who hears these words of mine and does them is like a wise man who builds his house upon a rock, and when the rains come and the floods come and the wind beats upon that house, it'll stand strong because it's on a strong foundation.' But he also said, 'Anybody who hears these words of mine and doesn't do them is like a foolish man who builds his house upon sand, and when the rains fall and the floods come and the wind beats upon that house, great will be his fall.'

"Well, you know, being a football coach, I knew exactly what Jesus was talking about, because we don't build a football team without a strong foundation. We must have a strong foundation of blocking and tackling and discipline to have a chance to ever have a good football team. So I understood what he was talking about. And at that time, I did not know that we were saved by faith, that it is a gift of God. Not through our works do we become a Christian, but because of faith. I did not know that.

"I was factual, as a football coach is, so I wanted to find out all the facts. So I started studying my Bible. And I started discovering the facts that God did love me, because in John 3:16 it says, 'God so loved the world that he gave his only begotten son, and whoever believes him shall not perish, but have everlasting life.'

"And I also learned that I was a sinner.

"I had no idea what sin was. I couldn't image how I could be a sinner—I'd been going to church, had pretty good basic morals, I thought, and the Bible said I'm a sinner. Then I learn that sin means we're separated from God. And the Bible went on to say, 'For the wages of sin is death. But the gift of God is eternal life through Jesus Christ our Lord.'

"Another thing I discovered was that Christ died for me. And, boy, that's a tremendous thing."

"The Bible says, 'But God commendeth his love toward us in that, while we were yet sinners, Christ died for us.' But the Bible also says, 'When you sin, the wages of sin is death.' Of course, the great thing that Romans 5:8 says is that 'Christ died for our sins.'

"The great story is that by faith, we are saved. In Acts 16:30, 31, Paul and Silas had been sent to prison. Of course, they were singing hymns—as they always did in prisons—because of what God had done for them. And late at night, you remember the story, when the thunder struck and all the jail doors flew open. And the guard saw it and he ran to get his knife to kill himself because in those times, if you lost a prisoner, you had to commit suicide. And Paul saw him and said, 'Wait a minute, we're still here.' He was so impressed with that that the guard asked, 'Sir, what must I do to be saved?' And Paul said, 'Believe in the Lord Jesus Christ, and thou shall be saved.'

"The whole message of the gospel that I was seeking was in First Corinthians 15:3, 4, it was the declaration of three facts: that Christ died, that Christ was buried and that Christ rose again. 'Because I live, he shall also live.' That was a great gospel.

"Of course, I committed my life to Christ at that time, one year before I took over the Dallas Cowboys as the head coach.

"St. Augustine says, 'Hearts are restless, O God, until we find our rest in you.' So that's what I was seeking all my life.

"At first, I was seeking it in the glory of football, of being successful as a football player, to find happiness and all the things I thought life had to offer. But when I found those things, I didn't find that was true. But when I accepted Jesus Christ, I knew what the answer was, because life is really about finding joy and peace much more than happiness.

"What I discovered after accepting Christ was that I was a churchgoer all my life, not a Christian. I didn't know that you could be a churchgoer and not a Christian. That kind of amazed me.

"But at that time, when I accepted Jesus Christ, I knew all this time that my priorities had been wrong. Because up until then, football was my No. 1 priority. My family was important to me, sort of, and God was involved somewhere in the shuffle. But after accepting Jesus Christ, God became first in my life. My family became so much more important to me than it ever had been before. And football took its proper place in my life."

"So this is the excitement of becoming a Christian. And I was so excited about becoming a Christian, I wanted to find someone to tell them about it. But I didn't know enough about the Bible to really tell them very much, so I attended an FCA summer conference program at Estes Park for about 1,000 coaches and athletes. It was a mountaintop experience in Colorado, and I knew that the FCA was where I should have my platform. I have been with the FCA ever since, witnessing to coaches and athletes throughout America.

"I was so excited about becoming a Christian, I wanted to find someone to tell them about it."

"But as I studied the Bible, I became really attached to the apostle Paul. . . . The apostle Paul must have been a great athlete, a great spectator, because he's always comparing athletes and Christians in his words. I thought that was great. I started reading about Paul and I started thinking about up to the time I became a Christian, I wanted to be a champion in a Super Bowl. Now, I wanted to be a champion for God. I wanted to know what it took to be a champion for God.

"And the apostle Paul led me to what I thought was very important, because if you read his words in the Bible, in Hebrews 12:1, he says, 'Since we have such a huge crowd of men of faith watching us from the grandstand, let us strip off anything that slows us down or holds us back, especially those sins that wrap themselves so tightly around our feet and trip us up. And let us run with patience the particular race that God has set before us.' What a tremendous verse for an athlete.

"Up to the time I became a Christian, I wanted to be a champion in a Super Bowl. Now I wanted to be a champion for God."

"Then, he went on to my favorite verse in the Bible, of how to motivate a football team or how to motivate a Christian. It's First Corinthians 9:24-27, and in the paraphrase edition it says, 'In the race, everyone runs, but only one person wins first prize. So run your race to win. To win a contest, you must deny yourself many things that keep you from doing your best. An athlete goes through all this trouble to win a blue ribbon or a silver cup, but we do it for a heavenly reward that never disappears. So I run straight to the goal with purpose in every step. I fight to win. I'm not shadow boxing or playing around. Like an athlete, I treat my body roughly, train it to do what it should, not what it wants to do, otherwise after enlisting others for the race, I myself might be declared unfit and ordered to stand aside.'

"What a tremendous verse that is. Now, if you want to motivate a football team to be successful, you can do it with that one verse. Because that's paying the price to be a champion."

"I think there's four things that are important—and I probably won't cover them all entirely today—of what it takes to be a champion on the athletic field and what it will take to be a champion for God.

"The first thing that I think it will take to be a champion is faith. Because what Paul says in First Corinthians is that in the race, everyone runs, but only person wins first prize, so run your race to win. Be a great Christian. Be a great champion for God. Be a great champion on the athletic field. When you define faith . . . what is faith? It's the confident assurance that something we want is going to happen. It is the certainty of what we hope is waiting for us, even though we can't see it up ahead.

"If you break those things down into that one definition, you'd see what an athlete looks for. You've got to have faith if you're going to be a great athlete.

"Roger Staubach was one of the greatest athletes I ever coached. The main reason that he was a great athlete, he had great belief in his ability to win. That's why he led us out of so many games in the final two-minute period and won the game for us, because of his leadership. It was strictly faith that did that, believing that it can be done, the positive attitude. I've been in Robert Schuller's church. I've been in his cathedral, and his theme is a power that he talks about, that comes only from God. The hour of power.

"God has given us so much talent that we don't use, it's incredible. We have so many opportunities to do more. But the thing that stops us are our fears, our anxieties, our doubts. That's what hinders an athlete from becoming a champion. In Second Timothy 1:7, God says, 'I do not give you a spirit of fear. I give you power, love and self-control.' That's one of the greatest verses I know of because fear comes from within us. It does not come from God. And I think this is important.

"As a Christian, anything is possible. 'For with God, nothing shall be impossible'—that's Luke 1:37. Reaching your full potential—'I can do all things through Christ, which strengthens me.' Phillipians 4:13.

The power of prayer—'Ask and it shall be given, seek and ye shall find, knock and the door will be opened to you.' That's why I think a Christian athlete like Roger Staubach, they can be so much greater if they are Christian—because of the power that comes within them, their ability to think positively.

> *"Roger Staubach had great belief in his ability to win. That's why he led us out of so many games in the final two-minute period and won the game for us."*

"But you know, faith is not easy. Robert Browning says, 'You call for faith and I give you doubt to prove that faith exists. The greater the doubt, the stronger the faith, I say, if faith overcomes doubt.' That's a tremendous verse there. Because we all have doubts, we're human, we're sinners. So we have our limitations. The greatest teaching in the Bible is Thomas. You remember, Thomas was a doubting Thomas. And the reason he was a doubting Thomas is because he'd question everything.

"After Jesus had been buried and came again, you remember the first time he appeared as a disciple, Thomas was not there. And I'm sure that all those disciples, after seeing Jesus and being so excited about it, they ran to tell Thomas, 'Hey, you weren't there. Where were you?' And Thomas says: I won't believe it unless I see the nail wounds in his hands and put my finger into them or place my hands into his side. Well, the next time Jesus appeared, you remember the situation. They were all there that time. And Thomas was back in the corner, looking around, and said, 'Is that really Jesus?' Of course, Jesus saw and said, 'Thomas, come here. Feel my hands. Stick your hands in my side, where the spear went in.' And, of course, Thomas fell on his knees and said, 'My Lord and my God.' But Jesus said something after that, in the next few verses. He said, 'Blessed are those who haven't seen and believe.'

"So this is the great thing that we're talking about. To be a great champion, you've got to have faith."

"The second thing I think you must have, is that you must train if you're going to be a champion.

"In our football team, we've been in the off-season program since April 1. Our guys work four to five times a week, just getting in good enough shape so we can step on the field in Thousand Oaks in July and withstand what we have to face for 20-23 games in the season. We have to train hard to be as successful as a champion.

"I think the same thing is true for a Christian. You remember what Paul said, 'Like an athlete, I treat my body roughly, train it to do what it should, not what it wants to do, otherwise after enlisting others for the race, I myself might be declared unfit and ordered to stand aside.' We have to train if we're going to be a champion for God, without question."

"The third thing I think you have to have is a goal, a plan of action, if you're going to be a champion.

"When we started in 1960 as an expansion club, I'll never forget it, you remember the AFL came in at that time and put a team in Dallas. We were out here in Los Angeles at that time for the league meeting. The draft was over with and they said, 'Dallas, you can have a team.' Of course, I got concerned because I didn't know who we were going to play with since the draft was over.

"I made a passionate plea in front of the owners. I said, 'Boy, you ought to stock us there because we've got to go into Dallas against the opposition and all.' So they came back out to announce what we were going to get and they said we could have three of the worst eight players on each team. And we started with 36 players—that's all we had. And we were so bad it was unreal. Our guys didn't even want to touch the ball, because when you touch the ball in football, things happen to you.

> *"When we started in 1960 . . . The draft was over with and they said, 'Dallas, you can have a team.' Of course, I got concerned because I didn't know who we were going to play with since the draft was over."*

"We played the Bears in the Cotton Bowl and they came in with George Halas and beat us about 45-0. When the game was over, here comes George across the field. I didn't know what he was coming for—condolences, I guess.

"Before he got to me, he said, 'Tom, you're going to lose every ballgame this year.' Of course, I knew that, but I hated people telling me it! I said, 'What do you mean, George?'

"He says, 'You're giving away every play. When you break the huddle, we know who is going to be carrying the ball, and our defense has been keying on you the whole game.' I couldn't argue because we hadn't done anything the whole game. I said, 'George, that's impossible.' I mean, you can give away one or two plays, but you can't give away every play in the game.

"He said, 'Since we don't play any more, I'll tell you what's happening. When Don Meredith goes in that huddle, three of those guys come out just laughing like everything and one of them comes out white as a ghost.'

"So I guarantee you, I started setting goals right then. We had to have a plan of action if

> *" When Don Meredith goes in that huddle, three of those guys come out just laughing like everything and one of them comes out white as a ghost.' "*
> —George Halas

we ever were going to get to the Super Bowl. So we started planning goals.

"We decided where we were right then, where we wanted to go and how we were going to get there. I think a Christian's that way if he wants to be a champion for God. Listen to what the apostle Paul says in Phillipians 3:13-14. He says, 'No, dear brothers, I'm still not all I should be, but I'm bringing all my energies to bear on this one thing: forgetting the past and looking forward to what lies ahead. I strain to reach the end of the race and receive the prize for which God is calling us up to heaven because of what Christ Jesus did for us.'

"We started with 36 players— that's all we had. And we were so bad it was unreal. Our guys didn't even want to touch the ball, because when you touch the ball in football, things happen to you."

"When I read that verse, I said, 'My goodness, the apostle Paul is possibly the greatest evangelist that ever walked the earth and he's concerned about reaching his goal.' I knew right then that we have to prepare ourselves for what God is planning for us, to receive the prize that God is offering us through Jesus Christ.

"We have to have our quiet time, our prayer, our Bible study, our witnessing. I work on it constantly because when I find myself not having any quiet time with God in the morning, if I go two or three days, I'm out of synch. But if I do it every day, then I'm always walking with him when I leave every morning. And you have to have a goal to be a champion."

"The last one I want to share with you this morning is the will.

"You know, you can keep the faith, which is most difficult; you can train hard enough so that you won't be declared unfit and ordered to stand aside, as Paul so ably put it, which is very tough; but to possess the will to become a champion may be the most important thing of all. This is what keeps athletes from becoming champions; they don't have the commitment, the will, to pay the price you have to do to be champions.

"We brought our rookies in last week, we had about 85 of them. We ran them around in shorts and saw what kind of athletes they were. But we don't play the game in shorts. We play the game in pads. Until I bring them out to Thousand Oaks in July and line up Randy White across from them, I'm not sure whether they have the will and the commitment to be a champion on our football team.

"One of my favorite players of all-time is Walt Garrison. Now, if you see Walt Garrison today, he's advertising snuff. I didn't teach him that. But he was a true cowboy, a rodeo cowboy.

"He came to us from Oklahoma State about 5-10, about 190 pounds. He wasn't fast, he wasn't quick—he wasn't very much of anything I could think of. Except he had a heart just about as big as he was. You couldn't get him out of a football game unless a doctor dragged him out.

"He went to our first two Super Bowls and he was our full-back in both of those games. Calvin Hill was our tailback. He gained 1,000 yards and was a big runner for us.

"We went up to play the Bears, this time in Wrigley Field, and they had a middle linebacker by the name of Dick Butkus. Butkus, on TV now he looks small, but when he was playing, he was about 245, 6-3, 6-4 and mean as a snake. He backed up that line and he grunted and growled.

"On this particular day, Butkus was keying on Hill, which was obvious. So every time Hill went someplace, he'd nail him and we couldn't gain a yard. But we were giving the ball to Garrison up the middle and getting six yards, seven yards, eight. You could tell Butkus was getting mad because he was calling Garrison everything he could think of. Finally, he wised up, which was within his range. So he keyed on Garrison the next play and we didn't know it.

"The hole opens and the only problem is Butkus was in it. Garrison, being a competitor, thinks he's going to run over him—which was his mistake. He just tore into him, and Butkus hit him right there and knocked him about four yards into the

"Old Garrison didn't even bat an eye. He said, 'OK, big shot. But I'll tell you this: If you bite my head off, you're going to have more brains in your stomach than in your head.'"

backfield, right onto his back, and then sat on him, straddling him.

"He looked down and said, 'You little shrimp. If you come through this hole again, I'm going to bite your head off.' And old Garrison didn't even bat an eye. He said, 'OK, big shot. But I'll tell you this: If you bite my head off, you're going to have more brains in your stomach than in your head.'

"So that's what it takes. If you can handle yourself under those circumstances as well as Garrison, you've got a will and you've got a commitment.

"But, you know, if you want to be a champion for God, you have to do the same things. You have to be committed. Because the people who are determined to do something for God, if you study history, are the men and women who have done something for God.

"If you go back to the Old Testament, read Nehemiah. With a trowel in one hand and a sword in another, he built the wall all the way around Jerusalem. He went to his king and said, 'God is calling me to do these things,' and I'm sure his king must have laughed at him. But he did it. Why? Because he had the will to do so first.

"The Christian has the perfect advantage when it comes to will. It's committing his own will to the will of God and letting the Holy Spirit direct him. What power there is in that type of situation.

"You remember the story of David. He wasn't born a king. As a little boy, remember, he went against Goliath. He went over there with that slingshot and he killed Goliath, a big nine-foot guy and he was just a kid without armor. Why did he do it? Because he took God with him. That's what's important.

"The apostle Paul was a perfect example of someone with the will. He ended up with his head chopped off. He spent time in every prison there was, probably.

"And Peter. He was told to quit speaking about this man Jesus, after Jesus had ascended. And Peter said, 'Whether it be right in the sight of God to hearken unto you rather unto God, judge ye, for we cannot but speak the things which we have seen and heard.'

"So, in order to be a champion for God, you've got to have a will."

"In conclusion, I would say this: If you want to be a champion, I don't care whether it's on the athletic field or anyplace else, you must have faith, you must train, you must have a goal and a will.

"But the important thing for us to remember this morning is that Paul knew the difference between a champion on the athletic field and a champion for God. You remember what he said in First Corinthians: 'To win a contest, you must deny yourself many things that keep you from doing your best. An athlete goes through all this trouble to win a blue ribbon or a silver cup, but we do it for a heavenly reward that never disappears.'

"So the challenge today for us, and the challenge for all our people, is to be a champion for God. If we can have enough of those, then we're going to win the battle. Because we're in a world today of a new morality; we have been since the '60s.

"And the only way that we're going to do it, the only solution to the drugs, the alcohol and all the things that plague us throughout America today, is Jesus Christ. The Bible is the answer for life, from Genesis to Revelations, because John 14:6 says, 'I'm the way, the truth and the life; no man cometh unto the Father, but by me.'"

In Loving Memory

Tom Landry
A Modern Legend
You Will Not Be Forgotten

(Photo courtesy of the Gen Long collection)